AWAKENING ^{TO}_{OUR} AWFUL SITUATION

WARNINGS FROM THE NEPHITE PROPHETS

JACK MONNETT

Nauvoo House Publishing   Heber City, Utah 84032

Also by Jack Monnett

Revealed Educational Principles & the Public Schools (1998)

John Taylor: Educator (2002)

Awakening to our Awful Situation
Copyright 2006 by Jack Monnett

Nauvoo House Publishing
Heber City, Utah 84032

EAN: 978-1-930679-98-6

This edition is printed on acid-free paper and meets the American National Standards Institute Z39.48 standard.

For Cleon
who understood the balance of
spiritual, academic, and public responsibility.

In politics nothing happens by accident.
If it happens, you can bet it was planned that way.

Franklin Delano Roosevelt

Table of Contents

Acknowledgements

This study has been aided immensely by the interest that has been shown in it by readers and those who have heard my talks alluding to some of the problems contained in the text. Their urging has made the work more fulfilling and has certainly made the hours spent researching and writing less tedious.

Much of the current research has been compiled from various internet sources while the majority of historical information has come from books listed in the bibliography and the resources of the Brigham Young University Library in Provo, Utah.

Chiefly contributing and giving direction to the study was Joel Skousen. His help with chapter reviews, suggestions, and source recommendations, was indispensable. Likewise, Ross Monnett has offered a constant flow of new information and encouragement. A critical analysis of the text with significant aid in the structure and organization of the book was made by Betty Bryner. Her tireless help was instrumental in meeting deadlines and arriving at a final draft for publication.

Patti Adams has given immeasurable help in the lay-out of the text and cover design. Her support, recommendations, and book savvy have proven key factors in producing *Awaking to our Awful Situation*. The inclusion of the technical expertise of Dr. Steven Jones and his analysis of the collapse of the World Trade Center Buildings is also greatly appreciated.

Several people have read preliminary copies of the book and have added comments and suggestions. Their help and encouragement have also been valuable in arriving at the finished text. They are: Reg Anderson, Rachel Degerman, Sharon Packer, Lewis Chappell, Lois Maxwell, Dr. Glenn Kimber, Zeldon Nelson, and Barbara Jean Whiteley.

And a final and most important thanks to my wife, Margie, for all of her support and patience. Her encouragement has been most helpful in bringing this book from thoughts and ideas to the printed pages.

Jack Monnett
November 1, 2006

FOREWORD

For good religious people, one of the most difficult tasks in today's sophisticated world is to perceive evil when masquerading as good. It is due, in large part, to wishful thinking. Good Christian conservatives are often a beleaguered, minority within a democratic society, and rarely gain the ability to effectively control the powers of government. Thus, when "one of their own," claiming to be true to the faith, gains political power, Christian conservatives almost always tend to place unconditional trust and approval in such a leader, even in the face of near constant betrayal. They never ask the crucial question: Why, if none of the true believers in constitutional limits can get elected, does the establishment suddenly back someone who was a "sudden convert" to the constitutional and limited government ideology? It is, as the old saying goes, "too good to be true."

Even on the side of evil there are great deceptions aimed at the gullible unthinking person: For example, the "fall of Communism and the Soviet Union was, in fact, "too good to be true." Evil never lays down its power when the going gets a little tough. Sophisticated evil leaders might do so as a ploy, to gain further advantage, but it's never real…unless accompanied by the signs of real repentance, and airing all the bloody linen from past repressions. Historically, this has happened only rarely, and then only to an individual who has a deep religious experience—never to an evil group of leaders as a whole!

So why would people fall for this grand deception—perhaps the greatest of all the deceptions the world has yet seen? Mostly it's a failure to learn or remember enough history to realize such things just don't happen in human nature. Perhaps people are prone to believe in these things because they provide justification for continued illusions of peace and prosperity.

Another reason people so easily believe in deception is that the establishment media often promotes these grand deceptions as truth. Most people seem to be all too comfortable to let establishment "experts" do their thinking for them. Mental laziness is also a factor—the failure to ask the key questions. Journalists fail to ask key questions because such questions lead to conclusions their editors have already told them are off-limits.

Ultimately, the cards are stacked against the common person who won't think critically, who doesn't really know history, and who relies on powerful controlled media forces to tell him what to think. But, not having critical thinking skills alone is not necessarily fatal to reaching truth. If a person has developed a refined conscience and *can sense* when something is wrong—even if denied the complete information—he or she can begin the search for better truth, and eventually find it. It is out there, in the alternative media. Perhaps this lack of spiritual perception is at the root of our declining state of reality.

In reality much of the blame must be laid at the feet of those who perpetrate deceptions in the first place, for they know what they are doing. Many people are conditioned to a certain value system that does not include deceit or expendability of human life and cannot conceive that anyone or any group could ascribe to such practices. What's more, their misunderstanding of the reality of Satan frequently hinders their judgment. Sadly, lack of thinking ability can't be easily solved by more education. There many over-educated people who are unable to see what's real in life.

Education is certainly no cure. If filled with errors and incorrect principles, education can actually inhibit one's ability to perceive truth. For example, almost all establishment sources, including education institutions, attack mercilessly any person who believes in conspiracy, and this despite the evidence that conspiracies have always been present in the world since its creation. Even those who observe solid evidence of conspiracy will almost apologize and explain away what they see rather than face the stigma of being labeled a "conspiracy nut-case."

Unfortunately, members of the LDS faith are particularly prone to this kind of denial and refusal to address the core political controversies of our time. Having fought their way out of a persecuted background, they have emerged into the warm sunshine of public acceptance and long for more. However, establishment recognition and praise has its price and the tough truths must be soft peddled and political correctness be praised.

What I admire about Jack Monnett is his willingness to tackle the tough subjects in life, even if the price is high. In this book, he has the courage to sound a warning about evil—not just the common criminal type of evil that plagues individual people, but systematic evil . . . evil that is planned, coordinated, and multi-faceted . . .evil that was specifically prophesied in the *Book of Mormon*.

Indeed the worst kind of evil is not to be found in any single rogue individual. What is much worse is a combination of power, wherein many evil persons unite their efforts under a central guiding hand—a secret combination, if you will. These conspiracies for power have a life that goes beyond the power and wealth of any of its individual members. That is why it has what I call a "generational effect." That is, it keeps growing generation after generation.

The mafia doesn't qualify in this regard. Because it is purely a conspiracy to get gain, its organization ruptures frequently into bloody killings and turf battles. Rarely does one man's power go beyond two generations before his family is eliminated and splits off into a separate branch.

The highest levels of secret combinations are run by Satan himself, and not always uniform in organization and structure. Sometimes competing conspiracies operate, sometimes the organizations morph into innocuous service organizations to mask their real purposes. They often use high ideals and naïve people to front for them. Every tactic is used in order to guard against discovery. Perhaps the most effective of all is to use allies within the top levels of the media to make sure the "conspiracy" word is always treated with derision.

The LDS faith is a great advantage in this world of deception. It's the only church with multiple scriptures warning the Saints to beware of these powerful secret combinations. The *Book of Mormon*, in particular, points out the way they operate, specifically touching upon their ability to use government and judges to provide cover and immunity.

Yet, strangely, most Mormons pay little attention to this threat. Part is because it is disguised and not obvious to the cursory glance. Part is because LDS people want desperately *not to believe* in the evils of government—they might have to do something about it.

But with those *Book of Mormon* warnings comes a grave responsibility to see the danger within and to warn others, lest we be partially responsible for the fall of liberty. No, it's not something you can leave to government, because the modern day Gadianton robbers have fully taken over large parts of government—particularly the illegal dark-side operations of federal agencies. We get a glimpse now and then of these evil operations when good federal officials see something and blow the whistle—which usually lands them in jail.

Jack's work provides just enough details (see Chapter 10) to jolt us into a realization of the scope of illicit activities sponsored by government. I must disabuse you of the temptation to consider each of the samples he cites as merely the work of "rogue government agents." This problem is systemic. The protection of lower level illegal acts comes from higher government officials, not outside agents, mafia criminals or supposed terrorists. Whistleblowers within government consistently complain that their appeals higher up the chain of command are met with outright hostility and career ending threats.

Worse, other officials with a sworn duty to protect whistleblowers are found guilty of direct collusion and foreknowledge of the crimes. They systematically engage in obstruction of the investigation directly and deter a successful prosecution through control of key judges. Again, these are not rogue agents, but a seasoned network of persons operating in collusion across supposedly independent branches of government.

What this book gives you is a glimpse into the bowels of evil operating just below the surface of the "freest country on earth." The author feels, correctly, that it's time to take a serious look at the consequences of continued blindness to this growing and prophesied menace.

Finally, there is a myth floating around that has inhibited many a person from accepting the reality of a modern-day secret combination of power. In essence it states, "Such a huge broad-based conspiracy of power within government would be impossible to control and keep secret—something would leak out if it were true."

As a matter of fact, the last part is true. A lot has leaked out, but the witnesses have been ruthlessly suppressed and the powerful forces we are dealing with have no mean ability to control what gets covered in the mass media. Modern media distorts not so much by outright lies, but by careful and purposeful omissions of key truths that would change the public's perception about many issues.

Second, the implication within the myth is that everyone involved in the conspiracy has a detailed knowledge about the conspiracy and its evil ends. Not so. A well ordered conspiracy uses multiple methods to insure against discovery, even among those who participate:

A) They hire predictable people who will do their bidding with a minimum of justification and explanation. They use a selection process for promotion into the higher ranks that involves compromising key moral principles, so that when they are tasked to do illegal acts, they won't balk.

B) They provide lots of money, perks and positive incentives, many times beyond legal compensation, to keep people loyal and unquestioning. Those who ask "too many questions" or express reluctance get fired.

C) Most agents and employees close to illegal activities see enough to wonder about the legality of what they are doing. They are fed a basic line that, "Yes, there is a power center, but it is benevolent. We have to do things in secret because "the people wouldn't understand." In combination with secrecy provisions, this satisfies most people looking for a way NOT to see evil.

D) When someone does press too hard to see inside the system, they or their family members get "leaned on," or otherwise threatened with any number of unpleasantries. Occasionally, these threats are carried out, and a chilling message gets telegraphed down the line, "This is what happens when you ask too many questions!"

E) Those at the very top echelons, probably numbering less than 100, who do know the whole conspiracy, are vetted through years of loyal service, and absolutely know the powers they are dealing with, and the consequences for betrayal. There have been *no defectors from these top echelons*—the only ones who could actually testify as to the breadth of the conspiracy.

Thus, while we will never have absolute proof of this great conspiracy to take down liberty and national sovereignty, we have enough evidence from hundreds of whistleblowers, many dead and some yet living, to sense that this threat is real and to begin to take effective action.

If after reading this comprehensive work you cannot sense that something is wrong, you will have to await the grand announcements of the Second Coming—when the secret acts of men throughout all the history of the earth will all be revealed. Even those of us who see much of what is going on behind the scenes will be shocked at how much we could not see. But at least we will not have been blind to the problem. That is Jack's goal—to open our eyes, in part, to the gravity of our situation.

Joel Skousen
Publisher, *World Affairs Brief*

Part I

We were warned—

Chapter 1

INTRODUCTION

The power of the Book of Mormon

A host of truths unfold to readers of the *Book of Mormon*. Members of the LDS Church gain a depth of understanding of the atonement of Jesus Christ found in no other standard work of scripture. We are able to visualize the Lord's dealings with people in their historical context over a thousand-year period of time—through righteousness and wickedness. We see prophets and their sacrifices and, unfortunately, the reluctance of people to heed their warnings. The *Book of Mormon* is available to all of the followers of Christ and all are free to ponder its message.

The book in your hands is just that—ponderings on the vitality of the *Book of Mormon* message for this generation. Unless otherwise stated, this book represents a collection of ideas fostered by the American prophets. It is neither a doctrinal statement nor does it portend to speak on behalf of the Church of Jesus Christ of Latter-day Saints. It does, however, insist that the *Book of Mormon* is relevant for today's readers.

There is no question that Moroni directed his comments to our dispensation when he referred to our "awful situation" and the grasp of secret combinations upon the world's population. His remarks are specifically directed to today's readers of the

Book of Mormon—members of the Church of Jesus Christ of Latter-day Saints. Because we are privy to Moroni's writing and have foreknowledge of diabolical schemes to "overthrow the freedom of all lands," we are given specific charges as we "awake to our awful situation."

The Prophets, the scriptures and us

In the coming chapters, we will review scripture, particularly from the *Book of Mormon*, and examine the direction and cautions it has for Latter-day Saints today. Coupled with scripture, we will refer to modern prophets and apostles of our dispensation to help us better understand our responsibilities. Because some of our latter-day duties are perceived as controversial, leaders over the past two decades have spoken in generalities about our responsibilities toward the United States Constitution and maintaining its guaranteed freedoms. They have, however, given particular direction to the saints to become familiar with scriptures, specifically the *Book of Mormon*. Although some may take exception with current church leaders, it is difficult to argue with Mormon or Moroni.

At a time when the saints were more insulated in their Rocky Mountain environment, Church authorities were quite vocal about the role of government and gave specific warnings to Church members. Those warnings and cautions are just as valid for our generation as when they were taught from the pulpit. We will also look at the statements and the reasoning of many of these leaders, together with modern scripture, to more clearly identify current trends and responsibilities. Understanding warnings and consequences of neglect taught by scriptural examples gives Latter-day Saints an edge in safeguarding liberties today.

Our responsibilities to learn and do

Two topics frequently misunderstood by members of the Church of Jesus Christ of Latter-day Saints in today's world are (1) secret combinations and (2) responsibilities to government. Because the specifics of these areas touch close to our everyday lives, both topics are often categorized as controversial and political. As such, they are not generally included in Relief Society, Priesthood or Sunday School class discussions. Consequently, understanding these topics and their affect upon us is sometimes muddy and open to personal interpretation.

We usually read and study by ourselves, therefore, all of us are on different levels of understanding. Our exposure to information—both in quality and quantity—makes us different people. Some have given these topics a great deal of their time while others have neglected them entirely. Combined with a mixed understanding of these issues is their emotional nature. A discussion of political leaders and issues often brings out heated feelings and we find ourselves leaning toward one side of an issue or the other. When we settle on the side we think is best, we tend to take offense with others who share their reasoning of opposing views. Rather than experiencing disharmony in our relationships, it is often easier to say little and move to subjects of more agreement. This is why Hugh Nibley once observed that the Saints "are strangely touchy on controversial issues."

But as uncomfortable as arguments and contention are, they are sometimes necessary to expose us to other views and facts. Although we may desire to "get along" with everyone and "gloss over" differences, it is from our differences that we learn. What a shame it would be if everyone had the same opinions and points of view! And because of the vital place that these topics hold in both Latter-day Saint history and scripture, commandments have been given to read the scriptures and to be involved in learning about government. Both topics are aimed at one primary objective: freedom—the same issue which precipitated the premortal conflict before coming to the earth.

Our knowledge-base is so much broader than the average believer in Jesus Christ. With others we enjoy the *Bible* as a standard work of our Church and we study both the Old and New Testaments—but we find even greater meaning to stories and scriptures contained in them because of modern revelation. Side by side with the *Bible* we study the *Book of Mormon*, the *Doctrine and Covenants* and the *Pearl of Great Price*. In the event that our scripture studies turn stagnant, there are opportunities as never before for members of the Church to read mountains of published works; attend Institute of Religion and BYU Continuing Education classes; discuss scriptures and principles in Sunday classes; and listen to addresses by both local and general leaders.

There is hardly an excuse for ignorance. Although all are not "gospel scholars," there is an expectation that each member of the Church—given sufficient time—knows the essential doctrines of Mormonism: the Godhead; the plan of salvation; the role of the Church; the place of living prophets; and a host of beliefs peculiar to the Church of Jesus Christ of Latter-day Saints.

Forewarnings to Latter-day Saints

It is difficult to maintain a consistent regimen of scripture reading without becoming aware of latter-day warnings. Threats to freedom, the preponderance of secret combinations, and the necessity of righteous government are themes that run throughout modern scripture. President Ezra Taft Benson commented that

> *If you use the scriptures as a guide, you know what the Book of Mormon has to say regarding murderous conspiracies in the last day and how we are to awake to our awful situation today. I find certain elements in the Church do not like to read the Book of*

*Mormon and Doctrine and Covenants: to such, they have too much to
say about freedom.* [1]

According to President Benson, freedom is the major
underlying theme of the *Book of Mormon*. If we read the
scriptures but do not recognize this theme, we have missed a
giant part of its specific message to our dispensation.
Indispensable to our learning is our individual effort to read and
study. To be sure, a certain amount of knowledge can be
absorbed by discussions and classroom attendance; but real
understanding and internalization of doctrine only comes through
diligent reading, studying, and prayer. President Marion G.
Romney, a past-member of the Church's First Presidency, asked
the rhetorical question: "Would you rather drink from the fount
or drink downstream after the animals had walked through and
muddied the water?" Reading the scriptures, he said, was the
fount of knowledge—while books about scriptures and classroom
discussions were merely secondary sources.

The Lord had individual effort in mind in 1832 when he
chastised members of the Church and told them that they were
under condemnation for treating "lightly the things [they had]
received."

> *"And they shall remain under this condemnation until they
> repent and remember the new covenant, even the Book of Mormon
> and the former commandments which I have given them, not only to
> say, but to do according to that which I have written*
> *"That they may bring forth fruit meet for their Father's
> kingdom; otherwise there remaineth a scourge and a judgment to be
> poured out upon the children of Zion."*
> *Doctrine and Covenants 84:54-58*

The "former commandments" were found in the *Doctrine
and Covenants* and were readily accessible to the Saints. More

explicit, the Lord was definite that the *Book of Mormon* was a call to action: "to do according to that which I have written."

While not neglecting the larger knowledge-base of Church members, this book will specifically look at the warnings given to Latter-day Saints in this dispensation that are contained in the *Book of Mormon* and general addresses delivered to the Church. The Nephite prophets filled their book with principles, stories and warnings for latter-day readers—knowing that our generation could learn from their mistakes, their history of intrigue, and their testimonies of the Savior.

The Book of Mormon's "big picture"

Mormon, and more particularly his son Moroni, had a more comprehensive view than the other prophets because of their charge to edit and condense all the previous records. Through their abridgement of the several plates, they viewed what we might term today "the big picture." This included not only witnessing the destruction of their own people but acquainting themselves with the historical antecedents, the prophecies, and the step-by-step decline of the Nephite nation. Although there is much to learn from an entire study of the *Book of Mormon*, it is the big picture—the direction of the commentaries and warnings written by the compilers of the book—that will occupy the majority of our space.

The Book of Mormon is about us

Perhaps there is no more poignant expression used by the prophets than Moroni's admonition: "When you shall see these things come among you that ye shall awake to a sense of your awful situation."[2] There is no question that he is talking to readers of the *Book of Mormon* in the latter days and is giving us the benefit of his insight and experience. Added to his own testimony of the decline and fall of the Nephite people is his reason for including the warning into his abridgement—that God commanded him to share his experiences and to alert readers to their peril.[3]

Moroni described the "awful situation" while he was finishing his father's book. Although his comments are found throughout the *Book of Mormon*, none is more riveting than his statement "I speak unto you as if ye were present, and yet ye are not, but behold, Jesus Christ hath shown you unto me, and I know your doing."[4] What he saw was alarming—but accurate!

The things he saw and warned us about are surprising to some—but they shouldn't be. Even though many of the calamities and "hidden things of darkness" that Moroni and others saw that are scheduled for our generation are generally unknown, we have been commanded to make ourselves aware of them. Modern revelation is careful to emphasize that we also are responsible to know and act upon the perils of our time.

"Truth" is one of the powerful subjects treated in Section 93 of the *Doctrine & Covenants*. In that section, Latter-day Saints are instructed that Christ is the Spirit of Truth—that he comprehends all truth, being a "knowledge of things as they are, and as they were, and as they are to come."[5] Truth, we find, is the essence of agency; that being aware of truth a person is able to make correct decisions. Then as the section draws to a close, the four key leaders of the Church—the three members of the First Presidency and the Presiding Bishop—are all chastised by the Lord because they failed to keep the commandment "to bring up [our] children in light and truth."[6] Not coincidently, the Lord ends this section with an admonition ". . . to obtain a knowledge of history, and of countries, and of kingdoms, of laws of God and man, and all this for the salvation of Zion."[7]

Simply put, the Lord told his saints that they needed to be aware of history and of world events. This is a reiteration of a revelation given just four months earlier wherein he commanded

the Church to "teach one another the doctrine of the kingdom."[8]
So that there would be no mistake about what constituted the
"doctrine of the kingdom," he outlined it in *Doctrine &
Covenants* 88:78-79.   In one complete sentence, following the
enumeration of spiritual and gospel subjects, he went on to tell
the saints to learn of ". . . things which are at home, things which
are abroad; the wars and the perplexities of the nations, and the
judgments which are on the land; and a knowledge also of
countries and of kingdoms—" In today's jargon, the Lord would
have commanded us to be aware of domestic and foreign
policies, international concerns, and relentless wars.   As he
defined "truth" in section 93, he said, "And whatsoever is more
or less than this is the spirit of that wicked one who was a liar
from the beginning."[9]   Placing current domestic and foreign
policies side-by-side with the U.S. Constitution, he taught us the
same principle: ". . . whatsoever is more or less than this, cometh
of evil."[10]

Thus, through the study of the backgrounds and events
making up today's world, we better understand Moroni's
warnings to our generation.   Wars, economic policies, homeland
security, peacekeeping missions, governmental policies, and
secret combinations all converge into what Moroni saw.

With national and international chaos, he also saw the
degraded state of the "natural man."   He saw secret
combinations; defiled churches lifted up in pride; great
pollutions; murder, robbing, lying, deception, whoredoms, and all
manner of abominations.   To those who would read the *Book of
Mormon*—members of the Church—he was even more definite.
He wrote that "there are none save a few only who do not lift
themselves up in the pride of their hearts."   His allusions to pride
are written in general terms so he told us how we would
recognize their manifestation in our lives.   He said that we, just as
in *Book of Mormon* times, would "wear very fine apparel."   To

that he may have added other identifiers such as driving expensive automobiles, living in large and spacious homes, and other signs of wealth that are prevalent today. He also described character traits of which we are familiar such as being caught up in envy, strife, malice, persecution, and "all manner of iniquities." He told us that just as in Jacob's time[11] our priorities for wealth would be askew and instead of using our surplus for aid to the poor and those truly in need, we would "love money and [our] substance, and [our] fine apparel."[12]

Book of Mormon warnings to latter-day readers are abundant. Those same concerns are shared today by leaders and prophets of this dispensation. Warnings are found throughout general conference addresses, in Church magazines, and in virtually all directives emanating from the Church. Warnings are given to us because Latter-day Saints are susceptible—just as others are—to the "awful situation" referred to by Moroni. Our day is one of marital infidelity; pornography; dishonesty; materialism; and an abundance of "worldly wisdom" lacking the spirit of God.

We live in a world abounding in sin. Describing a particularly wicked time in world history, Moses epitomized Noah's generation as a time in which "every man was lifted up in the imagination of the thoughts of his heart, being only evil continually."[13] Bringing that time closer to us, President Spencer W. Kimball wrote that

> *. . . when I review the performance of this people in comparison with what is expected, I am appalled and frightened. . . . we feel that truly we are living in conditions similar to those in the days of Noah before the flood.*[14]

Mormon, Moroni and other prophets saw all of this and knew that Satan would have tremendous power in our generation. Specifically, they compiled the *Book of Mormon* for us—to strengthen our testimonies of the Savior's atonement; to bring their descendants to Christ; and to warn their readers about severe latter-day perils.

Chapter 1—Endnotes

1   Ezra Taft Benson, *Teachings of Ezra Taft Benson*, Bookcraft: Salt Lake City. 1988. p. 81.

2   Ether 8:24

3   Ether 8:21, 26

4   Mormon 8:35

5   *Doctrine & Covenants* 93:24

6   *Doctrine & Covenants* 93:40-50

7   *Doctrine & Covenants* 93:53

8   *Doctrine & Covenants* 88:77

9   *Doctrine & Covenants* 93:25

10 *Doctrine & Covenants* 98:7

11 Jacob 2:12-20

12 Mormon 8:37-39

13 Moses 8:22

14 Spencer W. Kimball, "The False Gods We Worship," *Ensign*: June, 1976. p. 3.

Chapter 2

LOOKING AT MORONI'S WARNING

Wherefore, O ye Gentiles, it is wisdom in God that these things should be shown unto you, that thereby ye may repent of your sins, and suffer not that these murderous combinations shall get above you, which are built up to get power and gain—and the work, yea, even the work of destruction come upon you, yea, even the sword of the justice of the Eternal God shall fall upon you, to your overthrow and destruction, if ye shall suffer these things to be.

Wherefore, the Lord commandeth you, when ye shall see these things come among you that ye shall awake to a sense of your awful situation, because of this secret combination which shall be among you; or wo be unto it, because of the blood of them who have been slain; for they cry from the dust for vengeance upon it, and also upon those who built it up. For it cometh to pass that whoso buildeth it up seeketh to overthrow the freedom of all lands, nations, and countries; and it bringeth to pass the destruction of all people, for it is built up by the devil, who is the father of all lies . . .

Ether 8:23-25

What were Moroni's concerns for our generation?

Moroni's warning is for us. Although members of the Church of Jesus Christ of Latter-day Saints share the blessings of the House of Israel through adoption into Abraham's posterity,[1] we in the United States of America and other non-Semite countries belong to nations of Gentiles. Moroni's way of directing his words to our generation is to call us "Gentiles." We are the object of his concern.

That concern for the latter-day followers of Jesus Christ came to the forefront during Moroni's abridgement of the 24 gold plates found by the people of Limhi at the time of Mosiah. These plates told the story of the Jaredites—a people favored by the Lord and led to the American continent under the direction of a prophet. The Book of Ether is an extremely condensed record of the Jaredite nation but was useful to Moroni to reinforce the lessons of the Nephite record. Because of the parallel experiences of the descendants of Lehi with secret combinations, Moroni was able to emphasize both their power and their pervasiveness in the *Book of Mormon* record. Only a minute portion of Ether's work is included in today's *Book of Mormon*—less that a hundredth part—so it stands to reason that Moroni sifted and gleaned only the most vital sections of Ether's writings for today's readers.[2]

Setting the stage

Using the eighth chapter of Ether to prepare readers for his warning, Moroni included an account of Jared (not to be confused with the original Jared who led the Jaredites) who rebelled against his father King Omer. Unsuccessful in his first attempt to overthrow his father, Jared's daughter reminded him of the power of conspiracy and about ancient writings that were possessed by the Jaredites of "secret plans [to] obtain kingdoms and great glory."[3] Jared's daughter (we are never given her name) suggested that she could dance for Akish, evidently a man possessing some leadership, and entice him to organize a "secret combination." In her Salome-like approach, Akish desired to wed her—Jared only agreeing to her marriage after Akish agreed to deliver the head of his father, King Omer.

After telling the general story of Jared's intrigue, Moroni was quite explicit about the conspiracy—the secret combination—that arose as a result of the agreement between Jared and Akish. Not only did he discuss the terminal effect of the combination ("They have caused the destruction of this people of whom I am now speaking, and also the destruction of the people of Nephi"[4]) but just as importantly, he exposed the satanic origin of such combinations.

Akish gathered a body of men around him to join in fulfilling Jared's wish. With their leader, the participants swore upon their lives that they would never divulge the secrecy and anonymity of their plot and performed a series of oaths administered by Akish. These were not typical pledges but were particular covenants "handed down from Cain," and "were kept up by the power of the devil."[5]

Moroni saw no need to write the oaths for latter-day readers; however, we get a fairly clear idea of their severity in Moses' account of Cain and Abel. In the exchange with Satan prior to slaying Abel we read

> *And Satan said unto Cain: Swear unto me by thy throat, and if thou tell it you shalt die; and swear thy brethren by their heads, and by the living God, that they tell it not; for if they tell it, they shall surely die; and this that thy father may not know it; and this day I will deliver thy brother Abel into thy hands.*[6]

Although not including the explicit oaths of the Akish combination or those of his successors, Moroni leaves the topic on the chilling note that "it hath been made known unto me that they are had among all people."[7] Simply put, their existence is as prevalent today as in *Book of Mormon* times.

Because of their pervasiveness throughout history, it is instructive to read the contemporary accounts of *Book of Mormon* prophets about secret combinations. Their views of events as they transpired as well as the overview accounts by Mormon and Moroni leave little doubt of the impact of the combinations upon Nephite life. Foreshadowing problems in the promised land, just fifty years after leaving Jerusalem, the prophet Jacob described the role of Satan—that he "stirreth up the children of men unto secret combinations of murder and all manner of secret works of darkness."[8]

It was understood by the first Nephites that much of Satan's influence through his followers on earth would come through secret groups. Later, when Nephi recounted his vision of the latter-days and described the various plights of those who would occupy the promised land in our dispensation, he told his readers that "there are also secret combinations, even as in times of old, according to the combinations of the devil."[9] Thus Nephi, with both Mormon and Moroni, saw us—the latter-day inhabitants of their land—and warned us of the same things. Of the many things they saw, their alarm of secret combinations in our generation was one that stood at the forefront.

For the first several hundred years after their arrival, the land of promise was free of Satanic combinations. During the days of King Mosiah, when the city of Zarahemla was founded, 24 gold plates that held the record of the Jaradites were discovered by the Nephites. Mosiah, who was also a seer, translated the record but little was said by the prophets about the wickedness of the Jaradites until Alma gave specific instructions to his son Helaman about the Jaradite records.

Alma explained that the Jaradite history was valuable and that it would be beneficial to the Nephites to know "the secret works of those people who have been destroyed." Helaman was told to tell his people about "all their murders, and robbings, and their plunderings, and all their wickedness and abominations"[10] so that the Nephites would understand that the Lord punishes those who engage in such wickedness—that those involved in future combinations, just as the Jaradites, would also be destroyed.

In telling the Nephites about the Jaradites, Alma didn't want Helaman to give too much information. Just as Moroni would write later in the book of Ether, Alma warned Helaman not to divulge "their oaths, agreements in their secret abominations; yea, and all their signs and wonders." This was done for the benefit of the Nephites "lest peradventure they should fall into darkness and also be destroyed."[11] Thus it was that Helaman and future prophets kept the "secret plans of their oaths and their covenants from [the Nephites} and only their wickedness and their murders and their abominations" were made known. As from most bad examples, the story of the fall of the Jaradite nation proved to be a teaching tool for the Nephites.

The primary reason for inclusion into the *Book of Mormon* and into Helaman's teachings was simply to "teach [the Nephites} to abhor such wickedness and abominations and murders" and to clearly show that the Jaradites "were destroyed on account of their wickedness and abominations and their murders."[12]

True to his charge, Helaman taught the Nephites and his future readers about secret combinations.[13] The occasion for this instruction came when Paanchi sought to be the chief judge over the Nephites. Following a popular election wherein he lost his bid, Paanchi prepared to "flatter away those people to rise up in rebellion against their brethren." For his treasonous designs, he was tried and condemned to death. The followers of Paanchi felt that an injustice had happened and, rather than accepting the new chief judge, appointed an unprincipled man named Kishkumen to murder the new chief judge.

As far as we can tell, Kishkumen was the first to introduce a secret combination into the Nephite society. He returned to those who had commissioned him "and they all entered into a covenant, yea, swearing by their everlasting Maker, that they would tell no man that Kishkumen had murdered Pahoran."[14] After swearing their blood-oaths to each other, "Kishkumen and his band, who had covenanted with him, did mingle themselves among the people, in a manner that they could not be found."[15]

Through Kishkumen, the conspiracy that would eventually destroy the Nephite civilization took root. Those who knew Kishkumen's guilt had sworn with their lives that they would be true to their secret knowledge. Mingling and infiltrating through the Nephite culture, no particular suspicion was placed on them and, should there be questions, excuses and alibis were set forth by others of the band.

Following Pahoran's assassination, Helaman was elected to fill the office of the chief judge of the land. Still plotting to obtain the leadership, Kiskumen now determined to also kill Helaman. It was at this time that he united with a man named Gadianton "who was exceedingly expert in many words, and also in his craft, to carry on the secret work of murder and of robbery; therefore he became the leader of the band of Kishkumen."[16] Our *Book of Mormon* account explains that Kishkumen failed in his attempt to take Helaman's life and, instead, lost his own life. With Kishkumen's death, Gadianton fled with his followers and, from this juncture, became known in the Nephite record as the Gadianton Robbers.   Moroni added his perspective to the separation of Gadianton from the Nephites:

> *And behold, in the end of this book ye shall see that this Gadianton did prove the overthrow, yea, almost the entire destruction of the people of Nephi.*[17]

How could a group of robbers have destroyed the mighty Nephite civilization? In fact, don't we normally credit the Lamanite civilization with bringing down the Nephites?

The final wars certainly pitted the Nephites against the Lamanites; but those wars came at a time when the Nephites were already weakened and demoralized from within. The erosion of the Nephite nation was, for the most part, accomplished through the insidious infiltration of the Gadiantons into the very fabric of the Nephite culture. Because it was important for us to understand how this subversion could occur— so that we could recognize similar events in the latter-days— Helaman detailed the movements and the inroads of the secret combination.

Because of the secret nature of the Gadianton Robbers and their ability to lie and defend one another, it took awhile before the Nephites recognized that they were a distinct group. Helaman explained that had the secret society been identified before, they would have been destroyed early in their existence; however, they were unknown and thus allowed to grow.[18]

For the next twenty years the Nephites were concerned about everyday affairs: the growth of the Church; the rebelliousness of the Lamanites; and, above all, their personal finances. With ups and downs, it was generally a prosperous time in Nephite history and there was no particular concern about secret combinations. Then, out of nowhere, the chief judge Cezoram was murdered. When his son took his place as the Nephite leader, he also was murdered.

People undoubtedly were astonished at the assassinations but they were also quite surprised to learn about the huge numbers of followers the Gadianton band had acquired. Quietly, the secret society had gained followers among both Nephites and Lamanites and "now there were many, even among the Nephites, of Gadianton's band. "But behold, they were more numerous among the more wicked part of the Lamanites."[19] To rid themselves of the combination, the Lamanites used "every means in their power to destroy them off the face of the earth."[20] At this time, Satan exercised his influence with the Nephites and they joined "with those bands of robbers, and did enter into their covenants and oaths."[21]

How the Gadianton band operated

Helaman explained the essence of the covenants that were entered into on that occasion. Knowing the covenants that were made helps our generation to understand their ability to entice so many into membership into the secret order. The thrust of the covenant was this: "that they should protect and preserve one another in whatsoever difficult circumstances they should be placed, that they should not suffer for their murders, and their plunderings, and their stealings."[22]

Imagine! They could commit any acts they desired to acquire anything they wanted, and be beyond the reach of the law. How could they get away with this? Those that were not members of the conspiracy could not identify those who were a part of it, thus the subversive group could work in secret. It was impossible to know whether a witness was an honest person "covering" for a suspected person or whether it was another Gadianton. Even more disturbing and frustrating to the organized Nephite society was that the Gadiantons "did obtain the sole management of the government."[23]

In a situation where wicked persons were rewarded and righteous persons were plundered, how easy it was for the Nephites to drop their values and partake in the sins of the Gadiantons! It was in this manner that the Gadianton robbers "seduced the more part of the righteous until they had come down to believe in their works and partake of their spoils, and to join with them in their secret murders and combinations."[24]

Reading the effectiveness of the Gadianton band, a reader might postulate that there were very clever men who devised the schemes employed by the secret society. The leaders although undoubtedly clever, however, had little to do with the power of the group. Instead, Mormon wrote that Gadianton received his inspiration from "that same being who did entice our first parents to partake of the forbidden fruit."[25]

> *Yea, it is that same being who put it into the heart of Gadianton to still carry on the work of darkness, and of secret murder; and he has brought it forth from the beginning of man even down to this time.*
>
> *And behold, it is he who is the author of all sin. And behold, he doth carry on his works of darkness and secret murder, and doth hand down their plots, and their oaths, and their covenants, and their plans of awful wickedness, from generation to generation . . . .* [26]

Throughout the *Book of Mormon* we read that there were three great inducements for people to align themselves with the Gadianton secret combination: (1) power; (2) gain; and (3) freedom from punishment for their crimes.

The Gadianton robbers were a type of future Satanic control

When Alma had originally explained the secret combination of the Jaradites to Helaman, he also prophesied of its future growth and of its eventual destruction. Alma said that just as the Jaradite civilization had been destroyed, other nations that upheld secret combinations would suffer the same fate; but, that the Lord would give them all the opportunities possible to repent. Failing to repent, when these societies were "ripe in their iniquities" they would be met with destruction. A particularly interesting part of Alma's unfolding of Satan's work to Helaman in chapter 37 of his book also contains a reference to a future prophet:

> *(23) And the Lord said: I will prepare unto my servant Gazelem, a stone, which will shine forth in darkness unto light, that I may discover unto them the works of their brethren, yea, their secret*

works, their works of darkness, and their wickedness and abominations.

(24) And now my son, these interpreters were prepared that the word of God might be fulfilled, which he spake, saying:

(25) I will bring forth out of darkness unto light all their secret works and their abominations; and except they repent I will destroy them from off the face of the earth; and I will bring to light all their secrets and abominations, unto every nation that shall hereafter possess the land.

Gazelem, a future prophet possessing the interpreters—the urim and thummim—would expose the secrets and abominations of the secret combinations to future generations living in the promised land. The only other reference to this prophet is found in *Doctrine and Covenants* 78:9, a scripture originally given to the Church at a time when leaders needed to shield their identities and used other names. In this scripture, Joseph Smith was known as Gazelem—a fitting title because of his latter-day revelations concerning Satan's employment of secret combinations.

Therefore, all of the *Book of Mormon* prophets who discussed the disruptions and lawlessness of secret combinations during their particular administrations (Nephi, Alma, Helaman, Mormon and Moroni) simultaneously gave warnings to future readers of their records concerning the on-going role that would be played by the same oathbound groups. It is difficult to study the precepts of the *Book of Mormon* without arriving at this singular conclusion: that the Nephite prophets saw our period in history and saw that the same Satanic groups that caused their demise were actively using the same secret means to overthrow today's civilizations.

As this book progresses, unmistakable evidences of modern-day Gadiantanism will be presented. The era and government structure is removed from the ancient American examples; but the inducements and apparent success of the contemporary secret combination is as complete and as devastating. The Nephite prophets were right.

Today the term "secret combination" appears to be a term peculiar to the *Book of Mormon*, but it was clearly understood to early readers and during the formative years of the Church. In fact, the first definition of "combination" in *Webster's* 1828 dictionary includes the word "conspiracy." As evidence these combinations were on-going, eight months following the Church's organization the Lord referred to a plot against Joseph Smith. The plot, he said, was hatched in "secret chambers to bring to pass even your destruction." The danger, Joseph was told, was because the enemy was combined.[27]

The enemy being combined—or a combination of enemies—is the root of "secret combinations." If we have a known enemy, we know with whom we are dealing and may act accordingly. Multiple enemies who have made pacts with one-another in secret, however, are much more threatening and subversive. Added to the cloak of secrecy and unknown participants is the personal oversight of the author of the secret combination himself—Satan who controls and manages secrecy and loyalty through a system of blood oaths.

God's wisdom in revealing nature of secret combinations

Prefacing his warning, Moroni said that "It is wisdom in God that these things should be shown unto you that thereby you may repent of your sins." God's wisdom, his omniscience, dictates that we should know about the murderous conspiracies of the Jaradites and Nephites—and should know that the same conspiracies exist today. One asks, "Why?" "What is so important about these secret combinations or societies that I should know about them?" Many, in fact, have simply chosen to

ignore them because of their "political" or controversial nature—
but that approach is in direct conflict with God's wisdom.

As Moroni reviewed the secret combination that led to the
destruction of the Jaradites, he said that God's primary reason for
wanting readers to know about Satan's secret program is so that
we may repent of our sins. Why? Because we are members of
satanic societies? Probably not. Because we might allow
ourselves to become influenced or manipulated by them? That is
a definite possibility—but is that really a sin? God said, "Yes!"

How blissful life would be if we never suspected
individuals, organizations, or nations of acting with ulterior
motives. Blissful ignorance, though, is antagonistic to our
Heavenly Father's role for Latter-day Saints. An angel appeared
to King Benjamin and commanded him to tell the Nephites and
readers of the *Book of Mormon* that unless a person yields to the
Holy Spirit "the natural man is an enemy to God."[28] A further
latter-day warning reads that "it is the nature and disposition of
almost all men, as soon as they get a little authority, as they
suppose, they will immediately begin to exercise unrighteous
dominion."[29] Thus, human nature possesses some inherent
defects that are contrary to the Lord's program. God does not
intend that you and I pass through life with the acceptance and
gullibility of a Pollyanna. In fact, the Lord's counsel has been to
"be wise as serpents,"[30] and to seek "the word of knowledge, that
all may be taught to be wise and to have knowledge."[31]

Knowledge that we need

Adding to our knowledge, Moroni and other prophets
succinctly outlined the latter-day problem:

WHAT: Satan's plan to destroy freedom.
WHO: Oath-bound individuals who have entered into various
      combinations to uphold Satan's plan.

WHY: To overthrow the Lord's plan of agency and to control the posterity of Adam.
HOW: Through oaths and promises of power, gain, and immunity from legal consequences.
WHERE: Among all people—a world-wide effort of control generally accomplished through governments.

Moroni taught that the knowledge of secret societies existing for the sole advantage of power and gain will help us to repent of our sins. What sins? A primary sin of which we need to repent is that of allowing ourselves to be deceived. In fact, some might say that this sin also includes "willful disobedience"—the intentional ignorance of Satanic manipulation in economic, social and government affairs. Why would a person willfully ignore such interference? Let's look at reasons given for noninvolvement:

My stewardship is to my family; to provide for them and nurture them. That is a full-time responsibility and leaves little time for anything else.

We elect politicians to take care of major economic and social issues. They are in a position to know much more than I do. If I try to get involved, I'll just be in their way.

I stay in touch with newspapers and television news. If my elected representatives don't represent my views on issues, I will not cast my ballot for them in the next election.

These reasons are generally given by Latter-day Saints for exercising minimal involvement in affairs in which Satan's hosts are most involved. However, when Moroni said that gaining a knowledge of secret combinations "that thereby [we] may repent of [our] sins and suffer not that these murderous combinations shall get above [us},"[32] he implied that the reasons listed for inaction were insufficient. Instead, he taught that knowledge of the secret groups and their secret activities would keep us from being manipulated because we would "suffer not" that they would "get above" us.

The Lord wants us to understand and use this principle in our decision-making—to pray to discern motivations and the impact of decisions. Some may assume that "all is well in Zion" and that our "choice land above all other lands" is truth's standard-bearer to the world; however, as truth's standard-bearer we are given the grave charge to teach only truth. We cannot stand, even inadvertently, behind Satan's plan. President Ezra Taft Benson made the bold statement that "It is from within the Church that the greatest hindrance comes. And so it seems, it has been. Now the question arises, will we stick with the kingdom and can we avoid being deceived?"[33] What an indictment!

Throughout the scriptures prophets have referred to the power of Satan and his minions. Knowing that prophets receive divine direction for their followers, we can make literal assumptions that (1) Satan is real, and that (2) Satan uses people and organizations to further his purposes on the earth and to frustrate those who desire to follow the Lord. In doing this, he is not a novice who simply incorporates the work of a few bad or rogue elements into government and other decision-making bodies. Instead, he infiltrates and monopolizes entire systems. Is he successful? The Lord said that "if possible [he] shall deceive the very elect."[34]

Satan's plan is covert. Instead of openness, he revels in "hidden things of darkness" and in "secret chambers." Moroni wrote that it was "wisdom in God that these things should be shown unto you" because we might miss them unless we were specifically looking for them. Satan's plan of deceit is to teach that (1) God doesn't exist; (2) only "conspiracy nuts" look for plotting and ulterior motives against others; and (3) in reality, "all is well in Zion" and there is little need to be watchful or critical of the behavior of others. President Benson was explicit about attitudes within the Church that promote Satan's deception:

> *Satan is anxious to neutralize the inspired counsel of the prophet and keep the priesthood off balance, ineffective, and inert in the fight for freedom. He does this through diverse means including the use of perverse reasoning. He will argue, 'There is no need to get involved in the fight for freedom—all you need to do is to live the gospel.' Of course, this is a contradiction because we cannot fully live the gospel and not be involved.*[35]

Suffer not!

In Moroni's caution to "suffer not that these murderous combinations shall get above" us, we need to understand his vocabulary. "Suffer not" means literally "not to tolerate" and places both responsibility and accountability on his readers to stop the influence of Satanic combinations. This charge parallels verse 22 of his warning wherein he said that nations that "uphold" these organizations would be destroyed. "Suffer not?" "Uphold?" When have we ever willingly allowed such conspiracies to be a part of our lives? Overtly we have most likely done nothing to promote their being. Unwittingly, on the other hand, we may have upheld their existence and thus contributing to the power of secret groups. This is why Moroni's first warning told us that they were real and included their overall plan. Having knowledge that secret combinations do exist and are a part of our culture, we can begin to restrict and prohibit their advancement.

Both a military leader and a prophet, Moroni explained that the primary manifestation of subversive organizations was governmental. In *Book of Mormon* times, judgment seats were particularly susceptible to combination control thereby causing government chaos. Nephi, the religious leader following Helaman earlier wrote that the "Gadianton robbers filled the judgment-seats—having usurped the power and authority of the land."[36] This brought disastrous results to Nephite society.

> *Condemning the righteous because of their righteousness; letting the guilty and the wicked go unpunished because of their money; and moreover to be held in office at the head of government, to rule and do according to their wills, that they might get gain and glory of the world, and, moreover, that they might more easily commit adultery, and steal, and kill, and do according to their own wills—*[37]

And, as awful as the control of the secret combination upon the Nephites was, Moroni's warning also included the secret end goal which was the "overthrow of the freedom of all lands, nations and countries." The scope of Satanic control, according to the prophets, was virtually unlimited within the planet. Yet, some say that the governments in most lands—and particularly the United States of America—are democratic. People in their lands are the decision-makers, not powerful secret combinations. However, because we cast votes in a representative democracy, perhaps, after all, we are those who "suffer" "murderous combinations" to rule and "uphold" them in their nefarious activities.

That makes us, as participants in elections and representative government, accountable for our knowledge. And, of course, knowledge that such secret organizations exist is not sufficient in itself, but it is prerequisite to understanding their plans and goals. Any understanding that we have personally acquired has been individually sought, prayed for, and acted upon. Therefore, to carry out Moroni's charge, to "suffer not that these murderous combinations shall get above you" we must first know of their existence. It was President Benson who called the Saints' attention to the fact that a person lacking knowledge will also lack leadership in fulfilling Moroni's challenge.

> *An inferiority complex which people feel when they are not informed is a serious problem. They dare not make a decision on these vital issues so they let others think for them; then they stumble around in the middle trying to avoid being controversial and get hit by traffic going both ways. Each has a part in this struggle. We chose the right side in the War in Heaven—be on the right side here.*[38]

With a similar message, Apostle John A. Widtsoe cautioned, that many the world's problems could be laid at the feet of those who were neither cold nor hot, but "who always follow the line of least resistance, whose timid hearts flutter at taking sides." He pleaded with Latter-day Saints to remember the great heavenly councils and reminded them that just as there could be no neutrality there, "on earth there can be no neutrality."[39]

The sin of silence

As damaging as neutrality is the sin of silence—to say and do nothing. To a large extent, this is an attitude externally fostered upon us by today's society. "Who am I to disagree?" "So many experts express themselves in a particular direction— who am I to go counter to their wisdom?" This brings to mind the Lord's rebuke against those who fail to speak up: "With some I am not well pleased for they will not open their mouths . . . Wo unto such for mine anger is kindled against them."[40] Dr. Hugh Nibley commented on this attitude among Church members:

> *Many have noted the strong tendency of Latter-day Saints to avoid making waves. They seem strangely touchy on controversial issues. This begets an extreme lack of candor among the saints, which in turn is supported by a new doctrine according to which we have a prophet at our head who relieves us of all responsibility for seeking knowledge beyond a certain point, making decisions or taking action on our own.*[41]

Instead of waiting for direction, the role of Latter-day Saints is to take action—to act rather than to be acted upon. Our charge is to be "anxiously engaged in a good cause and do many things of [our] own free will." If we fail to do this, we are told that "he that is compelled in all things the same is a slothful and not a wise servant" and further, that if we wait to be commanded to do a certain thing—and then go about it half-heartedly—we will be damned.[42] In a subsequent scripture the Lord defined "anxious engagement" as it pertained to Latter-day Saints and secret combinations:

> *Therefore, that we should waste and wear out our lives in bringing to light all the hidden things of darkness, wherein we know them; and they are truly manifest from heaven—*
> *These should be attended to with great earnestness.*
> *Let no man count them as small things; for there is much which lieth in futurity, pertaining to the saints, which depends upon these things.*[43]

What a responsibility! It's not a "small thing" at all but a command pertaining to the future of the saints. Hardly something to be undertaken half-heartedly; instead it is a cause that we should "waste and wear out our lives" in fulfilling.

But, although the Lord describes the fervor with which we should approach our activities in combating evil, he is careful not to outline our course. Rather than telling us explicitly and prescribing a particular program to fight Satan's inroads, the Lord asks us to evaluate our time, our talents, and above all, to seek direction from the Holy Spirit.

A person incorporating the Lord's directives will not be silent.

Knowledge is a key to fulfilling responsibility

There are some, however, who insist that they will be ready as quickly as they are told to follow the direction of the Church and its leaders. In this way they will step forward at the precise moment to save their country from "murderous combinations" and restore the freedoms guaranteed in the Constitution and other founding documents. "Maybe the Lord will never set up a specific Church program for the purpose of saving the Constitution" offered President Benson. Instead, as "the Prophet Joseph Smith declared, it will be the elders of Israel who will step forward to save the Constitution, not the Church."[44] This substantially changes the onus from the Church to the individual. President Benson continued his conference address by chastising the priesthood:

> Brethren, if we had done our homework and were faithful, we could step forward at this time and help save this country. The fact that most of us are unprepared to do it is an indictment we will have to bear.

Combating "murderous combinations" and "suffering" them not to exist includes both knowledge and willingness to act against them. This means that Latter-day Saints are obliged to study current happenings and, as necessary, to raise active opposition to groups that match the criteria outlined by Moroni.

The use of the term "murderous combinations" is particularly odious to many. Taking the lives of others is not only heinous but legally condemned by capital punishment. Yet the combinations spoken of by Moroni were "kept up by the power of the devil . . . to help such as sought power to gain power, and to murder . . . ."[45] In fact, the foundation of the secret combination is murder. Summing up the original pact of Cain with Satan,[46] Cain said, "Truly I am Mahan, the master of this great secret, that I may murder and get gain."[47] "Murderous" is not simply an adjective to arouse detest against secret combinations, but it is their tactical nature. Remember, "murderous" is not only descriptive of taking a single life; it definitely also includes the perpetration of wars and the millions of lives that have been sacrificed because of unholy alliances and secret combinations. This will be explored in greater detail in the chapter entitled *Wars and Rumors of Wars* as well as in Part 2.

Because the quest of secret combinations is "power and gain," it stands to reason that their goal is to get "above" us. "Above" indicates that in a line of authority or chain of command, they maneuver the organization or its players to dictate directives to those on lower levels. Moroni warns that we should "suffer not that these murderous combinations shall get above" us and attain positions of influence and direction. Could that happen?

We know that it did happen throughout the *Book of Mormon* to the degree that it caused both the demise of the Jaredites and the Nephites[48] and, significantly, the caution is given also to Moroni's latter-day readers. In fact, not simply confining the damage of secret combinations to the geographical "promised land," Moroni said that they were "among all people" and "whatsoever nation shall uphold" them, "they shall be destroyed."[49] They were, and are, throughout the world!

The power and presence of secret combinations are the tools used to place them "above" us. This may be in an elected governmental sense, a governmental appointment, or in positions of wealth to influence decisions.

The adversary tempts with power, gain, and immunity from prosecution

But one asks, "Why would anyone knowingly involve himself in such an evil and subversive way?" Moroni tells us that primary motivations of the various combinations are to acquire power and gain, while Helaman details wanton stealing and murder without fear of retribution; thus, the chief reasons for personal involvement in secret combinations are the same— power, gain, and freedom from justice. Returning to the combination established by Akish, Moroni wrote "Now the people of Akish were desirous for gain, even as Akish was desirous for power wherefore the sons of Akish did offer them money."[50] Ultimately, all motivation of the secret combination rests in these three draws.

Methods employed by secret combinations

The power of secret combinations can be easily demonstrated—especially in today's political arena. As we look at men—or groups—labeled A, B, C and D, it is not difficult to see that collusion between them (unknown to the public) can breed power. A, B and C, for example, agree to place D in a position of power. This, of course, is beyond four individuals, and includes constituencies, influence, unpaid favors, applicable research, and rationalization. Once D has achieved power, he is able to place A, B and C in other strategic positions of power. The four from this point are able to work back and forth, either in concert or in feigned disagreement leading to consensus.

Another approach used extensively is the independent third-party endorsement. Financed by those desiring certain results from apparently impartial evaluators, various official sounding institutes, scientific journals, and other "nonbiased" experts give credence to otherwise unacceptable ideas. The collusion is real but unnoticed to the public.

Another ploy engaged by collaborators is known as "the Third Way." When making a decision of profound effect—usually involving freedoms—options are presented for discussion. Simplified, this generally includes a decision that is sustained by the majority of people; a decision that accomplishes the end goal but is void of protected freedoms; and a compromise solution that, while leaving some freedoms intact, effectively eradicates others. Attention is given both to the option that destroys freedoms and to the compromise. Because of the presentations and the "feel good" momentum that the compromise is much better than the alternative that would completely destroy freedoms, the compromise (significantly diminishing freedoms) is selected. For a while people wonder why the obvious decision wasn't made—that which the majority desired and that which would have protected freedoms—but take heart in knowing that it could have been worse.

Therefore, the purpose of "the Third Way" is to create a compromise that will start a process of corruption leading to the original goal. For example, if the goal is state control of the economy, then the target of the planners is to destroy free market capitalism. To accomplish this, government allows private ownership but places it under increasingly constrictive government controls. If failures arise—and they will because of government dictates—the capitalist system is blamed and even more draconian controls are placed into effect.

Similarly, and used at all levels, is the Hegelian Dialectic. The dialectic encourages controlled conflict between what Georg Wilhelm Friedrich Hegel (1770-1831) labeled the Thesis and the Antithesis to produce a Synthesis. According to Hegel, this was the pattern of existing world history and could be used to alter and focus the direction of future world history—an ideal approach for secret combinations. This might be the creation of conflict between races, between those with and those without wealth, between religions, between countries; and between virtually any differences. In the process of conflict, there are those who monetarily benefit (weapons sales, land acquisition, natural resources, etc.) while strong nationalistic and ethnic differences are minimized. The predetermined conclusion then becomes the Synthesis—only to again be used as part of a new dialectic further arriving at more refined predetermined ends.

Many become confused with Hegel's terms, therefore, a more understandable explanation may be: (1) use conflict creation that forces people into a situation that cries out for change; (2) control both sides of the conflict and provide unworkable solutions to discredit the opposition; and (3) when it is apparent that the goal cannot be achieved, force compromises that are inherently unstable so as to create future conflicts.

If we say, for example, that a goal of the secret combination is the condensation of humanity into a one-world government with as little distinction in attitudes as possible, the Hegelian Dialectic is a useful tool. By manufacturing contention between the thesis and the antithesis through "managed conflict," the result is a synthesis or a compromise with the values and identities of each being less defined. Thus, the United States and Russia may begin as a thesis and an antithesis—likewise, others may be Communism and Capitalism; the United States and Mexican-Americans; Blacks and Anglo-Saxons; and virtually any other set of groups that could be manipulated through political action or media into conflict.

Those who seek to build up combinations of this magnitude, have as their goal "to overthrow the freedom of all lands; nations, and countries." In the process of overthrowing freedom, Moroni said, the secret combination would "bring to pass the destruction of all people." This conspiracy against mankind was what President Woodrow Wilson had reference to when he said:

> *Some of the biggest men in the United States, in the field of commerce and manufacture, are afraid of somebody, are afraid of something. They know that there is a power somewhere so organized, so subtle, so watchful, so interlocked, so complete, so pervasive, that they had better not speak above their breath when they speak in condemnation of it.*[51]

As the reader will observe in later pages, Woodrow Wilson spoke from first-hand knowledge. In fact, wasn't his a fairly common reaction that many of us have experienced? Have we found ourselves saying, "How could this have happened by itself? Is there some collusion—some powerful force in the background making decisions? Hence the introductory quotation given at the beginning of this book by Franklin Delano Roosevelt: "In politics nothing happens by accident. If it happens, you can bet it was planned that way."

Power, gain, and immunity from prosecution are the forces driving secret combinations. "Power" denotes that its possessor has power over another—just as "gain" denotes that incoming surplus comes at the expense of another. And, just as members of the Gadianton band were free from punishment because of their control of Nephite judges, those in secret combinations today are generally immune from prosecution. The invidious society engendered by these combinations and the wanton destruction of God's children as a result of their activities caused Moroni to write that "even the work of destruction come upon you, yea, even the sword of the justice of the Eternal God shall fall upon you, to your overthrow and destruction if ye shall suffer these things to be."

The penalty for allowing secret combinations to exist

Those directly participating in secret combinations at the highest level (not to be confused with those working ignorantly under their direction) are oathbound to Satan. Just as Cain compacted with the devil, they have made a conscious decision to follow Satan. Those who uphold the combinations and suffer them to exist, however, are also held under severe condemnation. In Moroni's words, we are in line for "overthrow and destruction" because "the sword of justice of the Eternal God" will come down upon us if we "suffer these things to be." How can God hold us accountable for the spread and power of secret combinations? What is our responsibility?

The year 2005 saw a request from President Gordon B. Hinckley to read the *Book of Mormon*. In fact, as a Church we have always been commanded to read and study the scriptures— but 2005 saw particular emphasis. Along with the good, solid doctrine of the Church, the *Book of Mormon* contains the methods and the warnings about secret combinations from the Nephite prophets. Presidents, prophets and apostles have not only spoken about our responsibilities but they have encouraged members of the Church to go to writings of past prophets and scripture to more fully understand their duties. In 1966, a particularly direct statement was issued to the membership of the Church by President David O. McKay in the April General Conference. Speaking of the threat of Communism and secret combinations he offered the following admonition:

> *We therefore commend and encourage every person and every group who is sincerely seeking to study Constitutional principles and awaken a sleeping and apathetic people to the alarming conditions that are rapidly advancing about us. We wish all of our citizens throughout the land were participating in some type of organized self-education in order that they could better appreciate what is happening and know what they can do about it.*[52]

There is really little excuse for active Latter-day Saints not to understand their responsibilities regarding evil generally and secret combinations specifically.   Although all scriptures reference them, the *Book of Mormon* is the most direct.

Awakening to our awful situation

"Wherefore, the lord commandeth you when ye see these things come among you that ye shall awake to a sense of your awful situation because of this secret combination which shall be among you" is wording that is difficult to misunderstand. Reviewing the list of commandments given to the Saints in the Latter-days, this appears to be one of the most explicit with the sharpest consequences.   Moroni's previous verse warned of the negligence of unmasking secret combinations and allowing them to get "above" us. If guilty, he said that we would pay the price: "the sword of justice of the eternal God to fall upon [us]."

Moroni elsewhere stated that he saw us and the world in which we currently live—"Jesus Christ hath shown you unto me, and I know your doing"[53] he said. There is no equivocation here. Moroni does not say "if" these things come among you, or they "might" come to pass—instead he writes "*when* ye shall see these things."   They will happen. And when they do and we become cognizant of the bondage we are under (for the subversive goal is to "overthrow the *freedom* of all lands") there will be misery and feelings of helplessness that we haven't known. We will "awake to a sense of our awful situation" and as the *Book of Mormon* and all history teaches, bound by misery and slavery we will unitedly turn to God.

Freedom is the key

The "awakening" *will* come and we *will* witness certain things. They will not spring upon us suddenly, but, instead will be part of a constant theme that has undermined all of world history.   Coupled with all of the predicted evils will come increased deception and rationalizations by both media and government. The realization of our "awful situation" will not be apparent to everyone; but to Latter-day Saints and to those holding strong Christian ideals our awful situation will become more obvious and we will be able to discern our predicament. Earmarks of wickedness will tell us that our society is not right and will point to a larger force or conspiracy moving mankind away from freedom and toward bondage. These are signs. Moroni said that the signs will be universal and will be encroachments on freedoms that simultaneously engender maximum profits and gains for those of the combination. John Taylor taught as early as 1881 that

> *These things are beginning to spread among and permeate the nations of the earth. Do we expect them? Yes. The secret combinations were spoken of by Joseph Smith years and years ago. I have heard him time and time again tell about them, and he stated that when these things began to take place the liberties of this nation would begin to be bartered away.*[54]

Completely in agreement, President Henry D. Moyle of the First Presidency said in 1957, "A safe criterion by which movements political, social or religious can be judged meritoriously is by their impact upon our Godly attribute of free agency."[55] Restricted liberties, agency, freedoms—the power of the individual to act for himself—are all signs that are visible. Some will see such signs and become alarmed while others will be caught up in their own affairs and allow them to pass without giving a great deal of notice. (All is well in Zion!)

Freedom is generally protected by constitutional government. President George Q. Cannon of the First Presidency taught that combinations would "be of a political character, looking to the overthrow of governments and to the introduction of anarchy."[56] Counsel to the Saints has always been to jealously guard freedoms—particularly those freedoms of citizens that are guaranteed by the Constitution and the Bill of Rights. When these rights are curtailed or infringed upon in any way, we may be sure that the source is antagonistic to God's plan. His plan is clearly outlined:

> *The laws and constitution of the people, which I (God) have suffered to be established, and should be maintained for the rights and protection of all flesh, according to just and holy principles. That every man may act in doctrine and principle pertaining to futurity, according to the moral agency which I have given unto him.*[57]

Part Two of this book will deal more explicitly with breeches of constitutional guarantees and concerns that exist in today's world. For our purposes, it is sufficient to understand that our Heavenly Father directly intervened with the documents of the United States—and other countries that patterned constitutions after the United States—to protect the agency of the individual. When inroads are made into agency, they are the efforts of those working against God's plan.

Freedom has many manifestations. It is God-given and restricted to the person; no freedom possessed by one may encroach upon the freedoms or liberties of another. Our thoughts, motives, speech, possessions, and activities are the freedoms God desires us to maintain. Having real freedom during our sojourn on earth allows us to (1) be accountable for our actions; and (2) realize the joy that comes through making correct decisions.

Freedom is a two-edged sword, however, providing both opportunity as well as a forum for mistakes. The opportunities provided by the exercise of agency are limitless and depend only upon our closeness to the Lord's spirit, our imaginations, and our use of time. On the other hand, the open door to mistakes and unwise decisions is frightening to some. With that in mind, Dr.

W. Cleon Skousen once said that one of Satan's greatest tools was freedom. While it is vital for us to use properly in order to return to our Father in Heaven, it is also (at least initially) vital to Satan to entice us to transgress God's laws.

And because there are multitudes who misuse freedoms, they have lost much of their agency. A person who may exercise the right to borrow money may optimistically over-borrow and find himself burdened by debt. A person may desire to "try" habit-forming substances, only to find that he has acquired an addiction. A person exercising agency may indulge in sexual gratification outside the marriage covenant and find life encumbered by unwanted parenthood, sexual disease and unwholesome relationships. A person may decide that laziness is preferable to work and suffer loss of ambition, income and self-worth. The very nature of agency lends itself to both great rewards as well as great abuse.

Tandem with abuse of personal freedoms, there are those who fear freedom as a dangerous thing. Just as Satan's plan in the great premortal council appealed to vast multitudes of spirits—"I will redeem all mankind, that one soul shall not be lost"[58]—there are those today who are fearful of the consequences of poorly used agency. Spearheading fear and distrust of personal decision-making that can lead to unwanted consequences is the combination of which Moroni warned. This generally manifests itself in appeals to let others (often governments) assume decision-making and liabilities. In this scenario, freedoms are often bartered for security—a tactic we witnessed in the Grand Council.

Security often manifests itself as protectionism and is generally considered a very humane gesture. More than at any other time, today's society has fostered protectionism and imposed regulations to insure that people don't make "bad" decisions. Government regulations both regarding personal safety and the right to fail are apparent hallmarks of our society—a striking contrast to earlier generations.

Unfortunately, the various regulations and seemingly benevolent limitations placed on individuals usually encroach agency—the right to self-direction. Reflecting upon the necessity and the vitality of freedom of choice in the eternal plan, it can be seen that frequently our "do-gooder" tendencies inhibit rather than promote the Father's plan of agency.

The Lord established a model for freedom

In the latter-days, the Lord established a model government to protect freedoms—he "suffered" the creation of the Constitution of the United States of America. He said the "the law of the land which is constitutional, supporting that principle of freedom in maintaining rights and privileges, belongs to all mankind, and is justifiable before me."[59] The purpose of the Constitution, then, based upon "just and holy principles" was "for the rights and protection of all flesh."[60]

Lest we come to believe that this is singularly a national document for citizens of the United States of America, we need to focus on the words "all mankind" and "all flesh." Initially, principles of freedom found in the Constitution were given to the United States. Later, as the freedom climate spread, constitutions were drawn throughout the North and South American continents—all mimicking key provisions of liberty found in the United States Constitution of 1789. Likewise, the world environment has tended toward freedom and away from absolute control allowing "all mankind" to participate in varying degrees of freedom.

Recognizing intrusions that have abrogated and usurped agency from individuals is most marked where freedom has been most obvious and written about. Although "the freedoms of all lands, nations and countries" are at stake, Moroni's warning is most obvious to citizens of the United States of America. In their wisdom, the nation's founders itemized individual freedoms in the first ten amendments to the Constitution and labeled them the Bill of Rights. More of this will be found in the subsequent chapter entitled *Abuses to the Constitution and the Intents of its Framers*.

An important scripture to help us grasp the importance of the Constitution and our responsibilities toward it is found in *Doctrine and Covenants* 98: 4-7. It reads:

> *And now, verily I say unto you concerning the laws of the land, it is my will that my people should observe to do all things whatsoever I command them. And the law of the land which is constitutional, supporting that principle of freedom in maintaining rights and privileges, belongs to all mankind, and is justifiable before me. Therefore, I the lord justify you, and your brethren of my church, in befriending that law which is the constitutional law of the land; and as pertaining to law of man, whatsoever is more or less than this cometh of evil.*

Freedom's standard—the United States Constitution

The Lord is explicit about subjecting ourselves to law—but he qualifies law to be that "constitutional law of the land" and states that its intent is to "support that principle of freedom in maintaining rights and privileges." Hence, "befriending" the Constitution; to know and understand its provisions and intents is not merely an obligation, but a *sacred* obligation. Early in the Church's history, members were the targets of several unconstitutional acts: Joseph Smith and other leaders were continually incarcerated illegally; contrary to law, property was confiscated and Saints were ravaged and murdered in Missouri; Joseph and Hyrum Smith were killed while under protective custody; and the Saints were not allowed to practice the tenets of their religion once arriving in the Utah Territory. President John

Taylor, presiding over the Church at a tumultuous time when relations with the federal government were particularly rocky, reiterated our obligation that: "All laws that are proper and correct, and all obligations entered into which are not violate of the Constitution should be kept inviolate." Clarifying this position, he recalled Section 98 of the *Doctrine and Covenants* and further taught: "But if they are violate of the Constitution, then the compact between the rulers and the ruled is broken and the obligation ceases to be binding."[61]

Earlier Joseph F. Smith, later to become the Church's sixth president, made a similar statement:

> *The Lord Almighty requires this people to observe the laws of the land, to be subject to "the powers that be," so far as they abide by the fundamental principles of good government, but he will hold them responsible if they will pass unconstitutional measures and frame unjust and proscriptive laws. . . . If lawmakers have a mind to violate their oath, break their covenants and their faith with the people, and depart from the provisions of the Constitution, where is the law, human or divine, which binds me, as an individual, to outwardly and openly proclaim my acceptance of their acts?*[62]

Early leaders of the Church understood the divinity of the Constitution and recognized its purpose in "supporting that principle of freedom in maintaining rights and privileges." Their concern was that the protections granted and enforced through that document were being eroded in their day and, as time progressed, might become more clouded and abused.

No one speaks against freedom or liberty. Books are written and speeches are given touting freedom as the supreme privilege. America is known as the "land of the free" and countries throughout the earth pattern their constitutions and ideals upon freedom. If freedom, however, is such a popular ideal—why is it so difficult to obtain and to maintain? Liberty and freedom do not just "happen." Instead, the history of freedom is one of revolution, sacrifice, and bloodshed. And after paying such a dire price, why is freedom so difficult to maintain?

The Constitution of the United States is a freedom document. Except in its intent to "support that principle of freedom in maintaining rights and privileges," no general powers were granted. To the contrary, a primary purpose of the Constitution was to strictly limit the power of the federal government. The goal of its framers was to create a system of government that had so many "checks and balances" that inroads of despotism and tyranny would be confounded. Mosiah, in writing his book in the *Book of Mormon* also was concerned about freedom. When the Nephites asked for a king he explained that some kings were good, but in establishing a governmental system, it was best not to place all power in one person. He then suggested a system of judges, both higher and lower, to be chosen by the "voice of the people."[63] In some respects, his "checks and balances" were similar to ours of the United States—a bicameral legislature and representative government chosen by the people.

After some years, insurrections divided the Nephites and their system of government weakened. There were individuals who wanted personal leadership and acclaim and organized their own groups with proposed take-overs. The Gadianton Robbers continued to defy the Nephites and insidiously entered into their government. Freedom was good—but it certainly had its foes.

Attempts to undermine the Constitution

Likewise, freedom has it's foes in America and in other lands where it has been adopted. It would be folly to believe that liberty, once garnered, would be forever safe. Thomas Jefferson coined the phrase, "eternal vigilance is the price of liberty" and, with others of the Founding Fathers, continually warned citizens to treasure and preserve their liberties. Benjamin Franklin was more blunt but perhaps more prophetic. Speaking of the American Constitution, he said

> *I agree to this Constitution . . . and I believe, further, that this is likely to be well administered for a course of years, and can only end in despotism, as other forms have done before it, when the people shall become so corrupted as to need despotic government, being incapable of any other.*[64]

Why was Franklin so sure that the nation could "only end in despotism?" Unfortunately, freedom invites corruption. The Founding Fathers recognized the ideal of liberty, but also realized that there was a fine balance between the freedom to follow one's conscience and complete anarchy. Their ideal of freedom included the unfettering of agency but they also knew that unprincipled men would take advantage of granted freedoms and would endeavor to take control of the constitutional system. It was a pattern since the beginning of time.

Religion's responsibility to constitutional freedom
That was why righteousness and individual morality were so vital to not only the founding of the United States, but to its continuance. *That is why liberty can only function as a popular movement from the bottom up—not dictated from the top down.* Citizens must desire liberty and be willing to pay its price for it to be effective. If imposed on a group or a nation without that desire, the attitude is not one of freedom but one of selfishness. Under such conditions, rather than contributing to the whole in the preservation of freedoms, the pervasive attitude is generally "what's in it for me." In such an environment, government is more easily manipulated for personal ends—specifically, for "power and gain." That's why Franklin went on to say that "Only a virtuous people are capable of freedom. As nations

become corrupt and vicious they have more need of masters."[65] This agreed substantially with John Adams who wrote that

> *Our Constitution was made only for a moral and religious people. It is wholly inadequate to the government of any other.*[66]

Is it any wonder that Jefferson would say that "eternal vigilance is the price of liberty?" Vigilance is what Moroni had in mind when he wrote "suffer not that these murderous combinations shall get above you."

Befriending the Constitution

When the Lord established the Constitution of the United States, he foresaw the dangers inherent in maintaining the outlined rights and the spirit of the document. With his foreknowledge, he told us two ways that we should demonstrate our vigilance to preserve our freedoms. He instructed us (1) to "befriend that law which is the constitutional law of the land" because "whatsoever is more or less than this cometh of evil;" and (2) that "honest men and wise men should be sought for diligently, and good men and wise men ye should observe to uphold; otherwise, whatsoever is less than these cometh of evil."[67]

Both to arouse our attention and to help us understand the severity of our responsibilities, the Lord said "concerning the laws of the land, it is my will that my people should observe to do all things whatsoever I *command* them." To befriend the Constitution is a commandment! As some have observed, it is difficult to befriend either someone or something that is unknown—a friend is someone that we know well and with whom we share a certain intimacy. To befriend the Constitution of the land, a person must know it well and become intimately acquainted with it—else how can that person know if any proposal is "more or less" than the document itself allows. If it is "more or less" than the Constitution, the Lord says that it "cometh of evil" and, because of his command to befriend the document, indicates that we have a certain amount of complicity if we blindly allow undermining proposals to become law. President Ezra Taft Benson wrote

> *We have been instructed again and again to reflect more intently on the meaning and importance of the Constitution and to adhere to its principles. What have we done about this instruction? Have we read the Constitution and pondered it? Are we aware of its principles? Can we recognize when a law is constitutionally unsound? The Church will not tell us how to do this, but we are admonished to do it.*[68]

Responsibility to seek wise men

The second command is to seek honest, wise, and good men to govern the affairs of a country. This is in stark contrast to the electioneering, glad-handing, and "vote for me" spirit that make up today's political scene. We are told to seek candidates who have the qualities necessary for governance—not to simply wait to find out who wants the office. A great lesson can be learned from the correspondence of George Washington to Alexander Hamilton. A year prior to his acceptance of the presidency Washington wrote:

> *Every personal consideration conspires to rivet me (if I may use the expression) to retirement. At my time of life, and under my circumstances, nothing in this world can ever draw me from it, unless it be a conviction that the partiality of my countrymen had made my services absolutely necessary, joined to a fear that my refusal might induce a belief that I preferred the conservation of my own reputation and private ease, to the good of my country. After all, if I should conceive myself in a manner constrained to accept, I call heaven to witness, that this very act would be the greatest sacrifice of my*

personal feelings and wishes that ever I have been called to make. It would be to forego repose and domestick (sic) enjoyment for trouble, perhaps publick (sic) obloquy (ill repute); for I should consider myself as entering upon an unexplored field, enveloped on every side with clouds and darkness.[69]

Even following his election and embarking upon his journey to the capitol to assume his office, he wrote in his journal

About ten o'clock, I bade farewell to Mount Vernon, to private life, and to domestick felicity; and with a mind oppressed with more anxious and painful sensations than I have words to express, set out for New York, with the best dispositions to render service to my country in obedience to its call . . . .[70]

The Church is a skillful teacher of this principle. For callings to various assignments and church positions, wise men with authority meet together and review openings which need to be filled. After considering people who may occupy the positions, they engage in prayer and wait to receive spiritual confirmation. After their deliberation and prayers, callings are extended. Electioneering is nonexistent (can you imagine someone from a pulpit announcing, "All right, who wants to be the new bishop—the nominations are now open . . . ?) The Lord is extending the same selective stewardship to us; to seek honest, wise, and good people as candidates for public office. Honesty, wisdom, and goodness are the primary criteria—not whether candidates desire office or the glitter of public life.

Beware of piecemeal losses to freedom

Following the adoption of the Constitution of the United States, freedom generally reigned. Allegorically, President J. Reuben Clark said

Our fathers knew all the approaches of tyranny. They could hear its muffled tread afar off. They left us signs and warnings to quicken our ears, they set up for us bulwarks across his path. So well did they do their work that for scores of years tyranny did not leave its lair. Human freedom and happiness and prosperity filled the land and joy abode in the hearts of the people. We forgot that tyranny lived. Then it left its den in the night, and began stalking our liberties even as a wild beast creeps silently, through the darkness upon its victim.[71]

To be sure, there were some examples of violations to the Constitution's intent quite early. The Founding Fathers had concerns and, while they lived, they continually gave warnings and spoke out against encroachments they perceived. Jefferson felt that the Supreme Court was given too much power and proposed an amendment to weaken its influence; Washington saw party affiliation as particularly damaging and dividing to citizens; and James Madison was concerned that the "general welfare" clause of the Constitution could be taken too far by Congress giving the federal government power not intended by the framers. These abuses and potential abuses were feared but, generally, the Constitution kept tyranny in check. With the advent of wars, however, and the global presence of the United States, abuses have become exponentially greater. During the last seventy years America has witnessed a decline in its effectiveness to hold tyranny at bay.

Despite weakened freedoms, as much as ever in our nation's history we display our flag and sing the songs of freedom. Our hearts still flutter at parades when the military marches and the band plays *The Star-Spangled Banner*. Patriotism is alive. Moroni's caution to us, however, is that Satan is still very much a part of our generation and, as the "father of lies," we should not expect any dilution of our freedoms to be clearly labeled. Platitudes of equality, human rights, and national interests are frequently used in a patriotic sense—but without suspicion, they frequently tend to erode our personal liberties. Often those with the most unholy designs are those who are the most persuasive.   In fact, it was for this reason that the Constitution was originally adopted. Despite convincing rhetoric and public opinion polls, the Founders' understanding was that "In questions of power, then, let no more be heard of confidence in man, but bind him down from mischief by the chains of the Constitution."[72]

Chapter 2—Endnotes

1   Abraham 2:9-11

2   Ether 15:33

3   Ether 8:9

4   Ether 8:21

5   Ether 8:15-16

6   Moses 5:29

7   Ether 8:20

8   2 Nephi 9:9

9   2 Nephi 26:22

10   Alma 37:21

11   Alma 37:27

12   Alma 37:29

13   Helaman 1-7

14   Helaman 1:11

15   Helaman 1:12

16   Helaman 2:4

17   Helaman 2:13

18   Helaman 2:23

19   Helaman 6:18

20   Helaman 6:20

21   Helaman 6:21

22   Helaman 6:21

23   Helaman 6:39

24   Helaman 6:38

25   Helaman 6:26

26   Helaman 6:29-30

27   *Doctrine & Covenants* 38:12-13.

28   Mosiah 3:19

29   *Doctrine & Covenants* 121:39

30   *Doctrine & Covenants* 111:11

31   *Doctrine & Covenants* 46:18, 28-30

32   Ether 8:23

33   Ezra Taft Benson, *The Teachings of Ezra Taft Benson*,
          Bookcraft, Salt Lake City, 1988. pp. 496-407.

34   Joseph Smith—Matthew 22

35   Ezra Taft Benson, Ibid., p. 656.

36   Helaman 9:4

37   Helaman 7:5

38   Ezra Taft Benson, Ibid. p. 387.

39   John A. Widtsoe, Conference Report, April, 1941. pp. 16-
          17.

40   *Doctrine & Covenants* 60:2

41   Hugh W. Nibley, "Endowment History," (Unpublished
          manuscript). June, 1986. pp. 74-75.

42   *Doctrine & Covenants* 58:26-29

43   *Doctrine & Covenants* 123:13-15

44   Ezra Taft Benson, Conference Address, *Improvement Era*,
          June, 1965. p. 539.

45   Ether 8:16

46   Ether 8:15

47   Moses 5:31

48   Ether 8:21

49   Ether 8:20, 22

50   Ether 9:11

51   Woodrow Wilson, Address in New York City, September 4,
        1912.

52   David O. McKay, Conference Report, April 9, 1966. pp.
        109-110.

53   Mormon 8:34-35

54   John Taylor, *Journal of Discourses*, 22:142-143

55   Henry D. Moyle, *Relief Society Magazine*, 1957. Vol. 44,
        pp. 577-578.

56   George Q. Cannon, *Juvenile Instructor*, Vol. 25, p. 536.

57   *Doctrine & Covenants* 101:77-78

58   Moses 4:1

59   *Doctrine & Covenants* 98:5

60   *Doctrine & Covenants* 101:77

61   John Taylor, 1884, *Journal of Discourses* 26:350

62   Joseph F. Smith, 1882, *Journal of Discourses* 23:70-71

63   Mosiah 29:26-29

64   Albert Henry Smyth, ed., *The Writings of Benjamin Franklin*,
        New York: The MacMillan Co., 1905-1907. Vol 9, p.
        569. as quoted in W. Cleon Skousen, *The Majesty of
        God's Law*, pp. 544-545.

65   Albert Henry Smyth, ed., *Ibid.* 9:607.

66   John R. Howe, *The Changing Political Thought of John
        Adams*, Princeton, NJ, Princeton University Press,
        1966. p. 189.

67   *Doctrine & Covenants* 98:4-10

68   Ezra Taft Benson, *The Constitution: A Heavenly Banner*,
        p. 29.

69   Aaron Bancroft, *The Life of George Washington*. Boston:
        Waterstreet Bookstore, 1833. Vol 2, p. 81.

70   *Ibid.* p. 82.

71   J. Reuben Clark, 1938. *Vital Speeches* 5:176-177.

72   Thomas Jefferson, *Works* 9:470-471

Chapter 3

ABUSES TO THE CONSTITUTION AND THE INTENTS OF ITS FRAMERS

Most would agree that the constitutional intents of the most influential Founding Fathers were both noble and insightful. The core Framers were "wise men whom [the Lord] raised up unto this very purpose."[1] Literally, many sacrificed all that they had to insure that the foundation of the new nation was secure in freedom and that a righteous government was in place.

Their missions completed, they have left us to become acquainted with their work and recognize the principles they incorporated into our government. As a reward for their faithfulness, they were permitted to visit with Apostle Wilford Woodruff in the St. George Temple. Speaking in General Conference on September 18, 1897, Elder Woodruff related:

> *I am going to bear my testimony to this assembly, if I never do it again in my life, that those men who laid the foundation of this American Government and signed the Declaration of Independence were the best spirits the God of Heaven could find on the face of the earth. They were choice spirits, not wicked men. General Washington and all the men who labored for the purpose were*

> *inspired of the Lord. Another thing I am going to say here, because I have a right to say it, every one of those men that signed the Declaration of Independence with General George Washington called upon me, as an apostle of the Lord Jesus Christ, in the Temple at St. George two consecutive nights, and demanded at my hands that I should go forth and attend to the ordinances of the House of God for them.*

Temple ordinance work was completed at that time for the signers of the Declaration of Independence and for others of the Founding Fathers. While there, two of the Framers of the Constitution were ordained High Priests—George Washington and Benjamin Franklin—along with Christopher Columbus and John Wesley who also appeared to Elder Woodruff.

Despite the work of the Framers and their tireless educational efforts to teach the principles of good government to the new nation, much of their advice and many of their safeguards have been forgotten. This chapter will review specific areas of both the Constitution and the intents of the Founding Fathers. They were students of history and knew the various ways that freedom had been lost in other countries. They warned of tactics of unscrupulous men who would try to break through the defenses of the Constitution; some of the frailties of human nature that would seek security at the expense of freedom; and the tendency toward the piecemeal erosion of freedoms. Understanding the divine nature of the Constitution, Latter-day Saints recognize that any erosion of constitutional principles equates to a loss in personal freedom. Whether losses are caused by uninspired men or planned by secret combinations—both fulfill the Satanic agenda to stifle freedom and agency. This chapter will include much of their reasoning, as well as many of the encroachments that have gone against their warnings.

Declarations of war

Although Article 2 of the Constitution gives the nation's president the title of "Commander-in-Chief" of military forces, it explicitly outlines his duty and that of the Congress during times of warfare. When the Constitution was drafted and debated, the Founders had vivid memories of the confusion that existed during the Revolutionary War and the mixed signals that were often given to the military. They understood the value of one leader at the head of the nation that could make decisions quickly and unequivocally. On the other hand, there was a concern that one person could too easily abuse that power; therefore, certain restraints were placed on him by the Constitution.

Even though the President was given the title of Commander-in-Chief, the Constitution clearly outlined that "Congress shall have power to declare war." (Article 1, Section 8) In 1973, subsequent legislation known as the "War Powers Act" was approved by Congress—an act often referred to by the Executive Branch of government today; however, this Act also reaffirmed the role of Congress in declaring and initiating war except in "situations where imminent hostilities are clearly indicated by the circumstances." In other words, in the event of a national emergency and imminent hostility, the President could make rapid decisions; however, the Act also emphasized that, in such an event, the War Powers Act would "insure the collective judgment of both the Congress and the President" in such decisions. All of this means that the President of the United States—the Commander-in-Chief—has no singular authority to declare and maintain a state of war.

Congressman Ron Paul of Texas addressed the House of Representatives on October 3, 2002, regarding this key constitutional directive. He said:

Many Americans have been forced into war since [World War Two] on numerous occasions, with no congressional declaration of war and with essentially no victories. Today's world political condition is as chaotic as ever. We're still in Korea and we're still fighting the Persian Gulf War that started in 1990.

Congress is about to circumvent the Constitution and avoid the tough decision of whether war should be declared by transferring this monumental decision-making power regarding war to the President. Once again, the process is being abused. Odds are, since a clear-cut decision and commitment by the people through their representatives is not being made, the results may be as murky as before. . . . So far the proposed resolution never mentions war, only empowering the President to use force at his will to bring about peace. Rather strange language indeed! . . . . Since Iraq doesn't even have an Air Force or a Navy, is incapable of waging a war, and remains defenseless against the overwhelming powers of the United States and the British, it's difficult to claim that we're going into Iraq to restore peace.

History will eventually show that if we launch this attack, the real victims will be the innocent Iraqi who despises Saddam Hussein and are terrified of the coming bombs that will destroy their cities.

Not only is it sad that we have gone so far astray from our Constitution, but it's also dangerous for world peace and threatens our liberties here at home.

Representative Paul does not stand alone on this issue. The assumption of war powers by the executive branch of the United States government is troubling to many. In addition to a declaration of war, to insure that the Commander-in-Chief would not overextend his role in warfare, Article 1, Section 8, of the Constitution specifically delegated to Congress the responsibilities to

(1) " . . . make Rules concerning Captures on Land and Water" (i.e. rules concerning enemy imprisonment).
(2) ". . . provide and maintain a Navy"
(3) ". . . raise and support armies"

(4) "... make rules for the Government and Regulation of the land and naval Forces"

(5) "... provide for calling forth the Militia to execute the Laws of the Union, suppress Insurrections and repel Invasions"

(6) "... provide for organizing, arming, and disciplining, the Militia"

(7) "... the Erection of Forts, Magazines, Arsenals, dock-yards, and other needful Buildings"

Intentionally, the Framers limited the power of the Executive Branch of government relative to war and wartime decisions. Unfortunately, this is an area of the Constitution that is breeched today. In recent years, the President of the United States has made the following assumptive and erroneous declarations of his role as commander-in-chief:

> *Sending Americans into battle is the most profound decision a President can make.*[2]

> *The United States of America has the sovereign authority to use force in assuring its own national security. That duty falls to me as Commander-in-Chief, by the oath I have sworn: by the oath I will keep.*[3]

Indeed, this all-encompassing role of the President of the United States in war is one that the Framers of the Constitution both feared and warned the new country about.

Power to create money

As long as money had intrinsic value such as gold or silver coinage, or was backed by such and could be redeemed for precious metal—or any quantity of a specific commodity with value—it was safe currency. To ensure that the nation's currency would not be manipulated by private interests, the Constitution specified that Congress would "coin money, regulate the Value thereof, and of foreign Coin, and fix the standard of weight and measures." (Article 1, Section 8) Foreign money, particularly the silver Spanish peso, was often used in colonial America; therefore, it was given to Congress to determine trade value by its weight and purity.

As early as 1791, Secretary of the Treasury Alexander Hamilton—against the input of James Madison and Thomas Jefferson—recommended a central national bank under private control that would print and distribute money. Jefferson gave the following reasons for its opposition:

> *(1) that the subscribers to the bank would form a*
> *corporation*
> *(2) whose stock could be held by aliens*
> *(3) and be transmitted to a certain line of successors*
> *(4) thus placed beyond forfeiture and escheat*
> *(5) forming a monopoly in banking*
> *(6) placing it in a position to make laws paramount to the*
> *laws of states.*[4]

Despite his arguments, the First Bank of the United States was accepted and attained a twenty year charter from the federal government. It was created by selling 25,000 shares—18,000 which were purchased by English investors. Although popular abroad, United States citizens objected to the large amount of interest payments siphoned to the country with which they had just been at war. By 1798, Hamilton reconsidered the bank and wrote that "if currency or banknotes were to be issued and circulated as 'money,' it should have been done by Congress."[5]

Congress, however, did little to assume its responsibility to "coin money." There were countless abuses to sound monetary policy: banks were chartered by states indiscriminately; reserves were ignored and "fiat" money (banknotes without gold or silver reserves) was issued; and there was a great deal of currency confusion because money was printed by so many banks. Lacking a clear policy on banking and failing to carry out the congressional proscription of the Constitution, the monetary system of the United States was ripe for meddling.

In 1910, a secret meeting of financiers was held at Jekyl Island, Georgia, and the workings of the Federal Reserve System were formulated. At this meeting, it was determined that private interests would assume central banking within the United States. Plans were outlined at the Georgia estate to "sell" the private central banking system to both the federal government and to the citizens of the United States.

Through manipulation, the Federal Reserve Act of 1913 was enacted. Although many recognized the unconstitutionality of the act and the danger of placing the creation of money under private control, printing, establishing interest rates, and valuing money has been the prerogative of private banking since that time.

The right to bear arms

The Second Amendment to the Constitution reads:

> *A well regulated Militia, being necessary to the security of a free State, the right of the people to keep and bear Arms, shall not be infringed.*

This has been a popular issue to discuss because of its divisiveness. The printed media, television, and various radio talk shows have regularly highlighted the Second Amendment and featured both sides—those for more and those for less gun control. It never fails to create the heated feelings that the media enjoys and generally gravitates to a discussion between "guns cause crime and death, therefore control of guns is necessary;" and "the responsible use of firearms is not a danger and the Second Amendment to the Constitution was penned so that

Americans could take action in the event of a national emergency."

To have a clearer understanding of the issue, we need to identify those working for more gun control and analyze their reasoning.

Forces behind the control of firearms. In 1995, the United Nations attitude towards the private ownership of guns was published in the report, *Our Global Neighborhood* by the U.N.-funded Commission of Global Governance. The report stated the world danger in the "acquisition and use of increasingly lethal weapons by civilians; whether individuals seeking a means of self-defense, street gangs, political opposition groups, or terrorist organizations." This report was disturbing to many because "individuals" were pegged as responsible for the problem and, along with various illegal uses of guns that were already covered by other laws, "self-defense" was given as a reason for confiscation.

A steady stream of papers and pronouncements has documented the United Nations' concern about the issue of private weapons. Two U.N. officials, Jayantha Dhanapala of Sri Lanka (United Nations Undersecretary-General for Disarmament Affairs, 1998-2003) and Mark Malloch Brown (Administrator of the United Nations Development Programme) coauthored the global-policy report *Let's Go Out Into the World and Gather Up the Small Arms*, dated January 26, 2000. Referring to events in Albania, they said that through their departments, about 80% of the privately-held arms had already been confiscated.

In 2005, Senator David Vitter of Louisiana introduced Senate Bill 1488—a bill that would block the United Nations from pursuing gun control measures against citizens of the United States. Those U.N. measures, he said, included:

The establishment of an international tracking certificate which would be used to ensure UN monitoring control over the export, import, transit, stocking, and storage of legal small arms and light weapons—

Worldwide record keeping for an indefinite amount of time on the manufacture, holding and transfer of small arms and light weapons—

National registries and tracking lists of all legal firearms—

Why would the United Nations work against gun rights? These are issues, of course, that include gun ownership throughout all the countries of the world. In many nations, the right to gun ownership has ceased: Great Britain, Canada, Australia, Iraq, Albania, Russia, Rwanda, Zimbabwe, Sierra Leone, Afghanistan, China, Ukraine, and several other countries currently have bans on gun ownership. But why would the U.N. spearhead the elimination of privately held firearms?

One might say that in many of the countries listed above, civil unrest and instability would justify gun confiscation. The parallel to that, however, is that those who give up their arms are at the mercy of those who do not, thus inviting the looting, rape and murder that have highlighted foreign and international "take-overs" during the past half-century. Some of the "one-liners" by guns rights activists address this and other justifications.

Gun control is not about guns; it's about control.

Those who trade liberty for security have neither.

If guns cause crime, then matches cause arson.

Assault is a behavior, not a device.

The American Revolution would never have happened if the British had enforced gun control.

If guns are outlawed, only outlaws will have guns.

What part of "shall not be infringed" don't you understand? (from the Second Amendment)

A news release from the Libertarian Party gives some "food-for-thought" about the recent struggles in Iraq and the confiscation of personal weapons.

> *An allied military plan to confiscate weapons in Iraq may destabilize the nation further by giving the green light to street thugs and Baath Party loyalists who are terrorizing innocent civilians says the Libertarian Party.*
> *"Imposing this gun grab is like declaring war on Iraq for a second time," said Geoffrey Neale, Libertarian Party Chairman. "How many innocent men, women and children will be kidnapped, robbed or murdered because their U.S. 'protectors' turned self-defense into a crime?"*
> *He said, ". . . if criminal gangs don't comply with laws against looting, murder and kidnapping, they certainly won't comply with a new gun regulation. This weapons ban will just make all of their jobs easier by disarming their potential victims."[6]*

And what about the United States? Where does our country fit into the move to control personal firearms within our borders? On November 10, 2001, President George W. Bush said that, under U.N. Security Council Resolution 1373, "We have a responsibility to deny weapons to terrorists and to actively prevent private citizens from providing them." Unfortunately, his statement was so broad that any "private citizen" purchasing firearms could fall under his criteria.

The other issue, and the one generally used to promote gun control measures, is that "more guns cause more crime—fewer guns cause less crime." Because of the reoccurring frequency of this argument to restrict firearms—rather than to attack gun control on constitutional grounds—several studies have been made to either verify or debunk the claim. One of the most thorough researchers has been Attorney Don B. Kates, a member of the California State Advisory Committee to the U.S. Civil Rights Commission and currently a Research Fellow with the Independent Institute. Kates' research has uncovered some interesting statistics on the relationship—or lack of relationship—of gun ownership and crime in the United States. He tells us that current figures on the quantity of guns in the United States are not accurate because of the large number of individuals who are fearful of gun confiscation; yet, with reported sales and registrations, we can arrive at some major conclusions. In 1946, for example, there were approximately 48.5 million firearms owned in the United States. By 2003, that number had jumped to about 272 million—but the murder rates were essentially identical. During the decade of the 1990s with an additional 47 million guns added to the nation's stockpile, all forms of killings by guns actually decreased. One of the frightening abuses most often cited by those in favor of gun control is accidental shooting—firearms in the hands of children and inexperienced shooters—yet, those killings actually dropped by half during the 1990s. Other statistics of the 1990s show that with the millions of additional guns, there was a 25% decrease in the number of murders committed by firearms.[7] Virtually all research statistics either validate that there is no appreciable difference in gun violence or that gun violence decreases with more guns owned by citizens.

Concerns about gun registration. While some may agree that there are problems with the constitutionality of gun laws and their actual confiscation—they are less concerned about the accepted practice of registering firearms. After all, a person registering weapons is allowed to buy and keep them.

Considering registration, however, the histories of other countries are instructive. New Zealand began registering firearms in 1921. Using the registration data, in 1974, all personal revolvers were confiscated by the government. In 1996, Australia had a gun registration program in place. That year the government banned most semiautomatic rifles and shotguns with an end to destroying them—a process that is still continuing. To date, of the 4 million rifles affected, roughly 600,000 have been destroyed. Registration laws have had similar effects in Great Britain and Canada.

A much more troublesome case history took place in Nazi Germany. The Weimar Republic enforced gun registration in 1928, a program that Adolf Hitler both abused and amplified later. Dr. Stephen Halbrook researching his book *Target Switzerland*, found that Germany's extensive gun registration records were used to take all weapons from the Jews with the penalty of death levied for noncompliance. Later, during the invasions of Czechoslovakia and Poland—countries that also demanded gun registration—records were used to confiscate firearms and insure that any insurgency would be left without guns.

And in the United States? Although to date gun confiscation has been minimal, there are still incidents that demonstrate violation of the Second Amendment. One recent exception took place in New Orleans, Louisiana, with the destruction brought by Hurricane Katrina. Virtually all survivors who remained in New Orleans—particularly those protecting their homes and businesses—were accosted in door-to-door searches by the National Guard for the purpose of taking away all firearms. This quasi-military exercise, on order from Chief of Police Warren Riley and supported by Mayor Ray Nagin, took guns from honest citizens who sought to protect their homes and businesses from looters and vandals. Because many New

Orleans citizens were forced to stand by weaponless, the city suffered compounded losses that very probably could have been prevented.

Another disturbing breech occurred in New York City in 1991. There the City Council imposed a ban on guns that were previously declared legal. Even though Police Commissioner Lee Brown said that the guns in question had never been used to commit a violent crime in the city, the City of New York authorized a ban on the firearms. One man living in Staten Island said he had previously been told that the guns were legal; that it was his constitutional right to possess them; and that he had never been cited for an offense misusing guns. Nevertheless, his home was entered, searched, guns were seized, and he was arrested. The 2,340 New Yorkers that had previously registered their semiautomatic rifles and shotguns received letters from the New York Police Department stating that the guns in question had to be either taken out of the state; rendered inoperable; or surrendered.

Because of the various examples cited and the gathering momentum of anti-gun legislation, some concerned citizens have coined the pungent phrase: "The Founders included the Second Amendment to our Bill of Rights just in case our other rights are ignored by government."

A parallel to the use of arms in the *Book of Mormon* is found in 2 Nephi 5:14. Although the Nephites desired to live in peace and pursue agricultural interests, once they separated themselves from the Lamanites, they made preparations for war. They didn't want war—that was the last thing on their agenda but they knew that the answer to restricting warfare was preparation for war. Consequently, one of the first things they did was to "take the sword of Laban, and after the manner of it [they] did make many swords." It was in that same spirit that the Framers of the Constitution said that "a well regulated militia [was] necessary to the security of a free state" and that "the people's right to bear arms . . . shall not be abridged." The militia as defined in the Bill of Rights was not a standing army but was composed of citizens bearing privately owned arms. The paradox of battle is that the preparation for it will avert battle, while a lack of preparation will invite it.

Freedom of speech

Thomas Jefferson once said that the freedom of speech could "not be limited without being lost." The Founders desired the right to be critical, particularly as it related to government and decisions respecting the nation. This is a part of the First Amendment to the Constitution which contained other rights the Founders felt were inherent—such as the right to assemble peacefully, the freedom of the press, and the freedom to worship as they chose. Earlier, when the original pilgrims came to America, many of the same freedoms had been curtailed and England, as well as other European countries, had placed limits on them. In some countries there was a state religion and people were disallowed or legally sanctioned for following another belief. Prohibitions had been placed on speaking openly of these new beliefs and speaking against government. Freedom of speech meant that a person could express his feelings about religion, politics, or other controversial issues without fear of government repercussion. This seems so basic to American thought in the 21st century that, for some, it would be unthinkable to be without the freedom of speech.

I had a rather unique experience in the mid-1990s when I accepted an assignment to teach at a Chinese university. The Chinese students were aware of political activities in the United States and on several occasions wanted to discuss events and hear them from an American perspective. One day our President had done some personal things of which I was quite embarrassed that captured world attention. As those issues came up in class I expressed my disapproval of the President of the United States and made some strong comments that indicated I was quite disgusted with his behavior. The classroom became suddenly very silent. Finally, a student said, "You wouldn't say that if you were in America now, would you?"

I said, "Yes, I would." And I began to realize what the students were thinking. I said, "It's not uncommon for Americans to voice their disapproval of political leaders or anyone they feel has done something disgraceful." What I had taken for granted and expressed without giving a great deal of thought, was a monumental issue for those Chinese students.

The Amendment states that freedom of speech would not be abridged—or, as Jefferson said, would not be limited. The national heritage would include our right to express dissatisfaction. And, should we be in a group, laws would not inhibit "the right of the people peacefully to assemble, and to petition the government . . . ." Approaching the government frequently involves confrontation but not physical violence— hence, various marches, sit-ins, or other demonstrations that are guaranteed by our Constitution to allow our right to dissent and to make our objections known.

Recently, however, our right to express our disapproval with government, political leaders, or our own political ideals, has been severely abridged. In the August 6, 2004 issue of *The Nation*, reporter Jim Hightower wrote:

> *At the 2000 GOP nominating convention in Philadelphia candidate Bush created a fenced-in, out-of-sight protest zone that could only hold barely 1,500 people at a time. So citizens who wished to give voice to their many grievances with the Powers that Be had to:*
>
> *(1) Schedule their exercise of First Amendment rights with the decidedly unsympathetic authorities.*

(2) Report to the protest pen at their designated time, and only in the numbers authorized.

(3) Then, under recorded surveillance if the authorities, feel free to let loose with all the speech they could utter within their allotted minutes (although none—not Bush, not convention delegates, not the preening members of Congress, not the limousine gliding corporate sponsors, and certainly not the mass media—would be anywhere nearby to hear a single word that they had to say.)

Then, once ensconced in the White House, Bush's followers institutionalized the art of dissing dissent, routinely dispatching the Secret Service to order local police to set up Free Speech Zones to quarantine protesters wherever Bush goes.

The Free Speech Zone (FSZ) has become a modern abuse to the right the Founders guaranteed in the Constitution. As someone recently asked, "What if the Boston Tea Party would have taken place within time limits the British had set and in a quarantined area far from the sight of others or from the press?" Free speech, by its very nature, is confrontive and insists on dialog between opposing views. A few more modern examples follow:

Bill Neel was a retired steelworker who attended a 2002 Labor Day picnic where the President had gone to be photographed with workers. Bill made up a sign that he carried to the picnic: "The Bush Family Must Surely Love the Poor: They Made so Many of Us." The Secret Service told Bill that he had to leave and go to the designated FSZ—a ballpark behind a chain-link fence that was a third of a mile away. Bill said that he wouldn't leave so he was arrested for disorderly conduct and taken to the Pittsburgh jail. At Bill's trial the Secret Service testified that they had instructed the local police to confine "people that were making a statement pretty much against the President and his views." The district court judge threw the case out with the statement: "I believe this is America. Whatever happened to 'I don't agree with you, but I'll defend to the death your right to say it?'"

The President made an appearance in St. Louis in 2003. There were about 150 protesters who were taken to a FSZ where they could not be seen from the street. The media were not allowed to talk to any of the protesters nor were any of those in the FSZ allowed to leave the zone to talk to the media.

When the President came to Columbia, South Carolina, Brett Bursey was there with a sign that read "No War for Oil." Standing in a public area, he was told by local police to go to the FSZ—a half-mile from where people were gathered, even though he was still two football fields away from the President. When he refused to leave he was arrested because "the content of his sign was a problem." At his trial five months later the trespassing charge was dismissed—because there is no such thing as trespassing on public property at a public event. The federal attorney then intervened and said that Bursey had entered a "restricted area around the President;" yet Bursey was two hundred yards from the President in the midst of hundreds of other onlookers.

In May of 2003, about one-hundred Texans opposed to the war in Iraq were traveling to the President's ranch about five miles outside of Crawford. To get to the ranch, it was necessary to drive through the town of Crawford. However, a police blockade was set up and the protesters were told that they had to leave immediately or they would be considered a demonstration, for which they did not have a permit. Five of the group got out of their cars and began to explain that they had no intention of demonstrating in Crawford, that they were only driving though to organize themselves at the President's ranch. The five were arrested and taken to jail. Nine months later at their trial, the defending lawyer asked the arresting police "if someone who simply wore a political button reading 'peace,' could he be found in violation of Crawford's ordinance against protesting without a permit?" "Yes," he was told, "it could be a sign of a demonstration." All five were convicted.

Because of many documented examples of the abridgement of freedom of speech, several legal groups have begun to ask questions and to petition for guaranteed rights. The

American Civil Liberties Union and others have levied suits against the Secret Service for what appears to be a continued repression of basic protesting rights falling under the heading of "freedom of speech." Their briefs have cited cases in Arizona, California, Virginia, Michigan, New Jersey, New Mexico and Texas.

Non-Constitutional encroachments on freedom

Other abuses have not specifically violated constitutional provisions, but have been contrary to the Framers' intents. These misused government powers have generally been on four primary fronts: (1) redistributing wealth; (2) catering to special interests; (3) curtailing basic rights under the guise of national security— wars or threatened wars; and (4) executive orders from the executive branch of government. Each of these directions and mandates are accorded lofty rhetoric designed to commit citizens to their necessity.

(1) *The redistribution of wealth.* A temptation of governments perpetually has been to take from the "haves" and give to the "have-nots." Early Rome was notorious for heavily taxing working citizens for both the benefit of the ruling class as well as those who had very little. Because there were fewer tax-paying workers than those receiving benefits, their minority voice could not be heard above the demands of welfare recipients.

Thomas Jefferson taught that government should be prevented "from wasting the labors of the people under pretense of caring for them."[8] The Lord said quite succinctly, "Thou shalt not be idle; for he that is idle shall not eat the bread nor wear the garments of the laborer."[9] Nevertheless, under pretense of caring for the less fortunate, government has frequently made appropriations from the "haves" to the "have-nots." This has always been contrary to teachings of the Lord and his prophets.

As President David O. McKay emphatically stated, "It is not government's duty to support you." He went on to say

> *I shall raise my voice as long as God gives me sound or ability, against the communistic idea that the government will take care of us all, and that everything belongs to the government. . . .*
>
> *It is wrong! No wonder, in trying to perpetuate that idea, that men become anti-Christ, because those teachings strike directly at the doctrines of the Savior.*
>
> *No government owes you a living. You get it yourself by your own acts . . . .*[10]

Unfortunately, government has opted for a much different course. Pursuing wealth redistribution, it has adopted two specific approaches: a graduated income tax and deficit spending. The first, the graduated income tax, was originally restricted by the Constitution because it was a "direct tax"—a tax paid directly by the citizen. (Article 1, Section 9) Although the Constitution says a great deal about raising revenues for the government, the Founders were concerned about the application of a tax directly on the person rather than a tax on consumption which would allow the person to choose whether or not to pay the tax. (Hence, in this situation the tax would be "voluntary" such as the tax on tea and the stamp act imposed by the British.) In 1894, an income tax was considered by Congress but dismissed on the grounds that it was unconstitutional.

Then, in 1913, the Sixteenth Amendment to the Constitution was declared legal. It does, however, have a dubious history of ratification. Thirty-six states (three-fourths of the forty-eight states) were needed for ratification; however, the reporting procedure was fraught with irregularities and the actual number ratifying was apparently fewer than needed.[11] Nevertheless, the amendment was accepted and the federal income tax began in 1913.

With the income tax came a simplified method of redistributing the nation's wealth. Initially the new law taxed the richest one percent of the population one percent of their earnings above $3,000. Since then, it has grown to include all income earners with a graduated tax penalizing higher incomes with substantially higher percentages of income payments due. As President J. Reuben Clark observed, "At first it was light, but it grew by leaps and bounds. Always and ever, the more you feed a government, the hungrier it gets . . . ."[12]

President Henry D. Moyle also raised a warning voice about taxes:

> *The difficulty with all governments, and one to which our own has fallen heir, is that the majority, by virtue of its right to place limitations on man's free agency, has undertaken to infringe upon the rights reserved to the individual, for the direct and immediate benefit of the majority individually rather than for the establishment of law and order. For example: the Constitution expressly prohibits taking of personal property for public purposes without just compensation. Under the guise of taxation, the Constitution is violated and property is taken from one and given to another. This demonstrates clearly the power to tax is the power to destroy. That is the course which we now pursue.*[13]

As burdensome as taxes are, they do not contribute enough money to supply the United States government with the income necessary to offset its expenditures. Because of this, the second powerful method of redistributing the nation's wealth is deficit spending—the ability of the government to spend money that it doesn't possess. Deficit spending both allows the government to avoid raising taxes while lessening resistance to spending by removing and postponing immediate financial consequences. This two-pronged political tactic has been used frequently over the past several decades in the United States: (1) to garner votes by promising and delivering benefits; and (2) to lessen immediate financial pain by creating money and borrowing from the Federal Reserve without creating additional taxes.

Thus, deficit spending, is the difference between what is received in revenues and the amount it spends from the Federal Reserve Corporation. Some have erroneously believed that the government simply owes this money to itself as allowed in times of emergency under Constitutional law; however, the Federal Reserve Corporation is a separate and private entity that levies interest on money loaned to the government. The interest on the national debt is compounded and is a large part of the country's deficit—now in excess of $8 trillion.

Deficit spending increased substantially during the New Deal of the Roosevelt administration under the economic philosophy of John Maynard Keynes—and to a much larger degree in postwar economy. Keynesian economics encouraged deficit spending by governments so that money could be used whenever and wherever needed with the idea that if all segments of the economy were running smoothly, money would flow freely. Whereas years previous to the Roosevelt administration had generally reflected a surplus of money taken in by the government as opposed to money spent, each year of the Roosevelt presidency produced deficits.[14] To regulate the nation's money supply, interest rates were regulated—low interest rates encouraged borrowing and freer cash flow while higher rates encouraged slow down and stabilization.

Despite some seeming advantages of ready money to use as needed, both the Founding Fathers and LDS Church leaders have given directions to the contrary. Jefferson cautioned that

> *To preserve our independence, we must not let our rulers load us with perpetual debt. We must take our choice between economy and liberty, or profusion and servitude. If we run into such*

debts, we must be taxed in our meat and drink, in our necessities and our comforts, in our labors and in our amusements.[15]

To demonstrate the folly of deficit spending, many have simply made the comparison of personal finances to government spending.   When an individual uses credit for too many purchases, the bills eventually catch up and either that individual pays a dire price to liquidate his indebtedness or he takes out bankruptcy. Likewise, President Ezra Taft Benson—referring to deficit spending—said that "The end of such a course is national bankruptcy."[16] To understand the steamrolling affect of deficit spending, one only has to look back a few years to see its tremendous inroads. Ezra Taft Benson said in 1962 that

> *Added to the current debt at close to $300 billion, our total commitments now reach the almost incredible total of $750 billion, or three-quarters of a trillion dollars.   And even this stratospheric amount doesn't include another $250 or $300 billion we need to collect in future tax increases to make good on our present promises under the social security system.*[17]

Incredible?   Stratospheric?   Imagine President Benson's response to today's deficit in excess of $8 trillion.   In fact, in 2006 an author wrote that every child born in the United States

> *. . . shoulders a $156,000 debt. That's the estimated debt that every American owes the federal government, courtesy of the annual budget deficit, plus the national debt accumulated over the past century, plus promised but long-term unfunded commitments like his parents' Medicare and Social Security payments . . . . Not only that, but the burden is growing.   By the time [he] reaches working age, that amount could double or triple if nothing dramatic is done to alter the government's accumulation of red ink.*[18]

Apparently, unless a dramatic shift is made in policy, the government's spending deficit will be with us indefinitely.

(2) *Catering to special interests.* On the surface, the concept of lobbying doesn't appear to be a violation of the Founders' intents. Because members of Congress cannot be expected to be informed on all subjects, experts are brought in to elucidate and inform them about particular issues and the affects of certain laws. Of course, a major problem exists because lobbyists are not impartial and are paid by those who gain by passage of certain legislation. Because they stand to gain from the acts of Congress, they often add inducements for individual members of Congress to vote in their favor. The inducements can be quite creative, although the majority seem to relate to benefits following legislators' terms of office (rules have restricted many of the gifts, travel perks, and speaking fees they once received while serving in office) and to gifts through Political Action Committees (PACs). For the most part, Political Action Committees contribute to campaign funding to build the "war chest" for future elections—thus helping to reassure the reelection of incumbents.

Mark Twain observed that "It could probably be shown by facts and figures that there is no distinctly native criminal class except Congress." Though not a truism, those holding public office have disgraced their trust on several occasions— often through giving in to the pressures of special interest groups.

(3) *Curtailing of basic rights under the guise of national security—wars or threatened wars.* This will be covered more thoroughly in the chapter entitled *Wars and Rumors of Wars*, but because of its prevalence in subverting constitutional law, it must be included for consideration here. During times of perceived national emergencies citizens are somewhat prone to sacrificing

liberties. Attitudes emerge such as "It's the least I can do for my country;" or "It's a small price for the freedom I enjoy." Yet, often the forsaken liberties have little to do with the needs at hand, and very seldom are returned to the citizenry.

(4) *The use of executive orders from the executive branch of government.* Executive orders, sometimes referred to as presidential directives, are unilaterally made by the President of the United States. Although technically not a violation of "separation of powers" when they are restricted to the executive branch, they have increasingly breeched into all government branches. They frequently include new laws and carry the weight of congressional legislation; while also defining acceptable and unacceptable responses to the directives. In this way, both law and judicial direction emanate from the executive office—a dangerous combination of authority within the Constitutional system of United States government.

Through their studies of the necessity of "separation of powers," the Founding Fathers designed a series of checks and balances that would safeguard the independent function of the three branches of government: the executive, legislative, and judiciary.

A great fear of the Framers was a strong central government and lop-sided power coming from one federal political leader. Instead, they looked to the separate states for power and authority—hence the *United* States. John Adams felt that the only guarantee of rights lay in the separation of powers; a president that could have decisions overturned by Congress and constitutional balancing by the Supreme Court. James Madison in Federalist Papers 46, wrote that the "very definition of tyranny" was "the accumulation of all power, legislative, executive, and judiciary in the same hands." In this statement, Madison was likely paraphrasing Montesquieu who wrote that

"There can be no liberty where the legislative and executive powers are united in the same person."

Executive orders, however, increasingly bring the three branches of government under presidential direction and become law—constitutional or not—upon their publication in the Federal Registry. President J. Reuben Clark warned of the abuses and potential abuses of executive orders and said in the October General Conference of 1943 that

> . . . *they are outside our constitutional law and procedure. Behind them there are no popular urges—indeed, they not infrequently fly in the face of the peoples' desire; they are made without public notice or discussion, in violation of established law-making procedure; they are not made by representatives of the people with a responsibility running back to the people . . . .*
>
> *However, these "directives" involve more than the legislative usurpation. The units that frame them likewise enforce them,—thus becoming both legislature and executive. Furthermore, in cases of dispute, they not infrequently try, condemn, and pronounce judgment for violations, thus acting as a court in judging their own enactments. . . . This is tyranny in its most complete form; however beneficial it may happen temporarily to be in fact. It was Thomas Jefferson who said: "What has destroyed the liberty and rights of man in every government which has ever existed under the sun? The generalizing and consolidation of all cares in one body.*

This is the constitutionally debilitating affect of the executive order. Unfortunately, executive orders have continued at an escalating pace and have often opened a backdoor to legislation that the Founders had not intended. President Bill Clinton added an average of one executive order per week of his two presidential terms and effectively legislated from his office. One executive order set aside the Grand Staircase-Escalante National Monument—placing 1.9 million acres of southern Utah under federal control and eliminating productive use of the land;

another added the term "sexual orientation" to federal hiring policies. From the years 2003 through 2005, an additional 114 executive orders were issued.

The individual states and the Constitution

Although there may be some areas that are murky, a reading of the Constitution generally satisfies the question of the constitutional legality of a law. The first thing that must be done to determine constitutionality is to look at the jurisdiction of the federal government in making any decree. All principles and articles that are mentioned in the document were explicitly placed under the direction of the federal government with parameters and limits established by the Constitution. All other unmentioned aspects of government were reserved by individual states—thus, the intent of the Founding Fathers was to allow as much control as possible at lower levels of government. Objections to this responsibility could be overturned and given to the federal government by amendment to the Constitution but, barring amendments to the contrary, the states were to reserve that power. To be sure that there was no misunderstanding, the tenth amendment—the final of the Bill of Rights—declared that:

> The powers not delegated to the United States by the Constitution, nor prohibited by it to the states, are reserved to the States respectively, or to the people.

Therefore, if a particular item is not mentioned in the Constitution, given that there is no amendment absorbing it under the control of the federal government, it remains within the jurisdiction of the individual states. A primary example of this violation is found in the field of education—an area specifically omitted from the Constitution and left to be regulated by states. This will be covered in greater depth in the chapter entitled *Education: What is a Parent to do?*

Our responsibilities

Studying the intents of the Founders and their fears of abuse to the Constitution, we can more clearly understand Moroni's warning. We know why the Constitution was drawn— "for the rights and protection of all flesh according to just and holy principles"— and we know that the men called to do it were "wise men whom [the Lord] raised up unto this very purpose." This knowledge sets us apart from other citizens of our country who may feel that the Constitution is a good document and that it helped to create a powerful nation—but who lack the insight of the Lord's direct involvement.

Given our knowledge of the Constitution found in the *Doctrine and Covenants* and Moroni's warnings about Satan-inspired groups that would exercise power to destroy "the freedom of all lands, nations, and countries," we have a huge stewardship. Every generation has had its specific challenges. Our responsibility has always been to resist Satan. In this, resisting temptations and encroachments on freedoms would be more easily accomplished if we could identify our adversaries. Unfortunately, because of the nature of conspiracy, it is often impossible to name the key players influencing our loss of freedoms. As such, the "eternal vigilance" recommended by the Founding Fathers is most appropriate.

From all of the warnings contained in the *Book of Mormon* and given to us through modern prophets, we know that our task is awesome. We also know by our divine placement in this promised land and during this dispensation, that we have the capacity to succeed. These facts point strongly toward a belief peculiar to Latter-day Saints. Jerome Horowitz, in his masterful treatise on the United States Constitution, *The Elders of Israel and the Constitution*, relates:

It is also a Latter-day Saint belief, declared by Joseph Smith and reaffirmed by subsequent prophets, that the time would come when the Constitution of the United States would be all but destroyed. An expression used is that it would "hang by a single thread."

These predictions continue to the effect that the Elders of Israel will be instrumental in saving the Constitution, if it is saved at all. The Term "Elders of Israel," as used in this context, apparently refers to the Mormon people rather than to a specific priesthood group.

If the Latter-day Saints are to help save the Constitution, it is important that they understand it. It is not sufficient to declare that they believe it, without being familiar with its significant provisions and the principles on which it is based.[19]

What are our responsibilities? Forewarned, our generation knows what to watch for; how to recognize the involvement of unholy usurpers; and their ultimate goal to destroy freedom and agency.

Chapter 3—Endnotes

1   *Doctrine & Covenants* 101:80

2   George W. Bush, "State of the Union Address," January 28, 2003.

3   George W. Bush, "Address to the Nation," March 17, 2003.

4   Eustace Mullins, *The Secrets of the Federal Reserve*, Bankers Research Institute: Staunton, VA. 1983. p. 35.

5   Hamilton's Writings as quoted by W. Cleon Skousen, *The Making of America*, p. 424

6   News from the Libertarian Party, http://www.LP.org

7   Timothy D. Lytton, ed., "Suing the Gun Industry: A Battle at the Crossroads of Gun Control and Mass Torts," University of Michigan Press, Ann Arbor, 2005. pp. 2-65.

8   as quoted by David O. McKay, Conference Report, April, 1950, p. 35.

9   *Doctrine & Covenants* 42:42

10 David O. McKay, *Church News*, March 14, 1953, as quoted in Jerreld Newquist, *Prophets, Principles and National Survival*. Publishers Press. Salt Lake City: 1962. pp. 346-347.

11 Bill Benson and M. J. "Red" Beckman, "The Law That Never Was: The Fraud of the Sixteenth Amendment and Personal Income Tax." Constitutional Research Associates, South Holland, IL. 1985.

12 J. Reuben Clark, *Vital Speeches* 5:176-177, as quoted in Newquist, *Op. Cit.*, pp. 372-375.

13 Henry D. Moyle, *Relief Society Magazine*, 1957. Vol. 44, pp. 577-578.

14 Robert Lekachman, *The Age of Keynes*, Vintage Books, New York. p. 115.

15　　　Thomas Jefferson as quoted by David O. McKay,
　　　　　　　Conference Report, April, 1950, p. 35.

16　　　Ezra Taft Benson, BYU, February 28, 1962, as quoted in
　　　　　　　Newquist, *Op. Cit.*, p. 369.

17　　　*Ibid.*

18　　　Elaine S. Povich, *AARP Bulletin*, Vol. 47, No. 2, February,
　　　　　　　2006: Washington, DC. p. 10.

19　　　Jerome Horowitz, *The Elders of Israel and the Constitution*.
　　　　　　　Parliament Publishers. Salt Lake City: 1970. pp. 1-2.

Chapter 4

WHERE DO SECRET COMBINATIONS FIT INTO THIS?

Moroni gave us keys to identify the secret combinations of the latter-days. He told us that their power at the deepest levels came from Satan; that their motives were to acquire power and gain; and that their overall plan was to destroy the freedom of all lands and nations. Although apparently obscure to many, Moroni told us that we can recognize them and that we must not allow them to have the power to get above us. Eventually, however, he said that we would "awake to our awful situation" and recognize the grasp of the secret combination upon our lives.[1]

In 1970, Dr. W. Cleon Skousen wrote a review of the book *Tragedy and Hope* by Dr. Carroll Quigley of Georgetown University. Many previously had read Skousen's exposition of Communism entitled *The Naked Communist*, but this review was to take a much different turn. Rather than addressing Communism as the major global threat, he took several direct quotations from Quigley's book and stated that behind Communism and most of the disruptive influences throughout the world stood a coterie of super-wealthy international bankers. The book's title was *The Naked Capitalist.*

Quigley, he said, was neither seeking notoriety nor was he writing an expose; but wrote because of the historical significance of the world influence held by the elite bankers. He considered himself to be an "insider" and had been given access to many of their secret papers and plans; he felt that ultimately he was doing a humanitarian service to document their activities.

Dr. Quigley brought his readers' attention in *Tragedy and Hope* to the primary means of world influence—that those who control money effectively control governments, laws, wars, and resources. He explained that for over two hundred years, the elite banking families had worked to create a financial network throughout the world that could "manipulate the quantity and flow of money so that they were able to influence, if not control, governments on one side and industries on the other."[2]

> *The greatest of these dynasties, of course, were the descendants of Meyer Amschel Rothschild (1743-1812) of Frankfort, whose male descendants, for at least two generations, generally married first cousins or even nieces. Rothschild's five sons, established branches at Vienna, London, Naples, and Paris, as well as Frankfort, cooperated together in ways which other international banking dynasties copied but rarely excelled . . . .*
>
> *The names of some of these [other] banking families are familiar to all of us and should be more so. They include Baring, Lazard, Erlanger, Warburg, Schroder, Selingman, the Speyers, Mirabaud, Mallet, Fould [and] Morgan."[3]*

Working as a network with the debt and financing of nations, the Rothschild family soon was in a position to influence the leaders in every country in which they were present. A primary reason that they were able to wield such influence was because of their positioning in key financial centers throughout the world. Dr. Quigley wrote that

> *The powers of financial capitalism had far-reaching aim, nothing less than to create a world system of financial control in private hands able to dominate the political system of each country and the economy of the world as a whole. This system was to be controlled in a feudalist fashion by the banks of the world acting in concert, by secret agreements arrived at in frequent meetings and conferences. The apex of the system was to be The Bank of International Settlements in Basel, Switzerland, a private bank owned and controlled by the world's central banks which were themselves private corporations. Each central bank, in the hands of [international bankers] sought to dominate its government by its ability to control Treasury loans, to manipulate foreign exchanges, to influence the level of economic activity in the country, and to influence cooperative politicians by subsequent rewards in the business world.*[4]

By manipulating currency control—the amount of currency, the acceptance of corporate and government notes, interest rates, and the timing of notes that were due and payable—the bankers exercised a great deal of control over national and international affairs. One of the first major disruptions caused by such money manipulation was the first major "panic" experienced in the United States; one that had a near-devastating affect upon the early Church

President Andrew Jackson refused to renew the charter of the Second United States Bank in 1836. To a lesser degree than the Federal Reserve System of today, this was a private central bank that controlled much of the country's financial affairs. Jackson was able to see through the power and profits of the ownership and openly exposed the bankers as a "den of vipers." He further went on to announce that "I intend to rout you out and by the Eternal God I will rout you out. If the people only understood the rank injustice of our money and banking system, there would be a revolution before morning."[5]

Exercising presidential authority, he withdrew government funds that had been in the bank—$10 million—and deposited them into state banks. The immediate result was an unprecedented prosperity for the new nation: the national debt was paid, the economy bustled, and a surplus of $50 million was soon in the treasury.

It was at this time that the Kirtland Safety Society Anti-Banking Company—the Kirtland Bank—was chartered. The young Church, now located in Kirtland, Ohio, was growing rapidly and new converts were coming into the city in large numbers. Many had sold their homes and belongings in other areas and were now buying new farms and building new homes. The bank was an important part of the new community. Joseph Smith cautioned the leaders of the Kirtland Bank to avoid speculation and was especially cautious about the low "fractional reserve" requirement. Although the law allowed the bank to lend as much as 90% of its money without gold or silver in reserve, wiser men in Kirtland, including Joseph Smith, felt that higher reserves should have been maintained in the event of an emergency. Unfortunately, that emergency came when the international bankers began to manipulate the flow of money, thus precipitating the "Panic of 1837."

In the process of banking, there must be a constant flow of paper: stocks, bonds, securities, etc. When that flow is interrupted and money cannot be obtained from the bank for any part of the money flow, panic sets in.

> The Panic of 1837 was aggravated by the Bank of England when it in one day threw out all the paper connected with the United States.
> . . . Why did the Bank of England in one day "throw out" all paper connected with the United States, that is, refuse to discount or accept any securities, bonds or other financial paper based in the United States? The purpose of this action was to create an immediate

financial panic in the United States, cause a complete contraction of credit, halt further issues of stocks and bonds, and ruin those seeking to turn United States securities into cash.[6]

Because of this kind of external control, manufactured panics have occurred on several occasions in many countries. However, because of the misunderstanding of the nature of the collapse of the Kirtland Bank, members of the Church blamed Joseph Smith for its failure. A general apostasy, including five members of the Quorum of the Twelve, occurred with several charges placed against the Church for losses incurred by the panic.

Why would money be manipulated like this? When a panic or depression occurs, often quickly and unexpectedly, people are frequently overextended. Generally, panics are preceded by economic booms and people have invested as much as they are able with expectations of rapidly recovering their investments. Investors have pledged collateral for their investments; however, when the panic or depression comes, that collateral is often sold at undervalued amounts or confiscated by lending institutions. Because large banks—particularly those associated with the international banking cartel—have capital, they are able to buy properties, stocks, etc., at extremely low prices and recognize huge profits at the conclusion of the panic. Thus, the bankers have phenomenal control over not just money that has been borrowed, but all phases of a person's or nation's assets.

To understand the import of Dr. Quigley's statement that the group of which he writes seeks "nothing less than to create a world system of financial control in private hands able to dominate the political system of each country and the economy of the world," it is important to understand the process of creating and controlling money. In the United States, the Federal Reserve Corporation is the body that has assumed this role.

The Money System of the United States

Because of Congressional failure to follow constitutional safeguards respecting money and allowing it to be both printed and disseminated by a private corporation, the United States dollar has gone through major devaluation and created severe trade problems. The private printing of money ushered what is termed today as "fiat" currency—money that is based upon "good faith" rather than gold or silver reserves. W. Cleon Skousen plotted the dollar's plunge:

> *In 1913 the Federal Reserve replaced the national bank system, and Federal Reserve notes were issued with a promise to redeem them in gold on demand.*
>
> *On April 5, 1933, one month after his inauguration, President Franklin D. Roosevelt declared a national emergency and ordered all gold coins, gold bullion, and gold certificates to be turned in to the Federal Reserve banks by May 1. This order applied only to those residing in the United States. It did not apply to foreigners living abroad. Within the United States only those who had special gold collections or needed the gold for industrial or professional use were allowed to retain quantities of the yellow metal.*
>
> *As gold coins, gold bullion, or gold certificates were turned in, the American people received Federal Reserve notes redeemable in silver.*
>
> *On May 22, Congress enacted a law (48 Stat. 31) declaring all coin and currencies then in circulation to be legal tender, dollar for dollar, as if they were gold. It also empowered the President to reduce the gold content of the dollar to 50 percent.*
>
> *On June 5, Congress enacted a joint resolution (48 Stat. 112) that all gold clauses in contracts were outlawed and no one could legally demand gold in payment for any obligation due him.*
>
> *On January 30, 1934, the Gold Reserve Act was passed, giving the Federal Reserve title to all the gold which had been collected. This act also changed the price of gold from $20.67 per ounce to $35 per ounce, which meant that all of the silver certificates the people had recently received for their gold now lost 40 percent of their value.*

The next day the President proclaimed (48 Stat. 1730) that the dollar was to be fixed at 15 and 5/21 grains of standard gold and was to be maintained at this level "in perpetuity." This is still the definition of the "dollar" in the United States code. Russia and the central banks began buying up gold in huge quantities.

Thus there came into being a dual monetary system: a gold standard for foreigners and Federal Reserve notes (redeemable in silver) for Americans.

From 1914 to 1973 American currency went through the following erosion:

(1) From 1914 to 1934 every Federal Reserve note was redeemable in gold or silver

(2) Between 1934 and 1963 all Federal Reserve notes promised to pay (or be redeemed) in "lawful money," which meant silver. Then the wording on the Federal Reserve notes began to be changed to somewhat obscure language, which should have given Americans a warning that the government was planning something.

(3) In 1965 President Lyndon Johnson authorized the treasury to begin issuing debased "sandwich" dimes and quarters with little or no intrinsic value, and the quantity of silver in fifty-cent pieces was reduced to 40 percent.

(4) On June 24, 1968, President Johnson issued a proclamation that henceforth Federal Reserve silver certificates were merely fiat legal tender and could not be redeemed in silver.

(5) On December 31, 1970, President Richard Nixon authorized the treasury to issue debased "sandwich" dollars and half dollars.

(6) By August 1971 many of the European countries had collected so many billions in Eurodollars (foreign aid, money spent by the U. S. military abroad, etc.) that European banks had begun to get nervous about redeeming their money in gold. A threatened run on the U. S. Treasury resulted in the American gold window being slammed shut. This resulted in a collapse of the dollar on the world market. Since then it has fluctuated on the world market like any other commodity, since it is no longer redeemable in precious metal and therefore has no intrinsic value.

(7) In 1973, the U. S. dollar was officially devalued, changing the price of gold from $35 per ounce to $42.23 per ounce.

(8) On March 16, 1973, Congress set the American dollar completely afloat with nothing to back it up but the declaration of the government that it was "legal tender" or fiat currency.

(9) The world market immediately reflected serious erosion in the value of the American dollar. To buy an ounce of gold it took not $42.23 but $100, then $200. After that it moved higher and higher until it required $800 to buy an ounce of gold. Gradually, some confidence was restored in the dollar as the symbol of the American economy, and so it settled back down to a plateau of approximately $300 plus.

Today the American economy operates under a monetary system which is completely outside the Constitution. Its fiat money is continually manipulated both in value and in quantity. This has had a devastating impact on its purchasing power, which is now down to about 8 percent of its 1933 value. It has eroded the value of savings, insurance policies, retirement funds, and the fixed incomes of the elderly.[7]

With the rate of indebtedness increasing and the worth of the dollar declining at such a rapid pace, the money had to be going somewhere. William Guy Carr summed up the early profits of the Federal Reserve:

In 1914 the Federal Reserve System, consisted of twelve banks which had bought $134,000,000 worth of Federal Reserve stock. [It was generally assumed at that time that most of the stock was purchased with fiat money printed by the central bank.] According to Congressional Record of May 29, 1939; #8896, they had made a profit of $23,141,456,197. In 1940 the assets of the Federal Reserve were shown as five billion dollars. In 1946 they were declared to be forty-five billion dollars. The bankers made forty billion dollars profit out of the transactions of World War Two.[8]

Dr. Skousen's book referred to above, *The Making of America*, was published in 1985. Since that time the dollar has continued to lose value and has further exacerbated the insecurities he discussed. But how did all that happen? How could the United States, the greatest producing nation on the earth, have lost its edge? In fact, how could it have been lost to the point that the nation's economic system would no longer be viable?

The average person gives little thought to the world's system of money. It is a convenient medium of exchange and allows us to trade our services and production into currency so that our efforts can supply our needs and wants. It seems to work and not a lot of attention is drawn to it. From our study, that may be a good thing! If more concern were given to our money system and people realized the hollow value of the dollar, perhaps there would be less perceived stability.

Des Griffin in his enlightening book, *Descent Into Slavery*, reviewed the workings of banks, particularly the international bankers and the Federal Reserve.

> *We'll start with the need for money. The federal government, having spent more than it has taken from its citizens in taxes, needs, for the sake of illustration, $1,000,000,000. Since it does not have the money, and Congress has given away its authority to create it, the government must go to the creators of the $1 Billion dollars. But the Federal Reserve, a private corporation, doesn't just give its money away. The bankers are willing to deliver $1,000,000,000 in money or credit to the federal government in exchange for the government's promise to pay it back with interest! So the Congress authorizes the Treasury Department to print $1,000,000,000 in U. S. Bonds which are then delivered to the Federal Reserve.*
>
> *The Federal Reserve then pays the cost of printing the $1,000,000,000, perhaps as little as $1,000, and makes the exchange. The government then uses the money to discharge its obligations. What are the details of this fantastic transaction? Well, the government's debts are discharged all right, but the U. S. government has now indebted the people to the Federal Reserve bankers for $1,000,000,000 plus interest until paid! Since this and similar*

*transactions have been going on since 1914, the government is
indebted to bankers for nearly [8,000,000,000,000 (2006)]. On this
we pay about 7 percent interest, with no hope of ever paying off the
capital.*

      *You say this is terrible! Yes it is, but we have only shown
part of the sordid story. Under this debt-money system, those United
States Bonds referred to above have now become assets of the banks
in the system against which they can now make loans to individual
and commercial customers. Since U. S. banking laws require only a
10% reserve, this means the bankers can lend up to ten times the
amount of the Bonds they have on hand. On the one transaction of $1
Billion we discussed, they can lend $10 Billion to private customers
at interest. This gives them upwards of $10 Billion out at interest for
an original cost to them of as little as $1,000! And since Congress no
longer creates and issues money under the Constitution, the only way
our people and our businesses can get money to carry on trade and
expand farming and industry is to borrow it from the bankers!*[9]

As if creating money and receiving interest weren't
enough, it has been shown through repeated investigations and
research that more extensive manipulation has occurred. Griffin
continues:

      *This practice is so refined today that the Federal Reserve
Board need only to announce to the news media an increase or
decrease in their rediscount rate to send stocks up and down as they
wish. Using this method since 1914, the bankers and their agents
have purchased secret or open control of almost every large
corporation in America.*[10]

But it didn't need to happen. The Founders were quite
vocal about money in the new nation and left a set of principles
for Americans to follow. They understood that money, real
money, couldn't be created from nothing. Alexander Hamilton,
although a student of banking himself, taught that production by
citizens was "the most powerful instrument in increasing the

quantity of money in a state."[11] He further agreed that "Money is, with propriety, considered as the vital principle of the body politic.[12] After all, only with money, could the government meet its various obligations and fulfill its limited role.

Therefore, the Constitution laid out the terms of money for the Founders as well as for later generations. In Article 1, Section 8, Congress reserved the responsibility "To coin Money, regulate the Value thereof, and of foreign Coin, and fix the Standard of Weight and Measures." It was understood that the money coined was gold and silver, therefore, the next Section directed that "No State shall . . . make any Thing but gold and silver Coin a Tender in Payment of Debt." In other words, states (banks) could only accept gold and silver for payment of debts.

Gold and silver coins, however, were bulky and inconvenient. With that in mind, paper currency was issued by banks but carried the stipulation that it was "legal tender" and could be exchanged by the bearer for gold or silver. Gold and silver could not be manufactured or easily replaced. They were metals that had intrinsic value and were regulated by the free market. The Founders then used the power of Congress to "fix the standard of weights and measures" to the intrinsic worth of the metal.

When financing he Revolutionary War, the government had virtually no reserves or precious metals to anchor its money to; therefore, it authorized the printing of paper continental dollars to meet its wartime needs and to allow commerce to continue. Because the dollars had no backing, the "continentals" rapidly lost value until a common comparison to something without value for Americans was the statement: "not worth a continental." Following their debacle with fiat currency, the leaders of the new nation worked on plans to devise a new money system that would be secure and create confidence.

Thus the Framers of the Constitution placed money on a standard of gold and silver. Although paper money was often used, it was always backed with precious metal. One of the problems of paper money was the temptation of a bank to print more money than it had in gold and silver reserves. Permission to do this, unfortunately, was later codified into bank law and the system of "fractional reserves" came into being. Today's fractional reserve law states that a bank must only hold 10% of the cash that it receives; the balance may be lent out or invested for greater profits. Worse, carried into today's banking where both gold and silver are nonexistent, the only reserves a bank carries are Federal Reserve Notes—those issued by the Federal Reserve Corporation with only the "good faith" of their users.

Referring to a list of vital constitutional principles that are paramount to sound society, President Ezra Taft Benson wrote

> *I believe in honest money, the gold and silver coinage of the Constitution, and a circulating medium convertible into such money without loss. I regard it as a flagrant violation of the explicit provisions of the Constitution for the federal government to make it a criminal offense to use gold or silver as legal tender or to issue irredeemable paper money.*[13]

Unfortunately, with the total elimination of precious metals from the world's currencies, it would be virtually impossible—given today's current conditions—to return to the gold or even the silver standard because the currency of the United States and that of every other nation is fiat. With such currency, there is no stability—nothing with which to tie the dollar to a set value. As more money enters into circulation, the currency is worth less; hence ever increasing inflation. By law, interest rates are assigned by the Federal Reserve as is the amount of money issued. As a result of this money system,

The millions of working families in America are now indebted to a few banking families for more than the assessed value of the entire United States. And these banking families obtained this debt against us for the cost of the paper, ink and bookkeeping![14]

The power to create money has opened the doors to unimaginable wealth. Moroni said that the primary motivations of the combinations were power and gain—in our wildest dreams, we couldn't fathom the kind of temporal power and gain that Satan held out as a reward.

To understand how this power came to be accepted and embedded as part of the American way of life, it is instructive to review the presidency of Woodrow Wilson.

The Woodrow Wilson Administration

Much of the methodology of the elite international bankers is found in an examination of the presidency of Woodrow Wilson—the watershed years for much of the nation's and world's current direction. An amazing number of foundational events all occurred within a very short period of time.

1912   The election of Woodrow Wilson
1913   The enactment of the Federal Reserve
1916   The Graduated Income Tax
1917   Entry into World War One
1917   The Bolshevik Revolution
1919   The Treaty of Versailles
1919   The Council on Foreign Relations
1920   Proposal of the League of Nations

1912—*The election of Woodrow Wilson.* Students of politics have always been puzzled by the meteoric rise of Woodrow Wilson into the national political scene. From his presidency of Princeton University and partial-term as governor of New Jersey for two years, he became the President of the United States—against virtually all odds. In trying to make sense of it, Eustace Mullins and other historians have pointed to the proposed Federal Reserve (initially drafted as the Aldrich Plan and then proposed under both names—the Aldrich Plan under Republican leadership and the Federal Reserve under Democratic leadership) as a reason for his victory. Mullins wrote:

> *The Presidential campaign of 1912 records one of the more interesting political upsets in American history. The incumbent, William Howard Taft, was a popular president, and the Republicans, in a period of general prosperity, were firmly in control of the government through a Republican majority in both houses. The Democratic challenger, Woodrow Wilson, Governor of New Jersey, had no national recognition, and was a stiff, austere man who excited little public support. Both parties included a monetary reform bill in their platforms. . . . In retrospect, it seems obvious that the money creators decided to dump Taft and go with Wilson. How do we know this? Taft seemed certain of reelection, and Wilson would return to obscurity. Suddenly, Theodore Roosevelt "threw his hat into the ring." He announced that he was running as a third party candidate, the "Bull Moose." His candidacy would have been ludicrous had it not been for the fact that he was exceptionally well financed. Moreover, he was given unlimited press coverage, more than Taft and Wilson combined. As a Republican ex-president, it was obvious that Roosevelt would cut deeply into Taft's vote. This proved the case and Wilson won the election. To this day, no one can say what Theodore Roosevelt's program was, or why he would sabotage his own party. Since the bankers were financing all three candidates . . . . The result was that a Democratic Congress and a Democratic President were elected in 1912 to get the central bank legislation passed.[15]*

To this scenario, Dr. Skousen adds that

> *Two Morgan agents, Frank Munsey and George Perkins moved in behind Teddy Roosevelt with money and manpower from Wall Street. As Ferdinand Lundberg states [America's 60 Families, Vanguard Press, New York, 1938, pp. 110-112] "As soon as Roosevelt signified that he would again challenge Taft, the President's defeat was inevitable. Throughout the three-cornered fight, Roosevelt had Munsey and Perkins constantly at his heels, supplying money, going over his speeches, bringing people from Wall Street in to help, and, in general, carrying the entire burden of the campaign against Taft. . . ."[16]*

Thus, with the split vote, Wilson assumed the presidency of the United States and both he and his "adviser," Col. Edward Mandel House, placed their weight of office behind banking proposals. Col. House ("Colonel was an honorary title given to him by Texas governmental leaders) was much more influential than current historians generally give credit. He was educated in England—the son of a British financier who represented banking interests throughout the southern states. Skousen wrote that he "emerged as the virtual president during the Wilson administration. Two of his pet projects, the central bank and the graduated income tax, were both successfully adopted through the amazing capacity of House to pull wires behind the scenes."[17] Skousen additionally calls him "the chief architect for the formal creation of the CFR [Council on Foreign Relations]."[18]

The enactment of the Federal Reserve

The most important reason to have Wilson in the White House was to pass the issue of central banking—the Federal Reserve. Because of Constitutional safeguards placing the creation of money in the hands of Congress and away from private interests, it was necessary for the legislature to approve the proposed act. This would effectively give a money monopoly to the Federal Reserve. Chronicling events of the administration, Charles Sylvester Viereck wrote

> *The Schiffs, the Warburgs, the Kahns, the Rockefellers, the Morgans put their faith in House. When the Federal Reserve legislation at last assumed definite shape, House was the intermediary between the White House and the financiers.*[19]

Although there was strong objection by constitutionalists to the Federal Reserve Act, it was passed on December 23, 1913—two days before Christmas and at a time when many Congressmen had returned to their homes for what had been traditionally known as a "Christmas break." Only with many of those opposing the concept of the Federal Reserve gone, could it achieve passage.

Congressman Charles A. Lindbergh, Sr. (father of the celebrated aviator) was one of the bill's most vocal critics:

> *This Act established the most gigantic trust on earth. When the President signs this bill, the invisible government by the Monetary Power will be legalized. . . . The greatest crime of Congress is its currency system. The worst legislative crime of the ages is perpetuated by this banking bill. The caucus and party bosses have again operated and prevented the people from getting the benefit of their own government.*[20]

Lindbergh spoke loudly against the Federal Reserve to both Congress and his constituents. Although he had some degree of success, he was no match for the well-oiled machinery of the bankers. In 1917 he published the book, *Why is Your Country at War?* which documented the role of the Federal Reserve in bringing about World War One. Concerned about publicity and documented objections against the Federal Reserve System, President Wilson ordered the seizure and destruction of both the printing plates and all existing copies of the book in the spring of 1918.

Another author close to the events surrounding the Act's passage wrote in 1916:

> *In the Federal Reserve Law, they have wrested from the people and secured for themselves the constitutional power to issue money and regulate the value thereof.*
>
> *The House of Morgan has been supreme in legislation ever since [the contrived Panic of 1907] until now they have full legal control of the issue of money, and the complete control of the two dominant political parties.*[21]

The graduated income tax

The Constitution specified that no "direct" tax should be levied on the American people—a direct tax being one that is paid by the citizenry directly. Instead, government financing was to be borne through indirect means such as tariffs except in times of national emergencies. Added to the concern of the Founding Fathers that government would become too intrusive and meddlesome through direct taxation, is the warning contained in the Communist Manifesto. Its second plank to foster a socialist state was to enact a heavy "progressive"—or graduated tax on incomes.

Despite the warnings, an amendment to the Constitution was proposed to enact a direct tax on incomes. It was a graduated tax—those who earned more were to pay more and thus proposed as a minimal tax upon those of limited means and a heavy tax upon those of wealth. This was especially appealing because of the publicity given to the "robber barons" "monopolists, and "wealthy tycoons" who, it was intended, would shoulder the major tax burden.

From current research, it is apparent that the amendment was never properly ratified; however, the amendment was considered approved by Congress and the income tax was considered valid. Instead, however, of taxing the superrich as many had believed, a loophole was written into the tax code protecting charitable foundations and declaring them to be tax exempt. Rather than curtailing the growth of the elite bankers and industrialists, they were able to place their money into foundations and still maintain control of their expenditures. For those without the super-means of funding tax-exempt foundations, however, the income tax proved a deterrent limiting their ability to attain the status of the super-wealthy. Thus the common citizen became the object of income taxes—the direct tax that the Framers warned us about.

With the annual payment of income taxes, there was a constant source of money. Collected by the federal government, this money could be paid to the Federal Reserve System toward the national debt in times of war or other defined emergencies.

Entry into World War 1

Wilson's campaign slogan for his second term had been: "He kept us out of war." Although the United States was not at war during that time, ten months prior to the election of 1916, Col. House had cooperated with Sir William Wiseman, the Chief of the British Secret Service, on an agreement for the United States to enter the war as an ally to England and France. As we find so frequently during World War One, those with decision-making authority were closely tied to the Rothschild banking family. Wiseman was also a partner of Kuhn, Loeb & Company—a Rothschild controlled banking firm. Upon hearing of Wilson's prior commitment to the war, H. L. Mencken wrote that Wilson was "the perfect model for the Christian cad."[22]

President J. Reuben Clark, concerned about inroads into the Constitution by presidential appointments (such as Col. House) wrote in the *Church News*:

> *Again, and as another check upon the executive, in his conduct of international relations, the diplomatic representatives of the government must be, as we the people provided in the Constitution, nominated by the President and approved by the Senate. But the habit is growing of appointment by the President of quasi-diplomatic representatives, "ambassadors at large" they call them, who "going to and fro in the earth and walking up and down"—to use Job's phrase—bring their harvests to the President. President Wilson was the first to give this device considerable importance when he sent the ubiquitous Colonel House to Europe. Col. House (not approved by the senate) with the President's approval, committed us to enter World War 1 on the side of the Allies more than a year before Congress declared war.[23]*

Aligning personnel for WWI, Woodrow Wilson made two key appointments: Bernard Baruch as head of the War Industries Board and Eugene Meyer as head of the War Finance Corporation. These two worked intimately with Paul Warburg, the architect of the Federal Reserve and then-current Chairman of the Federal Reserve—the nation's banking system.

Now that the United States had a central bank, it was able to finance a war—a European war. The nations abroad had been nearly bankrupted through armament and defense programs; but by bringing the Federal Reserve to the United States, a fresh supply of money was in place for further exploitation. In 1914, the first year of operation of the Federal Reserve, the nation lent the Allied Powers $25 billion which—because it was not repaid—became a debt of the American people. Much more financing followed.

The inbreeding with the Rothschild machine was incredible. Bernard Baruch was a banker who had worked closely with Edward Harriman of Brown Bothers, Harriman Banking and Jacob Schiff—head of Kuhn, Loeb & Company, a banking house tied closely to the Rothschilds. Eugene Meyer was with Lazard Freres Banking (a major stockholder of the

Federal Reserve with the Rothchilds, Israel Sieff, Kuhn Loeb Company, Warburg Company, Lehman Brothers, Goldman Sachs, the Rockefeller family, and J. P. Morgan interests.) Bernard Baruch would later serve as a close advisor to Franklin D. Roosevelt and Harry S. Truman, and as Chairman of the Atomic Energy Commission overseeing the Manhattan Project— the atomic bomb. Eugene Meyer would later become a member of the Federal Reserve Board appointed by Franklin Roosevelt.

As startling as the connection was in the United States, the interrelationships beyond the Atlantic were just as surprising. Jacob Schiff, the business associate of Bernard Baruch, had two brothers, Philip and Ludwig Schiff who were major bankers to the German government during the war. Paul Warburg, a naturalized United States citizen in 1911, had two brothers also in Germany, both major bankers to the government. One brother, Max, was also the head of the German Secret Service.

At the conclusion of the war the various leaders met at the Treaty of Versailles to sign an armistice. The Allies dictated the terms of the Agreement with Germany left accountable for costs in war reparations and a severely emasculated military— conditions that many feel led directly to World War Two. Curiously, at the signing of the agreement by the national powers, Paul Warburg sat with the Americans and Max Warburg sat with the Germans.

The Bolshevik Revolution

During this time, the international bankers looked abroad as well as at home to further their interests. The monarchy of Russia proved to be an unstable leadership and following a contrived series of events that eventually brought riots to the capitol city of Petrograd, under Allied pressure, Czar Nicholas II resigned in March of 1917. A few months later, the governing

Kerensky regime allowed exiled Communists (having been exiled following the failed coup of 1905) to reenter the country.

It is important to understand that the Communists of the Bolshevik Revolution, contrary to accepted history, did not overthrow the czarist rulers of Russia, but were invited into the country following the abdication of Nicholas II. The Communist government was not a popular movement of the people, but instead was a well-financed plan to begin a new Russian regime.

Lenin was in Switzerland and Trotsky was in New York at the time of the czar's abdication. With the new fledgling leadership not quite positioned, they were able to establish the rudiments of a Communist government through plotting and "buying" a following. Both, with the blessings of the United States (particularly Col. Edward Mandell House and several elite banking families) Lenin and Trotsky had taken large sums of money into Russia—Jacob Schiff gave $20 million; Paul and Max Warburg contributed $6 million; and J. P. Morgan (including Harriman, Milner, Rockefeller, Rothschild) added another $5 million.

Gary Allen in *None Dare Call It Conspiracy* sums up the players in the building of the Russian Communist government:

> *In the Bolshevik Revolution we see many of the same old faces that were responsible for creating the Federal Reserve System, initiating the graduated income tax, setting up the tax-free foundations, and pushing us into WW1. . . . this is anything but coincidental . . . .*

Why would they be interested in planting their interests in Russia? There were several reasons—all equating to "power and gain." Allen goes on to reveal that the new government "transferred 600 million roubles in gold between the years 1918 and 1922" to Jacob Schiff's banking firm.[24] In addition, the

Rockefeller group was able to acquire rights to oil and soon built a refinery in the country.

As for power, do you remember the Hegelian Dialectic? Prior to the creation of the Soviet Union, America had no major enemy—none to challenge the traditionally accepted ideals of the United States. With the creation of a Communist state, the use of the Hegelian Dialectic using the thesis, antithesis, and synthesis, could begin to compromise American values and attitudes.

The Treaty of Versailles

As discussed elsewhere, the Treaty of Versailles was a weak document that enforced the armistice of WWI. It called for war reparations payments by Germany far in excess of the country's ability to pay without simultaneously injuring its own economy. By forcing Germany to the brink of economic collapse, the country was left with two stark realities: (1) that it must inflate its currency, at least temporarily, to meet its debt; and (2) that a future war would completely relieve its debt obligations and allow Germany to create its own economy while simultaneously siphoning the wealth of other European countries. (This plank of the Treaty, incidentally, was written by John Foster Dulles—another with links to key international bankers.) As said so often among historians and economists, "The Treaty included the seeds of World War Two."

The Council on Foreign Relations

While attending the Paris Peace Conference, many of the delegates met separately to begin a new organization. According to the Council on Foreign Relations Handbook of 1936, they met "to discuss setting up an international group which would advise their respective governments on international affairs." A few days later it was decided that "separate organizations cooperating with each other" would allow for more direct input into respective governments—thus the Council on Foreign Relations (CFR) was formed in the United States; the Royal Institute of International Affairs in Great Britain; and the Institute of Pacific Relations in the United States to deal with Far Eastern affairs. At the same time, other groups were organized in both Paris and Hamburg.

The lead person in organizing the Council was none other than Col. Edward Mandell House. The founders, for the most part, were those who had been present at the signing of the Treaty of Versailles. Financing for the Council came from J. P. Morgan, John D. Rockefeller, Bernard Baruch, Paul Warburg, Otto Kahn, and Jacob Schiff.

The CFR and other policy-making groups influencing government decisions will be treated later in this chapter.

Proposal of the League of Nations

One of the provisions of the Treaty of Versailles was the formation of the League of Nations—a forerunner to the United Nations. The League required mandates that were ostensibly designed to promote peace. Although the League was technically in operation from 1920 through 1940 and exercised significant interplay between member nations—the United States never became a part of it. The "treaty" provision of the League called for all nations to unite in a pledge to protect each other, a provision which Congress wisely saw as interventionist and contrary to the politically isolationist policy that the Constitution prescribed.

From the time of George Washington's Farewell Address, Americans had been warned of the danger of entering into treaties and alliances with foreign countries. There were two primary reasons given for avoiding these "entanglements:" (1) because national interests would rarely be the same, and (2) because alliances would necessarily encroach upon sovereignty, leaving the United States incapable of making unilateral decisions.

Despite the fact that the League of Nations failed to gain approval in the United States, it planted seeds for further consideration of the United Nations during and following WW2. From this point, a single world government would be a continuing goal of the international banking cartel.

The Post Wilson Era: The Expanding Influence of the Bankers

Following the Woodrow Wilson Administration, leaders representing key banking-industrial interests were already in prominent positions. A planning guide for the elite was found in a book written by Colonel House prior to his affiliation with President Wilson. The book, *Philip Dru: Administrator*, outlined a plan whereby his utopian-socialist views could be adopted into government. He said that it would be the job of a "conspiracy" to: (1) establish a central bank; (2) implement a graduated income tax; and (3) control both political parties of the United States. The first two goals were met during the Wilson Administration— the third would be accomplished through the Council on Foreign Relations and other policy-making groups.

Before studying the CFR, a short background of secret policy-making groups in Great Britain is instructive. Dr. Carroll Quigley turns to the English roots of the conspiracy as fundamental in understanding its breadth in today's world. The beginnings were at Oxford in 1870 with the appointment of John Ruskin. Quigley writes that ". . . he hit Oxford like an earthquake not so much because he talked about fine arts, but because he talked about the empire and England's downtrodden masses, and above all because he talked about all three of these things as moral issues."[25]

Ruskin permanently influenced men who throughout their lifetimes, would further his ideals. Some of these men were

Cecil Rhodes, Arnold Toynbee, Alfred (Lord) Milner, Sir George Parkin, Philip Lyttleton Gell, Sir Henry Birchenough, Reginald (Lord Esher) Baliol Brett, (Sir) John B. Seeley, Albert (Lord) Grey, and Edmond Garrett. These names are of interest because of the individual and collective roles they played in creating the Ruskin Utopia. Of these, the most influential was Cecil Rhodes. Having made a fortune with the financial support of Lord Rothschild in the South African diamond mines, by the mid-1890s he was worth about $5 million.

At that time Rhodes made two major decisions: (1) he bestowed money "to bring all the habitable portions of the world under their control" through the medium of "the Rhodes Scholarships at Oxford in order to spread the English ruling class tradition throughout the English-speaking world as Ruskin had wanted;"[26] and (2) he established a secret society to bring about the desired social reform.

Dr. Quigley wrote:

> In this secret society Rhodes was to be the leader; Stead, Brett (Lord Esher), and Milner were to form the executive committee; Arthur (Lord) Balfour, (Sir) Harry Johnson, Lord Rothschild, Albert (Lord) Grey, and others were listed as potential members of a 'Circle of Initiates;' while there was to be an outer circle known as the 'Association of Helpers' (later organized by Milner as the Round Table Association.)

Milner went on to serve as governor-general and high commissioner of South Africa. In his post, he recruited heavily from Oxford, and through his direction, "these men were able to win influential posts in government and international finance and become the dominant influence in British imperial and foreign affairs up to 1939."[27] From 1909 to 1913 "they organized semi-secret groups, known as Round Table Groups, in the chief British dependencies and in the United States."[28] These groups, because they held the same purposes, worked side-by-side with the organizations begun by Colonel House at the conclusion of WWI. The groups were the Royal Institute of International Affairs, the Council on Foreign Relations, and the Institute of Pacific Relations.

Speaking of the Rhodes' groups, Quigley continued:

> *At the end of the war in 1914, it became clear that the organization of this system had to be greatly extended. . . . In New York it was known as the Council on Foreign Relations, and was a front for J. P. Morgan and Company in association with the very small American Round Table Group. The American organizers were dominated by the large number of Morgan 'experts' . . . who had gone to the Paris Peace Conference and there became close friends with the similar group of English 'experts' which had been recruited by the Milner group.*[29]

Thus the secretive background of the Rhodes' Round Tables was the foundation for the fledgling American Council on Foreign Relations. Augmented by the previously listed financial support, additional money from recently created tax-exempt foundations, and existing membership in key positions, the CFR quickly became a quiet, influential body in domestic and international affairs.

Although we know a great deal about the CFR because of its journal and various comments made by members, a great deal lies in the area of speculation. The content of meetings remains a closely guarded secret and according to CFR bylaws, a condition of membership states that members refrain from disclosing particulars of Council meetings. Despite the secrecy, however, we do have access to its roster of membership, the pervasiveness of its influence, and many of its stated goals.

The foundation of the Council on Foreign Relations took place on May 19, 1919 at the Paris Peace Conference with

Colonel Edward Mandell House assuming the main organizational role. With him were Walter Lippmann, John Foster Dulles, Allen Dulles and Christian Herter. As an indicator of the influence this organization was to have, Walter Lippmann became the syndicated columnist that was the voice for the establishment; Allen Dulles became the Director of the Central Intelligence Agency; and John Foster Dulles preceded Christian Herter—both serving as Secretary of State under President Dwight Eisenhower. The formal organization of the group is listed in CFR records as 1921.

By the end of WW2 and the inception of the United Nations, 74 members of the CFR were in the original contingency sent to San Francisco to represent the United States. Among the group were Alger Hiss (who led the contingent, drafted the original United Nations Charter, was suspected of being a soviet spy and was convicted of perjury), Harry Dexter White (Assistant Secretary of the Treasury, Director of the International Monetary Fund, and an admitted Soviet agent), Owen Lattimore (described by a Congressional committee as a "conscious, articulate instrument of the Soviet international conspiracy") John J. McCloy (past chairman of the Rockefeller Chase-Manhattan Bank), Harold Stassen, Nelson Rockefeller, John Foster Dulles, Philip Jessup, Dean Acheson and others all filling key decision-making positions.[30]

An interesting aside demonstrating the CFR's interest in the United Nations is the report by Secretary of State and CFR member (and the son of a of an establishment banker) Edward R. Stettinius to President Harry S. Truman. Recapping the events leading to the foundation of the world body, he wrote

> *With the outbreak of war in Europe it was clear that the United States would be confronted, after the war, with new and exceptional problems. . . . Accordingly, a committee on Post-War Problems was set up before the end of 1939, at the suggestions of the*

> *CFR. The Committee consisted of high officials of the Department of State.*[31]

A committee on post-war problems? Two years before the United States entered the war? The State Department? (Incidentally, all but one member of the Committee was a member of the CFR.) Apparently, the Council on Foreign Relations knew much more than other Americans about the far-reaching effects of the war and was intent on resurrecting the League of Nations. In fact, three years following its organization, the CFR journal, *Foreign Affairs* carried an endorsement for world government:

> *Obviously, there is going to be no peace or prosperity for mankind as long as [the earth] remains divided into 50 or 60 independent states until some kind of international system is created. . . . The real problem today is that of world government.*[32]

Since WW2, the Council on Foreign Relations has assumed even greater leadership in national policy decisions. The organization generally has a roster of about three thousand members; all especially invited and interviewed for membership. Frequently, they hold appointed positions in government. For example, during Ronald Reagan's administration, 347 positions were held by CFR members. Under George Bush, Sr., there were 382, under Bill Clinton there were 387, and there are similar numbers in the current administration. In October of 1993, the *Washington Post* said of the Clinton White House:

> *The President is a member. So is his secretary of state, the deputy of state, all five of the undersecretaries, several of the assistant secretaries and the department's legal advisor. The President's national security advisor and his deputy are members. The director of Central Intelligence (like all previous directors) and the chairman of the Foreign Advisory Board are members. The*

secretary of defense, three undersecretaries and at least four assistant secretaries are members. The secretaries of the departments of housing and urban development, interior, health and human services and the chief White House public relations man . . . along with the speaker of the House . . . .

The above article is reminiscent of a description of the secret combination given by Helaman: "And thus they did obtain the sole management of the government."[33]

Perhaps the continuity of CFR personnel in the various administrations—both Republican and Democrat—explains why the same policies and decisions seem to carry on from one President to the next. Recall that Colonel House (in his book *Philip Dru: Administrator*) said that one of the chief goals of his political conspiracy was to control both political parties in the United States. The CFR, to a large extent, does that. All candidates for President of the United States—both Republican and Democrat—since Dwight D. Eisenhower, with the exception of Barry Goldwater and Ronald Reagan have been members of the CFR. On another level, we might contemplate James Madison's statement in the Federalist Papers that "the accumulation of all powers, legislative, executive and judiciary . . . may justly be pronounced the very definition of tyranny." All three branches of government at the highest levels are well represented by the Council on Foreign Relations.

The interweaving throughout government agencies has caused many to label the CFR "the invisible government"—also the title of a book written by Dan Smoot and descriptive of the organization's functions. Smoot, a respected columnist and author at a time when much of the CFR activity was coming to light, wrote that

. . . I am convinced that the Council on Foreign Relations, together with a great number of other associated tax-exempt

organizations, constitutes the invisible government which sets the major policies of the federal government; exercises controlling influence on government officials who implement the policies; and through massive and skilled propaganda, influences Congress and the public to support the policies.

I am convinced that the objective of this invisible government is to convert America into a socialist state and then make it a unit in a one-world socialist system.[34]

A constant theme of the CFR and the international bankers—and mentioned again by Smoot—is globalism or a one-world government. As evidenced by the leaders' support of the League of Nations; the drafting and spearheading of the United Nations Charter; and fostering the adoption of treaties and alliances world-wide—it is apparent that globalism is still a primary focus. Council of Foreign Relations President Richard N. Haass wrote a paper entitled *Sovereignty and Globalisation* under the date of February 17, 2006. Some excerpts are:

> *"States must be prepared to cede some sovereignty to world bodies if the international system is to function."*

> *"Sovereignty must be redefined if states are to deal with globalization."*

> *Globalisation implies that sovereignty is not only becoming weaker in reality, but that it needs to become weaker. States would be wise to weaken sovereignty in order to protect themselves, because they cannot insulate themselves from what goes on elsewhere. Sovereignty is no longer a sanctuary.*

> *Necessity may lead to reducing or even eliminating sovereignty when a government, whether from a lack of capacity or conscious policy, is unable to provide for the basic needs of its citizens.*

The goal should be to redefine sovereignty for the era of globalisation, to find a balance between a world of fully sovereign states and an international system of either world government or anarchy.[35]

Clearly, the goal of the CFR has not changed. Government leaders at the top echelons of decision-making do not have United States' sovereignty as their top priority, but rather have the mindset that a global government or world power is necessary to control world events. Is it any wonder that the United States has found itself embroiled in the affairs of other nations and has been a part of "peacekeeping" efforts across the globe?

For many years, the Chairman (and now the Honorary Chairman) of the CFR was David Rockefeller—the Director of the Chase-Manhattan Bank. His links to the international bankers cannot be disputed; nor can his influence in foreign affairs. In 1973, he was instrumental in the organization of another powerful, decision-making group: the Trilateral Commission.

The Trilateral Commission included representatives, far fewer in number than those of the CFR, from the United States, the Western European Bloc; and Japan. The stated purpose of the group was to examine common problems and "to support proposals for handling them jointly, and to nurture habits and practices of working together among these regions." Although the word "commission" indicates that the group was established by a government or other empowered body, it was not. As other names used by the world leaders, it sounded as though it had more official direction than it did.

The growth of the Commission's influence, however, is instructive in demonstrating its affect on American—and world—living. Its first director was Zbigniew Brzezinski who worked hand-in-hand with David Rockefeller to fill the membership of the Commission and lay out its future agenda. In

1980, there were 289 members of the group from the three regional areas, hardly indicative of their influence. Antony C. Sutton and Patrick M. Wood in their groundbreaking book, *Trilaterals Over Washington* summarized the backgrounds of the U. S. members of the organization in 1977: there were 28 bankers and directors of multinational companies; 34 academics and media specialists; and 47 politicians, attorneys, trade unionists, etc. Similar backgrounds were found to exist in other countries represented by the Trilateral Commission.

In 1976, three years following the inception of the Commission, Jimmy Carter became the President of the United States. He was a member of the Trilateral Commission. His running-mate, Walter Mondale, was also a member. Again, Helaman's description of the secret combination of his period comes to mind: "And thus they did obtain the sole management of the government." President Carter made the following appointments—all from the Trilateral Commission:

> Cyrus Vance: Secretary of State
> Zbigniew Brzezinski: Assistant to the President for
>   National Security Affairs
> Harold Brown: Secretary of Defense
> W. Michael Blumenthal: Secretary of the Treasury
> Andrew Young: Ambassador to the United Nations
> Warren Christopher: Deputy Secretary of State
> Brock Adams: Secretary of Transportation
> Lucy Wilson Benson: Under Secretary of State for
>   Security Affairs
> Richard Cooper: Under Secretary of State for Economic
>   Affairs
> Richard Holbrooke: Under Secretary of State for East
>   Asian and Pacific Affairs

W. Anthony Lake: Under Secretary of State for Policy
    Planning
Anthony Solomon: Under Secretary of the Treasury for
    Monetary Affairs
C. Fred Bergsten: Assistant Secretary of the Treasury for
    International Affairs
Paul Warnke: Director, Arms Control and Disarmament
    Agency
Robert R. Bowie: Deputy Director of Intelligence for
    National Estimates
Sol Linowitz: Co-Negotiator on the Panama Canal Treaty
Gerald Smith: Ambassador at Large for Nuclear Power
    Negotiations
Elliot Richardson: Delegate to the Law of the Sea
    Conference
Richard Gardner: Ambassador to Italy[36]

The overwhelming influence and the rapidity of assuming national leadership was astounding. Coupled with federal appointees, the Trilateral Commission also included the House Majority Whip; the Senate Majority Whip; and the Chairmen of both the House Conferences—Democrat and Republican.

In addition to the Council on Foreign Relations and the Trilateral Commission, other organizations controlled by the international bankers include the Bilderberger Conference, the Committee of 300, the Club of Rome, and the Pilgrim Society.

Because of the secrecy under which these groups operate, we are far from having all the data of their accomplishments and plans. Dr. Carroll Quigley's statements from *Tragedy and Hope* substantiate a great deal of our information, as well as statements from those who have been direct players in the events. The information presented in this text definitely points toward a conspiracy at the highest levels. We have examined vignettes of various events and movements of the Rothschild family; activities of international bankers; and government intrigue within the Woodrow Wilson administration. Do they add up to a secret combination? Again, examine the scriptural indicators we were given—primarily from Moroni's description in Ether 8— and see if some conclusions can be drawn. As some would ask, "Can we connect the dots?" To unmask secret combinations Moroni asks us to use the following criteria:

> Is it secret?
> Is it a combination?
> Is it a "murderous" combination?
> Does it attempt to get "above" us?
> Is its goal "power and gain?"
> Does it bring the "work of destruction" upon us?
> Does it seek "to overthrow the freedom of all
>   lands, nations, and countries?
> Is Satan at the foundation?

Is it secret?

From the beginning of the House of Rothschild, secrecy was a key issue. It is generally accepted by historians that the Order of the Illuminati founded by Adam Weishaupt in 1776 was, to a large degree, funded by Mayer Rothschild and important links in its membership were maintained. In 1798, John Robison, Secretary General to the Royal Society of Edinburgh and a professor at the University of Edinburgh, was asked to join the secret order. Piqued, he began a study of the order and wrote *Proofs of a Conspiracy* in 1798. According to Robison, a teaching of the order was

> *The great strength of our Order lies in its concealment, let it never appear in any place in its own name, but always covered by another name, and another occupation.*[37]

Total secrecy! Likewise, in their own affairs, the Rothschilds were quite secretive. The family was noted for using spies, secret communications, and shielding business exploits from non-family members.

Throughout later dealings and networkings of the family, there were several appointments emanating from the Rothschilds in various countries. In many cases, governments and other industrial/banking concerns have not known that they were, in fact, dealing with the House of Rothschild in those dealings. A case in point in the United States: it was not known for certain until following J. P. Morgan's death that he was acting under the direction of the family in buying railroads, shipping lines, and acting as a chief agent for the Federal Reserve.

Upon the death of Mayer Amshel Rothschild, his will specified definite instructions for his family which were intended to perpetuate secrecy.

(1) The family was to intermarry with first and second cousins—keeping the fortune within the family. Later, marriages also included families of other international bankers.

(2) Mayer Rothschild forbade any public inventory of his estate and any divulging of its value.

(3) A family partnership was to be entered into with the men of the family to manage its affairs. Women of the family would receive their interest in the estate subject to male management. Should any of the children have disagreed with this provision, they were given the alternative of being cut off from any inheritance. The deathbed provisions insured secrecy— that all family dealings were under family control and unknown to those outside the family.

Summarizing the Rothschild personality, two authors have written:

> *One cause of [Nathan Rothschild's] success was the secrecy with which he shrouded, and the tortuous policy with which he misled those who watched him the keenest.*[38]

> *Today the family grooms the inaudibility and invisibility of its presence. As a result, some believe that little is left apart from a great legend. And the Rothschilds are quite content to let legend be their public relations.*
> *Though they control scores of industrial, commercial, mining and tourist corporations, not one bears the name Rothschild . . . and never do publish a single public balance sheet, or any other report of their financial condition.*[39]

Continuing actions of the international bankers demonstrate the same emphasis on secrecy. The reader will find that most dealings are (1) done in secret; (2) done behind the scenes as opposed to being done openly by accepted leadership; and (3) done with ulterior motives rather than those given to the public. Examples of this secrecy are the organization of the Federal Reserve and its initial planning at Jekyl Island, and secret appointments to individuals and banks to work as unsuspected representatives. Dr. Carroll Quigley said in *Tragedy and Hope*, that the international bankers are "devoted to secrecy and the secret use of financial influence in political life."[40]

At a 1991 Bilderberg meeting (another powerful world-wide group controlled by the same leadership but open to fewer participants) an unauthorized tape recording was made of David Rockefeller's address. He told the elite group that "It would have been impossible for us to develop our plan for the world if we had been subjected to the light of publicity during those years. But the world is now more sophisticated and prepared to march towards a world government."[41]

Secrecy is definitely a hallmark of the Rothschilds and their liaisons: the international bankers.

Is it a combination?

The definition of a combination is a conspiracy—more than one entity working toward a common goal against an unknowing person or entity: hence the statement of the Lord to Joseph Smith, "behold, the enemy is combined . . . a thing which is had in secret chambers . . ."[42] The danger of combinations lies not in interests working together, but operating secretly and unknown to those with whom they are dealing. Thus, a secret combination is two or more entities working in conjunction against the interests of another that is ignorant of their plotting.

By the very nature of "secret combinations," they are kept from public knowledge and shrouded with hypothesis and supposition. Consequently, much of the knowledge of their existence comes after the events and changes they have perpetrated have already taken place. Most of our knowledge comes from members of the organizations later telling us what has transpired and how it happened. Some researchers have pieced various evidences together and then watched for breaks in the surrounding secrecy to verify that events have occurred. And, even though many of the groups in question have guarded agendas and minutes, we are able to look at membership rosters and determine the make-up of most of these groups. Therefore, even though much is known, because of our data-finding methods, we cannot know all that combinations have done or are currently doing. Fortunately, though, we do know enough to apply Moroni's criteria.

From the inception of the House of Rothschild and its extension into other banking houses, there has been apparent increased government collusion—generally kept from the public-at-large. From panics in the United States, England and France; to financing both sides of wars involving the United States, Germany, England, France, and Italy; to financing the Bolshevik Revolution and the growth of Communism in Russia; the international bankers and the House of Rothschild have, literally, changed the face of the world.

Unable to accomplish this simply through their family banking cartel, ties were forged—generally through marriage—with other banks on a global scale. In addition to money control, ownership of utilities, transportation and media, politics from virtually all places and persuasions have been employed. By manipulating both events and attitudes, the combinations have dictated the direction of nations as well as the average person's activities and beliefs.

Is it a murderous combination?

The history of the House of Rothschild and others joined to the combination, was built on a foundation of wars and managed conflict. The initial money to begin the Rothschild banking houses came from hiring and "renting" Prussian mercenaries under control of the Hesse-Cassel Dynasty to England to fight in the American War for Independence in 1776. It is said, in fact, that American patriots fought more German Hessians than British. From brokering the troops, Mayer Rothschild earned $3 million to finance his sons' banking establishments in various parts of the world.

In lending money to governments, war has proven to be the greatest source of gain for the bankers. W. Cleon Skousen wrote that the policies and tactics of the international bankers have deliberately aligned themselves "with dictatorial forces which have committed crimes against humanity in volume and severity unprecedented in history."[43] Through a continual pattern, the Rothschild aligned banking houses, have instigated wars for substantial banking gains. Prior to United States entry into global conflicts (WWI), the bankers maneuvered European nations to a perpetual state of war and countries maintaining standing armies. As those coffers were diminished, the United

States was seen as source of war renewal. Through the implementation of the Federal Reserve and manipulation of international events, the vision of world war was realized.

The adjective "murderous" as it applies to secret combinations, however, must be discussed on two levels. As shown, there is certainly no apprehension to engage massive numbers of soldiers in warfare as well as to take the lives of even greater numbers of innocent civilians. The second confirmation of "murderous" as descriptive of combinations lies in the nature of the oaths entered into by members of the Satanic groups. In Moses' recounting of Satan's oath with Cain, he first has Cain "swear unto me by thy throat, and if thou tell it you shalt die." Then, as Cain draws others into the secret combination, they make the same deathly pact.

The scope of this chapter does not include political assassinations or unexplained deaths of influential people—many of which have been attributed to the same source. On a limited basis some of these will be discussed in later chapters. The record of manipulated wars during the past two hundred years that have taken millions of lives, however, certainly qualifies the elite international bankers to be labeled a "murderous combination."

Does it attempt to get above us?

When Moroni wrote ". . . suffer not that these murderous combinations shall get above you," he allowed us some interpretation of the word "above." Generally we would agree that those above us make decisions for us and exercise some degree of control over us. In a well-ordered government or society we would expect that to be the case; however, once understanding the motives and unscrupulous control of secret combinations, Moroni warns his latter-day readers inhibit their growth and progress.

The power of secret combinations in the United States and throughout the world is huge! Decisions are made that unduly influence and control the lives of billions of people. As early as 1970, Dr. Skousen paraphrased Carroll Quigley's work in saying that he "clearly sets the stage for the coming conflict between traditional Americans and the powerful secret combination of the Global Establishment." *Tragedy and Hope*, allows us to see "the mammoth machine which Dr. Quigley believes is now too big to stop. When one contemplates the interlocking global ramifications which this power structure had developed, it is little wonder that Dr. Quigley feels so tremendously confident about its ultimate and irrevocable victory."[44]

Money is a powerful tool—one that common people as well as kings and leaders have both worshiped and sought since the days of Cain. Money or emblems of wealth have too frequently bought betrayal against personal values—for the common man as well as for the leader. Thus, decisions for the public have often not been in the interest of the public, but for the benefit of only a few. Our examples have included unpopular decisions by those "above" us, frequently to the detriment and loss of the public at large. Many decisions for wars, monetary policies, foreign aid, taxes, and wealth redistribution could be included in those decisions and will be covered in greater depth in future chapters and in Part Two.

Is its goal power and gain?

This identifying characteristic needs little discussion. International bankers, simply by their extensive holdings and wielding of power to extend gains, match Moroni's description. On a deep level at the highest echelons, these are personal rewards for carrying out covenants with Satan.

Does it bring the work of destruction upon us?
Thomas Jefferson warned

> *If the American people ever allow private banks to control the issue of their money, first by inflation and then by deflation, the banks and corporations that will grow up around [the banks,] will deprive the people of their property until their children will wake up homeless on the continent their forefathers conquered.*[45]

It is not difficult to trace the "work of destruction" under the influence of international bankers in the United States. Quite obviously, the great loss of lives in wars and other intrigue would be the most revealing statistic. Another traceable part of the nation's decline is the siphoning of both personal and national wealth away from the United States—much held by foreign investors with Japan and China holding the largest investments in treasury notes. In this regard, an examination of the history of the national debt is especially revealing. Prior to the inception of the Federal Reserve Corporation and the ability to create money, the national debt was tied to existing currency backed by gold—consequently, the debt was limited. Even in times of war and severe national emergency, money was borrowed using bonds and treasury bills either through banking lenders or the public. That money was then returned. When the Federal Reserve Act became law, the private owners of the corporation were allowed to create money from debt—essentially it could be created from nothing allowing large amounts of deficit spending.

Prior to the Federal Reserve, the national debt was backed by gold reserves and from 1900 through 1914 averaged about $2 billion. The expenditures of the First World War coupled with unlimited borrowing power allowed the debt to increase an additional $25 billion. The great depression following the 1929 stock market crash—another managed crisis brought about by the international banking cartel—added another $33 billion to the

national debt. World War Two saw another $222 billion added.
The Clinton White House years added $1.2 trillion to the debt,
and the current George W. Bush administration has continued to
add to the debt at a pace of $2.16 billion daily—now tallying
about $8 trillion.

A common misconception about the national debt is that
Americans have only spent their own money before it was
received and that the debt is simply owed to themselves.
However, as one author has written, "If that were true, every
man, woman, and child in the United States would own at least
$15,000 in government bonds.[46] In truth, the money is owed to
international bankers, with over fifty percent owed to foreign
investors who collect annual interest. It has been variously
estimated that between 40% and 100% of collected income tax is
spent to pay finance charges on the debt. Jefferson's statement at
the outset of this heading seems quite prophetic.

Financial decline has also had attendant changes on the
American culture. With debt, inflation, and higher tax payments,
the number of two-income families has risen dramatically.
Because of this, a channel of thought reasons: with father and
mother both in the workplace, less supervision is evident in the
home; to compensate for parental absence, taxes have been raised
and more programs have been governmentally implemented for
augmentation of child service agencies and public schooling;
because of government spending in these agencies, curriculum
and procedure is often mandated counter to parental wishes . . .
and so issues have compounded—unfortunately, often at the
expense of the family.

Does it seek "to overthrow the freedoms of all lands, nations, and countries?"

Ultimately, Satan's greatest triumph will be to withdraw
personal freedoms, thereby leaving us devoid of agency. Taking

freedom has been most successful as a piecemeal process—a bit-by-bit curtailing of liberty that seems noninvasive until it is finally realized that freedoms that were once assumed are now either qualified or gone. Much as the analogy of the frog: if placed in boiling water it will immediately jump out of the pot but placed in cool water that gradually comes to a boil, it will allow itself to become boiled by degrees until it is unable to free itself. Likewise, by allowing freedoms to be taken in small doses, they also may have devastating long-term effects.

A country's freedom is determined by its inherent right to act independently in making national decisions. Following a century and a half of British rule, the Founders understood the principle of sovereignty and its necessity to maintain individual freedoms. Yet, reviewing statements by the Council on Foreign Relations and various leaders of the international banking cartel, it is apparent that world government is their intent as opposed to national sovereignty and independent freedom.

Earlier in this chapter a statement appeared by the current President of the CFR wherein he called for limits to be placed on sovereignty—the freedom of a country to make independent decisions on behalf of its citizens. He indicated that an authority greater than the nation should evaluate and determine how much sovereignty a country should enjoy. He said

> *Necessity may lead to reducing or even eliminating sovereignty when a government, whether from lack of capacity or conscious policy, is unable to provide for the basic needs of its citizens.*[47]

Haass justifies international government by alleging that some countries are simply unable to take care of themselves and must be restricted from making poor choices by a larger, more inclusive government. Who would make up that larger government? One can only ask, "would the same leaders make decisions for those nations that have made United Nations' decisions for Korea, Vietnam, Kosovo, Iraq, and Afghanistan?"

That a global government is the intent of the international bankers cannot be disputed from their writings and expressed goals. If an international government were to become a reality, however, the sovereignty of a nation as well as the citizenship of a nation would be subservient. Local and national concerns would give way to those of differing beliefs, values and encroachments. Freedoms that are protected by local control and often taken for granted could then come under the discretion of the larger and more autonomous authority. Under another's judgment, freedoms that American's claim to be God-given, could be revoked or denied.

Some nations have already become subjects of world government. An arbitrator, Dr. Jan Oberg, was interviewed in 1998 after United Nations activities began in Kosovo. When asked to evaluate events there, he said:

> *Compared with one or five years ago, the present situation is worse for all parties. Innocent civilians—about 10% of the Kosovo-Albanians and 10% of the Kosovo-Serbs—have lost their homes, belongings, human rights and safety. . . . Serbia has lost important parts of its control and sovereignty and it has more international interference than ever . . . .*
>
> *. . . the political goals and the vision of an independent, peaceful and democratic Kosovo is gone.*
>
> *Some of you may think that the US/NATO would do something here to support you—forget it. Any "help" that comes when the war has broken out, is no help—it's interference. . . . the "peace" you will be offered is compatible with their interests, not necessarily with yours.*[48]

Could the same thing ever happen in the United States? Most would say that the idea is unthinkable—that there would never be a time that those of another country would enter our nation for "peacekeeping."   Yet, Moroni said that the combination would exercise control over "all lands, nations, and countries" which would effectively include the United States. Strobe Talbott, an editor of *Time Magazine* and former Deputy Secretary of State, editorialized on July 20, 1992, that, "In the next century, nations as we know them will be obsolete; all states will recognize a single, global authority. National sovereignty wasn't such a good idea after all . . . ." This brings more meaning to former Secretary of State Henry Kissinger's words to the Bilderberger Conference held in Evians, France, in 1991. Referring to the Rodney King riots taking place in Los Angeles at the time, Kissinger said

> *Today, America would be outraged if UN troops entered Los Angeles to restore order. Tomorrow they will be grateful! This is especially true if they were told that there were an outside threat from beyond, whether real or promulgated, that threatened our very existence. It is then that all peoples of the world will plead to deliver them from this evil. The one thing every man fears is the unknown. When presented with this scenario, individual rights will be willingly relinquished for the guarantee of their well-being granted to them by the World Government."*

Moroni's description seems terribly accurate: it "seeketh to overthrow the freedom [sovereignty] of all lands, nations, and countries; and it bringeth to pass the destruction of all people."

Is Satan at the foundation?
Because Satanic connection generally falls under the heading of "secrecy," we would not expect any group to openly declare that it is Satanic. Yet, because of the explicit scriptural references in Genesis, Moses, Helaman, Ether and other prophetic books, we know that Satan plays the leading part in secret combinations.

But we also know that all players in Satanic conspiracies do not derive their power directly from Satan. As we have studied the international bankers, it is evident that several, even of the more important actors, have not known the depth of their activities. Some, when they have recognized their aid to the secret combination, have repented and recanted their previous support. Because a person may currently be or may have been a part of activities that bring about Lucifer's plan, does not mean that person is a direct follower of Satan.

Here are two assumptions that we can make about Satan's role:

(1) Secret combinations have no aversion to murder. Millions of lives have been lost in manipulated war—even the lives of those who had no direct part in either its offense or defense. Regarding the international bankers that we have studied, virtually all of their profits and power have emanated from contrived warfare. In searching for an adjective to describe the secret combination of the latter-days, Moroni used the term "murderous." Nothing could be more descriptive. The first sin recorded in scripture was the murder of Abel by Cain, directly taught to Cain by Satan. Again, the example of the Jaradite combination founded by Akish began with oaths to Satan and the murder of King Omer. Secret combinations throughout the *Book of Mormon* resorted not only to trickery and deceit, but relied most heavily upon murder. Murder is an earmark of Satanic influence and signals that the followers of the secret combinations have no regard for eternal life and accountability before God for their actions.

(2) Satan's lure to his followers has never deviated from power, gain, and immunity from the repercussions of sin. Cain learned that following Satan brought him to the "great secret,"

that he could murder for gain. Describing the fundamental workings of secret combinations, Moroni wrote:

> *And they were kept up by the power of the devil to administer these oaths unto the people, to keep them in darkness, to help such as sought power to gain power, and to murder, and to plunder, and to lie, and to commit all manner of whoredoms.*[49]

The Gadianton Robbers of the *Book of Mormon* are never known as anything but wealthy and powerful. Aligning oneself with them assured financial success. The international banking cartel that we have studied is the epitome of power, gain, and immunity from the penalties of crime. No group on the earth today is wealthier nor has more power.

Modern prophets have been reluctant to label any one or any group as having direct ties to Satan. We are given the tools of discernment—the Holy Ghost, Moroni's warnings, and the knowledge of Satan's rebellion in the pre-mortal existence to give us direction. Further, because the Lord will hold us accountable for upholding and suffering the secret combinations to exist, he will certainly reveal their acts, their purposes, and ways that we may be effective in combating their influence.[50]

Chapter 4—Endnotes

1   Ether 8

2   Carroll Quigley, *Tragedy and Hope—A History of the World in Our Time*, The Macmillan Company: New York. p. 51.

3   *Ibid.* pp. 51-52.

4   *Ibid.* p. 324.

5   Eustace Mullins, The *Secrets of the Federal Reserve*, Staunton, VA. 1983. p. 50.

6   *Ibid.* p. 51.

7   W. Cleon Skousen, *The Making of America*. The National Center for Constitutional Studies. Washington, DC.: 1985. pp. 424-426.

8   William Guy Carr, *Pawns in the Game*, 2nd ed. National Federation of Christian Laymen, Toronto, Canada. p. 62.

9   Des Griffin, *Descent Into Slavery*. Emissary Publications. Clackamas, OR.: 2001 ed. pp. 283-284.

10   *Ibid.* p. 284.

11   Alexander Hamilton, *The Federalist Papers, No. 12*. The New American Library of World Literature: New York. 1961. pp. 84-91.

12   Alexander Hamilton, *The Federalist Papers, No. 30. Ibid.* pp. 188-193.

13   Ezra Taft Benson, compiled by Jerreld Newquist, *An Enemy Hath Done This*. Parliament Publishers. Salt Lake City: p. 145.

14   Griffin, *Op. Cit.* p. 284

15   Mullins, *Op. Cit.* pp. 18-19.

16   W. Cleon Skousen, The *Naked Capitalist*. Private printing: Salt Lake City. p. 18.

17   *Ibid.* p. 20.

18   *Ibid.* p. 51.

19   Charles Sylvester Viereck as quoted in Mullins, *Op. Cit.* p. 27.

20   Mullins, Ibid. p. 28, "Charles A. Lindbergh to the House of Representatives," December 23, 1913.

21   Henry L. Loucks, *The Great Conspiracy of the House of Morgan and How to Defeat It*, Arno Press.New York: 1975. p. 4.

22   Mullins, *Op. Cit.* p. 88.

23   J. Reuben Clark, *Church News*, November 29, 1952. quoted in Newquist, *Op. Cit.* p. 95.

24   Gary Allen, *None Dare Call it Conspiracy.* Rossmore, CA: Concord Press, 1971.

25   Quigley, *Op. Cit.*, p. 130.

26   *Ibid.* pp. 130-131.

27   *Ibid.* p. 132.

28   *Ibid.*

29   *Ibid.*, pp. 951-952.

30   Skousen, *The Naked Capitalist. Op. Cit.* pp. 53-54.

31   *Ibid.*, p. 52.

32   Philip Kerr, *Foreign Affairs*, December 15, 1922.

33   Helaman 6:39. Griffin, *Op. Cit.* pp. 283-284.

34   Dan Smoot, "The Invisible Government," Dallas, *The Dan Smoot Report, Inc.*, 1962. p. xi.

35   Richard N. Haass, "Sovereignty and Globalism," February 17, 2006. www.cfr.org/publication/9903/sovereignty_and_globalisation.html.

36   Antony C. Sutton and Patrick M. Wood, *Trilaterals Over Washington.* The August Corporation. Scottsdale, AZ.: 1978. pp. 21-24.

37 John Robison, *Proofs of a Conspiracy against all the Religions and Governments of Europe: Carried on the Secret Meetings of Free Masons, Illuminati, and Reading Societies: Collected from Good Authorities.* Philadelphia: Printed for T. Dobson. 1798. p. 112.

38 John Reeves, *The Rothschilds, Financial Rulers of the Nations.* 1887. p. 167.

39 Frederick Morton, *The Rothschilds*, Fawcett Crest, 1961. pp. 18-19.

40 Quigley, *Op. Cit.* p. 52.

41 Griffin, *Op. Cit.* p. 306.

42 *Doctrine & Covenants* 38:12-13.

43 Skousen, *The Naked Capitalist, Op. Cit.* p. 39.

44 *Ibid.* p. 107.

45 as quoted in Ken Bowers, *Beneath the Tide: Who Really Runs the World*, Private Printing, 2005. p. 21.

46 Griffin, *Op. Cit.* p. 50.

47 Haass, *Op. Cit.*

48 "Interview with Jan Oberg in Kosovo-Albanian "ZERI" in Pristina" by Blerim Shala, *The Transnational Foundation for Peace and Future Research*, No. 1687. December 22, 1998.

49 Ether 8:16

50 Ether 8:23-24

Chapter 5

WARS AND RUMORS OF WARS

War is a debilitating tool that can be used against a country—either aggressively or defensively. Because of the war-theme constantly running in the *Book of Mormon*, many first-time readers have been so taken by the battles and heavy death tolls that they have missed many of the sublime truths and gospel principles taught. In short, in both past and present history, the topic of war has been ever-present and has often overshadowed virtually all other activities.

Yet when asked, the large majority of people say that they don't want war. There seems to be no natural inclination to fight, to build up armies, and to sacrifice life. Generally, Latter-day Saints and others follow the scriptural dictum, to "renounce war and proclaim peace."[1] Nevertheless, the world seems to be in a constant state of war and war preparation.

Results of war

In addition to the large loss of life and inflicted injuries through war, there are other devastating results that sometimes escape notice. Here are some peripheral considerations that the citizens of a country assume during war conditions:

(1) While under perceived threat from another country, citizens often allow expedient measures to be taken to which they would not consent during times of peace. Once approved, these measures are frequently maintained following a war.

(2) Citizens tend to look to one person for clear direction (a commander-in-chief) rather than a body to debate the merits of each action (Congress) hence giving more power to the executive branch of government.

(3) Wartime justifies deficit spending because of immediate necessity. Heavy expenditures are not questioned.

(4) Because the horror of war affects an entire country, citizens are more disposed to take measures to prevent future wars. These include maintaining standing armies; peacetime stockpiling of munitions and warheads; and seeking peace options such as the United Nations.

With these considerations, William Manchester in his biography of General Douglas McArthur entitled *American Caesar* told about McArthur's reaction to the enormous cold war budgets of 1957, and quoted him as saying

> *Our government has kept us in a perpetual state of fear—kept us in a continuous stampede of patriotic fervor—with the cry of grave national emergency. Always there has been some terrible evil to gobble us up if we did not blindly rally behind it by furnishing the exorbitant funds demanded. Yet, in retrospect, these disasters never seem to have happened, seem never to have been quite real.*[2]

The "patriotic fervor" that McArthur alluded to is a prime result of "wars and rumors of wars." War has often been used as a rallying point to increase esprit de corps and even nationalism among the citizenry of a country. Another military leader, Marine Major General Smedley Butler retired in 1931 to speak out against the things he had learned and participated in. After receiving two Congressional Medals of Honor and staging a senatorial campaign, he began lecturing throughout the United States on the unpopular theme: *War is a Racket.* He would begin: "For a great many years, as a soldier, I had a suspicion that war was a racket; not until I retired to civilian life did I fully realize it. Now that I see the international war clouds gathering, as they are today, [just prior to WW2] I must face it and speak out."[3]

After giving the number of lives lost and the financial costs of the First World War, General Butler would discuss the inordinate profits of the war industries. As opposed to other earnings, he documented suppliers to troops profiting "twenty, sixty, one-hundred, three-hundred, and even eighteen-hundred per cent." After reviewing the business of war and the minimal worth that lives of service personnel were to those making war decisions, he would conclude by discussing the returning soldiers, their sacrifice and that of their families:

> *When he returned home minus an eye, or minus a leg, or with his mind broken, they suffered too—as much as and even sometimes more than he [the soldier.] Yes, and they, too, contributed their dollars to the profits of the munitions makers and bankers and shipbuilders and the manufacturers and the speculators made. They, too, bought Liberty Bonds and contributed to the profit of the bankers after the Armistice in the hocus-pocus of manipulated Liberty Bond prices.*[4]

War's patriotic fervor often leads to loss of freedom

Generals McArthur, Butler, and several other military and political leaders have sought to call attention to the issue of war. Undoubtedly, as in the American Revolutionary War and several *Book of Mormon* wars, there are times when war brings about divine purposes and patriotism is invoked for higher ideals. Those wars and incidents must be scrutinized, however, so that we know that we are engaged in a just cause. Once united against a common foe, all other concerns pale and the nation's entire momentum is placed behind perceived national interests—either right or wrong. This, unfortunately, often leads to a loss of freedom. The following anonymous statement has sometimes been attributed to Julius Caesar:

> Beware the leader who bangs the drums of war in order to whip the citizenry into a patriotic fervor, for patriotism is indeed a double-edged sword. It both emboldens the blood, just as it narrows the mind. And when the drums of war have reached a fever pitch and the blood boils with hate and the mind has closed, the leader will have no need in seizing the rights of the citizenry. Rather, the citizenry, infused with fear and blinded by patriotism, will offer up all of their rights unto the leader and gladly so. How do I know? For this is what I have done. And I am Caesar.[5]

Edward Gibbon's *Fall of the Roman Empire* bears out that Roman citizens had more controls and taxes placed on them during times of war—and that generally, even with the return of peace, the controls remained. In fact, war and threatened war has been a continuing rationale given for restricting freedoms. Because of fear—in the name of patriotism—freedoms are frequently relinquished.

How to start a war

Our concern in this text, however, is not simply the devastation and subsequent problems precipitated by war, but the manipulation of war by insidious powers that use war to achieve their own ends. "Power and gain" are the goals of the great secret combination of the latter-days and the use of war has become one of its most favored tools. Because of its positioning on both sides of conflict; huge profits gained through lending money to finance wars; control of various munitions manufacture and needed wartime raw materials; financing of postwar rebuilding efforts; and political control of subsequent agreements—war has become the most useful tool of the secret combination. No wonder that the Lord would refer to our day as one of "wars and rumors of wars"[6] and Moroni would call the secret combination "murderous."

As a short introduction to the manner in which wars can be manipulated, the example of the Russo-Japanese war will be used. This war was used to beat down the Russian Empire to pave the way for the Bolshevik Revolution and the triumph of Communism.

> *After the Tzar blamed the Jews for the unsatisfactory state of affairs in Russia, Baron Ginzberg was instructed to work to bring about the destruction of the Russian Empire. It was agreed that to start the Russo-Japanese War the Rothschild interests in Europe would pretend to be friendly with Russia. They would finance the war on Russia's behalf while secretly the Rothschild's partners, Kuhn-Loeb & Co. of New York would finance the Japanese government. The defeat of Russia was to be made certain by the Rothschilds withdrawing financial aid when it was most needed. Chaos and confusion was to be created within the Russian armed forces in the Far East by sabotaging the lines of transport and communication crossing Siberia. This caused both the Russian Army and Navy to run short of supplies and reinforcements.*

> *The Japanese government was financed by international loans raised by Jacob Schiff of New York. Schiff was senior partner in Kuhn-Loeb & Co. He cooperated with Sir Ernest Cassels of England and the Warburgs of Hamburg.*
>
> *The hypocrisy of Jacob Schiff can be better appreciated when it is explained that from 1897 he had financed the Terrorists in Russia. In 1904 he helped finance the revolution which broke out in Russia in 1905. He also helped to organize on an international basis the financing of the Russian Revolution which broke out early in 1917, and gave him and his associates their first opportunity to put their Totalitarian Theories into effect.*
>
> *The Russo-Japanese War was fomented by the international bankers in order to create the conditions necessary for the success of a revolutionary effort to overthrow the power of the Tzars.*[7]

The intrigue of the Russian War was neither unusual nor was it an isolated situation. Maintaining secrecy with various partners located in different world locations, the bankers were able to pit country against country, make promises, and to determine through their support which side would be the victor.

The following examples of manipulation by the world finance cartel will help us understand their influence in the United States. Similar stories of civil war, social unrest, and various provoked and unprovoked attacks throughout the world could be added.

World War 1

In the summer of 1914, World War 1 began in Europe. The forces of Great Britain, France and Russia lined up against Germany, Austria-Hungary and Turkey. Two years later, the United States entered the war.

The agenda during the Wilson Administration was crammed with several far-reaching goals. One of the major thrusts was the implementation of what came to be known as the *League of Nations*. A year prior to the declaration of war, the

President gave a speech entitled *League to Enforce Peace* wherein he laid out plans for a world government which, he said, would prevent wars like that raging in Europe from happening again. On April 6, 1917, Congress declared a state of war and the United States entered into World War 1—"the war to end all wars," and "the war to make the world safe for democracy."

The sinking of the American ocean-liner *Lusitania* by a German U-boat is often credited as being the primary motivator for the United States entering WW1. As often happens, what was told to the public was much different from facts that are known today. Americans were told that a German submarine indiscriminately sunk an American pleasure-cruiser killing over 1,200 passengers while the United States claimed neutrality from the German-English war. History books, however, are generally silent about the following circumstances surrounding the *Lusitania*:

(1) that merchant and other ships were considered war ships because of England's dictum to use them as such—in fact the Lusitania was registered in the British Navy as an auxiliary cruiser—

(2) that the Lusitania was owned by J. P. Morgan and that instructions had been given to fill much of the ocean-liner with explosive primers and ammunition (an estimated three tons)—

(3) that the Germany embassy had sent announcements to fifty major newspapers warning Americans not to sail on the Lusitania and that the United States State Department had ordered the newspapers not to publish them—

Col. House, visiting England at that time, recorded in his diaries that he had spoken the day of the ship's sinking with Sir Edward Gray and King Charles upon the subject of the *Lusitania*—and he was queried about America's reaction if the boat were sunk. House's diary reads, "I told Sir Gray if this were done, a flame of indignation would sweep America which would in itself carry us into the war."[8]

Referring to submarine warfare, and specifically the torpedoing of the *Lusitania*, Germany was dressed in a very poor image preceding the First World War. This was enhanced by the media—the twenty-five largest newspapers owned by the J. P. Morgan group—all editorializing about the "inevitability of war." With reference to the *Lusitania* and other events surrounding WW1, Arthur Ponsonby of the British Parliament admitted "There must have been more deliberate lying in the world from 1914 to 1918 than in any other period of the world's history."[9]

The armistice concluding WW1 was signed on November 11, 1918, at the Treaty of Versailles. In attendance were the financial leaders that had served as advisors to the United States, Great Britain and Germany. The provisions of the treaty were harsh and many felt, even at the time of the signing, that the treaty contained the seeds of future conflict. Lord Curzon, the British Foreign Secretary, remarked, "This is no peace; this is only a truce for twenty years."[10] He felt, as did others, that the treaty's terms would force Germany into future rebellion—which it did exactly twenty years later. Likewise, the economist John Maynard Keynes an advisor at the treaty signing, felt that "reparations provisions of the treaty were utterly unrealistic. . . . the Versailles Treaty aimed at the destruction of [the German economy] at precisely the time that it imposed tremendous reparations obligations upon a curtailed territory and a weakened economy."[11]

Despite all of the problems and infringements engendered by the war; the life-taking and economic prohibitions; and the poor treaty as a final solution—the international banking cartel succeeded in its agenda to control finances in the United States. First establishing the Federal Reserve system, then controlling the war economy, and finally planting the seeds of world government—the money interests maneuvered themselves into positions of decision-making and world leadership. Author Gary Allen described the new national leaders assuming authority during and as an outgrowth of World War 1:

> *During the "war to end all wars," insider banker Bernard Baruch was made absolute dictator over American business when President Wilson appointed him Chairman of the War Industries Board, where he had control of all domestic contracts for Allied war materials. Baruch made lots of friends while placing tens of billions in government contracts, and it was widely rumored in Wall Street that out of the war to make the world safe for international bankers he netted $200 million for himself.*
>
> *While insider banker Paul Warburg controlled the Federal Reserve, and international banker Bernard Baruch placed government contracts, international banker Eugene Meyer, a former partner of Baruch and a son of a partner in the Rothschilds' international house of Lazard Freres, was Wilson's choice to head the War Finance Corporation, where he too made a little money*
>
> *It should be noted that Sir William Wiseman, the man sent by British Intelligence to help bring the United States into the war, was amply rewarded for his services. He stayed in this country after WW1 as a new partner in the Jacob-Schiff/Paul Warburg-controlled Kuhn, Loeb bank.*[12]

Summarizing the effects of the war, Winston Churchill agreed that the terms had been unrealistic. He further wrote that even if America had *not* entered the war, ". . . peace would have been made with Germany; and there would have been no collapse in Russia leading to Communism; no breakdown of government in Italy followed by Fascism; and Nazism never would have gained ascendancy in Germany."[13] Given that appraisal, one is forced to ask, "then why did the United States enter the war?" The major result was not a safer Europe and it certainly was not the "war to end all wars." Instead, the results of the war were the development of greater government bureaucracy; a springboard to further intervention abroad; a dramatic increase in deficit spending and national debt; and a pretext for world government.

In 1953, long after the conclusions of World Wars 1 and 2, Congress determined that some tax-exempt foundations had overstepped their bounds by influencing American opinion. The Reece Committee was organized to investigate the foundations. A primary subject in the investigation was the Carnegie Endowment for International Peace and its influence surrounding WW1. Using the minutes of the foundation, the committee wrote in its 1954 report that there were specific questions that were addressed by the trustees:

> *Is there any means known to man more effective than war, assuming you wish to alter the life of an entire people?*

> *How do we involve the United States in a war?*

> *How do we control the diplomatic machinery of the United States?*

And then

> *These trustees in a meeting about 1917 had the brashness to congratulate themselves on the wisdom of their original decision because already the impact of war had indicated it . . . could alter life in this country. . . . they even had the brashness to . . . dispatch a telegram to Mr. Wilson, cautioning him to see that the war did not end too quickly. . . .*
>
> *The concern became, as expressed by the trustees, seeing to it that there was no reversion to life in this country as it existed prior to 1914.*[14]

In other words, as far as the Carnegie Endowment for International Peace was concerned, World War 1 had been a triumph—not because Germany had been defeated but because thought and lifestyle changes in America. War was the vehicle to bring about the change that the internationalists had desired. The First World War reversed the non-interventionist policy that had dominated American thought since the nation was founded and became the watershed for perpetual warring coupled with the dialogue of perpetual peace.

World War 2

Significant information exists showing that many wars have been contrived—planned by the few to involve the many. Although popular history generally teaches about war in simple terms, it can be demonstrated that a manipulated orchestration such as the sinking of the *Lusitania* in World War 1 aroused enough public indignation to create support for the war. Thus the war became a popular movement rather than an unpopular administrative decision. Likewise, there is compelling circumstantial evidence that the attack on Pearl Harbor which precipitated America's entry into World War 2 was a manipulated event to stir public support for a war against the Axis Powers.

The Freedom of Information Act has allowed historians and researchers to examine original documents, minutes and diaries which have given a much different interpretation to the events of December 7, 1941 than read in traditional history books. No longer considered to be a "sneak attack" by many, it now appears that there was ample goading of the Japanese into attacking the Pearl Harbor fleet, and sufficient intelligence to know when and where the attack would take place. Unfortunately, this information was withheld from the command of the Pacific Fleet and the Pearl Harbor massacre occurred. Here are some of the recently found facts surrounding the "day of infamy:"

(1) Admiral James O. Richardson, Commander-in-Chief of the United States Fleet, was first given the Pearl Harbor command. He objected to the vulnerability of the location, the number of ships to be harbored, and the safety of his men and went directly to the President. He was relieved of his command.

(2) On October 7, 1940, Lt. Commander Arthur H. McCollum of Naval Intelligence sent a memo to the President listing eight steps to take which would lead to an attack by Japan upon the United States. All were completed by the time of the attack on Pearl Harbor.

(3) The memo called for a complete embargo on all trade with the United States and Japan and cessation of oil access from Holland—Japan's source of oil.

(4) The intent of the President and his closest advisors was war in Europe against Germany. Japan, as one of the Axis Powers, was seen as a "back door" into the war. An October 18, 1941, entry into the diary of Secretary of the Interior Harold Ickes reads, "For a long time I have believed that our best entrance into the war would be by way of Japan."

(5) The Japanese war codes had been broken and deciphered prior to the attack. On September 24, 1941, Naval Intelligence in Washington, D. C. intercepted a message to Japan's consul-general located in Honolulu asking for the positioning of all naval ships docked at Pearl Harbor. This information was not forwarded to the command at Pearl Harbor.

(6) The November 25, 1941, diary entry of Secretary of War Henry Stimson reads that the President indicated that a Japanese attack would happen within a few days and asked, ". . . how we

should maneuver them into the position of firing the first shot without too much danger to ourselves.   In spite of the risk involved, however, in letting the Japanese fire the first shot, we realized that in order to have the full support of the American people it was desirable to make sure that the Japanese be the ones to do this so that there should remain no doubt in anyone's mind as to who were the aggressors."

(7) On November 25, 1941, Winston Churchill communicated with President Roosevelt that the Japanese would strike on America toward the end of the first week in December.

(8) On November 26, 1941, the two aircraft carriers docked at Pearl Harbor were sent out with fifty planes "as soon as possible" leaving the already vulnerable harbor further weakened in its defenses.

(9) The *New York Times* article of December 8, entitled "Attack was Expected," said that the United States knew of the attack a week earlier.   (Secretary of State Cordell Hull had given the information to reporter Joe Lieb.)

(10) Winston Churchill in writing later of the war said, "A Japanese attack upon the U. S. was a vast simplification of their problems and their duty. How can we wonder that they regarded the actual form of the attack, or even its scale, as incompletely less important than the fact that the whole American nation would be united."

For further research about the entry of the United States into war with Japan and the attack at Pearl Harbor, the reader is encouraged to read Robert B. Stinnett, *Day of Deceit: The Truth about FDR and Pearl Harbor,* and Frank P. Mintz, *Revisionism and the Origins of Pearl Harbor.*

Prior to the World War, citizens of the United States had looked upon the European War with interest but collectively determined to remain aloof. World War 1 had taken its toll in both lives and money, and Americans had no desire to enter another war. Yet, because of the attack on Pearl Harbor and a loss of 2,400 lives, a new resolve and affirmation of patriotism spread over the country. The country stood uniformly behind its Commander-in-Chief.

Apparently, the same political maneuvering was used by Germany during WW2. Interrogated during the Nuremburg War Trials, the following dialog ensued between Reichsmarshall Hermann Goering and his questioner Dr. Gustave Gilbert:

> *Goering: Of course, the people don't want war. Why would some poor slob on a farm want to risk his life in a war when the best he can get out of it is to come back to his farm in one piece. Naturally, the common people don't want war—neither in Russia, nor in England, nor in America, nor, for that matter, in Germany. That is understood. After all, it is the leaders of the country who determine the policy and it is always a simple matter to drag the people along, whether it is a democracy, or a fascist dictatorship, or a parliament, or a communist dictatorship.*
>
> *Gilbert: There's one difference. In a democracy the people have some say in the matter through their elected representatives. And in the United States only Congress can declare wars.*
>
> *Goering: Oh, that is all well and good. But voice or no voice, the people can always be brought to the bidding of the leaders. That is easy. All you have to do is tell them they are being attacked and denounce the pacifists for lack of patriotism and exposing the country to danger. It works the same in any country.*[15]

Why war? As Gibbon's study of Rome elucidates, power and control are more easily accepted by a citizenry when they are "infused with fear and blinded by patriotism." With a clear understanding of this principle, President J. Reuben Clark warned the Saints in general conference just prior to the formal declaration of the Second World War. Discussing Satan's plan of "the complete destruction of our Constitution" and the desired limits on "the free agency which the Lord gave to man," President Clark stated that many infringements on agency would take place "largely done during the war under the plea of war necessity [and would] be continued after the war under the excuse—if we are not then too cowed to require an excuse—that this new political order is necessary that we may rehabilitate the world."[16] Four years later, drawing toward the conclusion of the war, President Clark said that the co-conspirators of WW2 had "planned out what postwar America is to be, and I also know that unless the rest of us are awake, they will have their way."[17]

The staggering total of deaths attributed to the war, both military and civilian, was in excess of 51 million and the monetary cost of the war was in the neighborhood of $341 billion. This was a tremendous price to pay for a war that Americans did not want to enter. But many of the costs were not categorized so easily. As President Clark had warned, attitudes were developed and molded leading to a much different society than prewar America.

(1) Women had entered the workplace in great numbers and many desired to continue working—leading to both two-income families and independence from spouses

(2) The idea of gathering nations together to discuss differences was accepted to a greater degree than the previous League of Nations. A month following the

armistice in Europe, the United Nations charter was signed in San Francisco.

(3) A noticeable move from isolationism to internationalism including massive government spending and aid to foreign countries followed the war.

(4) A marked increase in consumerism followed World War Two both because of two-income families and because of a new attitude toward decreased savings.

Obviously, the war was not completely responsible for the above changing attitudes, but it was a catalyst in their introduction and redirection.   These mind-sets have all contributed to erosion of both the family as well as the country. Examining the seeds of the various movements planted during WW2 and comparing them with continuing movements today, the links are clearly visible. Spiraling divorce and single-parent families; non-marriage; relinquishment of national sovereignty; alliances compelling military involvement; unreimbursed foreign aid; easy credit; and tremendous personal debt—all trace their national surges to the Second World War.

Just as WW1 had sown the seeds of WW2, the Second World War set the stage for the cold war which would continue between the United States and Communism for the next forty-three years. A principle key for alarming nations into accepting a status of maintaining standing armies and spending huge amounts of money on preparatory warfare was fear of atomic and nuclear attacks. War and armament spending during the cold war amounted to more than five trillion dollars.

Japan and the atomic bomb

Conditioning or accustoming the American people to accept the expenditures of a cold war, it was necessary to create a mental picture of that which was to be feared. Because war allows for destruction, the conclusion of WW2 was selected for the first implementation of the "Manhattan Project:" the atomic bomb. Historically, the atomic bomb has been justified because (1) nothing else could make Japan bow to defeat; and (2) it saved the lives of untold American servicemen (some estimates were as high as a million) by shortening the length of the war. Because of these traditional American attitudes and the far-reaching effects of both atomic and nuclear destruction, the following circumstances surrounding the atomic bomb should be understood:

(1) Japan was defeated prior to dropping atomic bombs on Hiroshima (August 6, 1945) and Nagasaki (August 9, 1945). Admiral William Leahy in his book, *I Was There*, wrote

> *A large part of the Japanese Navy was already at the bottom of the sea. The combined Navy surface and Air Force action even by this time had forced Japan into a position that made her early surrender inevitable.*
>
> *It is my opinion that the use of this barbarous weapon at Hiroshima and Nagasaki was of no material assistance in our war against Japan. The Japanese were already defeated and ready to surrender because of the effective sea blockade and the successful bombing with conventional weapons.*
>
> *My own feeling is that being the first to use it (the atomic bomb) we had adopted an ethical standard common to the Barbarism of the Dark Ages. I was not taught to make war in that fashion, and wars cannot be won by destroying women and children.*[18]

Another informative study of WW2, *Reflections of a Hiroshima Pilot* by Ellsworth Torrey Carrington also tells of the diminished war capabilities of Japan two months prior to dropping the atomic bomb. Carrington wrote

> *. . . The major told us that the fire-bombing of Japan had proven successful far beyond anything they had imagined possible and that the 20th Air Force was running out of cities to burn. Already there were no longer any target cities left worth the attention of more than 50 B-29s, and on a big day, we could send up as many as 450 planes!*[19]

Through this period of time, reports were received on several occasions that Japan was considering surrender and had begun outlining terms of the agreement. The Air Force's U. S. Strategic Bombing Survey concluded in their report of July 1, 1946, that

> *The Hiroshima and Nagasaki atomic bombs did not defeat Japan, not by the testimony of the enemy leaders who ended the war did they persuade Japan to accept unconditional surrender. The Emperor, the lord privy seal, the prime minister, the foreign minister, and the navy minister had decided as early as May, 1945, that the war should be ended even if it meant acceptance of defeat on allied terms.*[20]

On October 5, 1945, David Lawrence, the founder and editor of *U. S. News and World Report* wrote an editorial stating that "The United States should be the first to condemn the atomic bomb and apologize for its use against Japan. Spokesmen for the Army Air Forces said it wasn't necessary and that the war had been won already. Competent testimony exists to prove that Japan was seeking to surrender many weeks before the atomic bomb came."

(2) Hiroshima and Nagasaki were not military targets. President Harry S. Truman wrote in his private papers that, "In

1945 I had ordered the Atomic Bomb dropped on Japan at two places devoted almost exclusively to war production."[21] The choice of the selected targets, however, does not bear out Truman's rationale.

Of Japan's 66 largest cities, 59 had been mostly destroyed through previous bombing raids. Through the bombings, about one-half million people were dead and another twenty million were left homeless. It is interesting that although the devastation was so terrific prior to August of 1945, both Hiroshima and Nagasaki had been left untouched. Were they in reality military targets, it stands to reason that they would have been part of the destruction preceding the atomic bomb.

Kensaburo Oe who would go on to win the Nobel Prize for Literature in 1994, authored an essay included in the anthology, *Hiroshima's Shadow* which took a closer look at Truman's claim. "Strictly military damage was insignificant" he wrote. It was true that

> *The Headquarters of the Japanese Second Army were located in Hiroshima and approximately 20,000 men—of which about half, or 10,000 died in the attack. In Nagasaki, there were about 150 deaths among military personnel in the city. Thus, between the two cities, 4.4% of the total death toll was made up of military personnel. In short, more than 95% of the casualties were civilians.*[22]

(3) The cities of Hiroshima and Nagasaki were not warned in advance of the atomic attacks. In their Introduction, the editors of *Hiroshima's Shadow* explain that

> *One of the myths of Hiroshima is that the inhabitants were warned by leaflets that an atomic bomb would be dropped. The leaflets . . . were dropped after the bombing. This happened because the President's Interim Committee on the Atomic Bomb decided on May 31 'that we could not give the Japanese any warning.' Furthermore, the decision to drop 'atomic' leaflets on Japanese cities*

was not made until August 7, the day after the Hiroshima bombing.
They were not dropped until August 10, after Nagasaki had been
bombed."[23]

Commenting on Japanese civilian lives lost in World War
2, President J. Reuben Clark said in the October, 1946 General
Conference of the Church:

> *. . . Then as the crowning savagery of the war we Americans*
> *wiped out hundreds of thousands civilian population with the atom*
> *bomb in Japan, few if any of the ordinary citizens being any more*
> *responsible for the war than were we, and perhaps most of them no*
> *more aiding Japan in the war than we were aiding America. Military*
> *men are now saying that the atom bomb was a mistake. It was more*
> *than that: it was a world tragedy. . . . And the worst of this atomic*
> *bomb tragedy is not that not only did the people of the United States*
> *not rise up in protest against this savagery, not only did it not shock*
> *us to read of this wholesale destruction of men, women, and children,*
> *and cripples, but that it actually drew from the nation at large a*
> *general approval of this fiendish butchery.*[24]

Compounding the tragedy of the event was the lack of
protest; the silent acquiescence and acceptance. President Clark
and others in the Church raised their voices against the apparent
non-military action.

As troubling as the bombing was and the devastation
surrounding it, was the allegiance of its designers to the world
money figures. Both the administrations of Presidents Roosevelt
and Truman listed significant numbers of bankers, their protégés,
and others affiliated with the non-profit foundations which they
had fostered. Both Col. Edward Mandel House and Bernard
Baruch continued the same roles they had filled with President
Wilson into the Roosevelt administration.

The ravages of war

James Madison, the chief architect of the Constitution, wrote that

> *Of all the enemies to public liberty war is, perhaps, the most to be dreaded, because it comprises and develops the germ of every other. War is the parent of armies; from these proceed debts and taxes; and armies, and debts, and taxes are the known instruments for bringing the many under the domination of the few. . . . No nation could preserve its freedom in the midst of continual warfare.*[25]

What an insightful statement! *"No nation could preserve its freedom in the midst of continual warfare."* Yet, war has continually been the heritage of planet Earth. The history of civilization demonstrates that virtually all societies have perished and been destroyed by wars—even those that have been noted for conquering and triumphs in war have eventually been brought into submission by other military powers. An excellent primer on the effects of war—both long-term and short-term—is the *Book of Mormon*. What are war's effects?

War creates division—it fosters attitudes such as "our country is better than your country;" or "our cause is greater than your cause." This division—sometimes given the more patriotic title of "nationalism"—is generally touted as a positive virtue but, although patriotic in championing ideals and national values, frequently leads to prejudice and the preclusion of the recognition that all members of the human race are children of a single Heavenly Father. In the *Book of Mormon* we find that, although there are wonderful examples of Nephites and Lamanites working together when listening to the words of prophets and enjoying the personal visit of the Savior, for the most part the book describes contention. Love of one group too frequently led to hatred of the other group. Consequently examples such as the Nephite exclusion of Samuel the Lamanite; King Lamoni's complete distrust of anything Nephite; and attitudes of both Nephites and Lamanites crying for the blood of the other during Mormon's and Moroni's administrations, permeate the *Book of Mormon*. Wartime division usually comes at the expense of the opposing power.

Where does the United States fit into the equation of war? President Spencer W. Kimball taught that

> *Warlike peoples pervert patriotism. We are a warlike people, easily distracted from our assignment of preparing for the coming of the Lord. When enemies rise up, we commit vast resources to the fabrication of gods of stone and steel—ships, planes, missiles, fortifications—and depend on them for protection and deliverance. When threatened, we become anti-enemy instead of pro-kingdom of God; we train a man in the art of war and call him a patriot, thus, in the manner of Satan's counterfeit of true patriotism, perverting the savior's teaching: 'Love your enemies, bless them that curse you, do good to them that hate you, and pray for them that despitefully use you, and persecute you;' we forget that if we are righteous the Lord will either not suffer our enemies to come upon us—and this is the special promise to the inhabitants of the land of the Americas—or he will fight our battles for us.*[26]

Isn't this what the *Book of Mormon* teaches?

War gives virtual dictatorial powers to the Commander-in-Chief breeding expediency and quick decisions. Naturally, citizens look to a common leader for direction and tend to place more confidence in decisive actions—thus allowing the central figure of government more powers than could exist in peacetime.

Coupled with the spirit of nationalistic division and the authority by what may be perceived as a majority of citizens, a leader is often not only given the power to advance military force, but may include encroachment on personal liberties.

History bears this out in the lives of dictators such as Caesar, Napoleon, Hitler, and others raising war's standard.

War fosters immunity to the repulsion of bloodshed and the hurt of others—military as well as civilian casualties. Nearing the final scenes of the *Book of Mormon*, the prophet Mormon wrote

> *And it is impossible for the tongue to describe, or for man to write a perfect description of the horrible scene of the blood and carnage which was among the people, both of the Nephites and the Lamanites; and every heart was hardened, so that they delighted in the shedding of blood continually.*[27]

Likewise, in today's world an apparent numbness exists to the deaths and suffering of others. A favorite sandbox phrase among children following WW2 was "bombs over Tokyo" as sand creations were destroyed; childhood heroes are "Rambo," "GI Joe," and other military or quasi-military victors; television and video games highlight and even score points for bloodshed; and books and movies on war are perpetually among best sellers and best attended. In this way, a conditioning effect is built for immunity to the horror of taking life.

Civilian casualties during war

Unfortunately, in a similar way, war casualties spill over to those who have neither culpability nor have engaged in fighting. As we draw nearer to our time in history, civilian casualties have increased and made up an ever greater share of war dead. During WW1, roughly five percent of casualties were civilian; while in WW2, about half of the reported deaths were civilian. The Vietnam War showed an even greater percentage of civilian casualties with roughly 1,300,000 Americans and Vietnamese who were enlisted in the armed forces killed, and between 2,000,000 and 4,000,000 Vietnamese civilians killed. In addition, as in most wars following WW2, some 350,000 tons of unexploded warheads and ammunition were left in Vietnam causing both ongoing decimation of property and lives.

The preemptive strikes beginning the Iraq War guaranteed that an even higher percentage of deaths would be civilian. War, then, is not simply soldiers fighting soldiers; instead, modern warfare reminds us of the Nephite prophets decrying Lamanite warfare in which they frequently killed Nephite women and children. There is little difference between warfare among *Book of Mormon* peoples and ourselves—except in numbers.

Of the postwar United States, J. Reuben Clark had predicted that the government would insist that our responsibility would be humanitarian—that money and influence should flow from the United States to rehabilitate the people of the world. Sold as a gesture of humanity, the United States set out on a course of gifting large amounts of money to nations throughout the world assuring continued global involvement. True to President Clark's warning, in total, by 1962 seventy-five countries had petitioned the United States for money—none being turned down. By that time over $80 billion had been given in foreign aid—and gifts became significantly larger as years passed. Prior to the Second World War the national debt stood at $2 million; today it is well over $8 trillion with $2.18 billion being added daily since September 30, 2005. (See www.brillig.com/debtclock for current national debt totals and statistics.)

The Korean War

Japan had occupied Korea during the Second World War and, at Japan's defeat, the United States had remained in South Korea there until 1946 as an occupational force. As a wartime agreement, Korea was divided with the northern half proclaiming communist rule while South Korea remained an ally of the United States. As Germany, Vietnam, and all countries that have been divided as spoils of war, contention between North and South Korea quickly arose. Finally, in 1950, North Korea invaded South Korea and the United States became a part of the conflict. For the first time United Nations troops were summoned and they fought under the American leadership of General Douglas McArthur.

The Korean War was fought between 1950 and 1953, and was the first modern war in which the United States was considered "interventionist." This was the first war that the communist government centered in Russia and China indirectly fought the United States and set the tenor for the cold war. Although this is often called the "forgotten war," the casualties were extremely high.

United Nations troops reported 17,000 deaths.
United States military reported 142,000 deaths.
North Korea reported 520,000 deaths.
South Korea reported 1.3 million military deaths
        and 3 million civilian deaths—about 10% of South
        Korea's total population.
China reported 900,000 deaths.

The cost of the war has been difficult to determine because of on-going military occupation and maintenance of Army and Air Force bases in Korea, but it is generally agreed to be in the neighborhood of $440 billion.

Essentially the same US leadership was in control of the state department and war decisions that had acted during the Second World War. Dwight D. Eisenhower was elected President of the United States in 1952—being the first member of the Council on Foreign Relations to hold the position. This war was highly significant because it demonstrated the first "police action" of America's military entering into a war without a formal declaration. The Korean War set the stage for entry into Vietnam both through its undeclared war action and the formation of SEATO—the Southeast Asia Treaty Organization wherein the United States pledged mutual military support in the event other treaty members were attacked. These were exactly the "entangling alliances" of which George Washington had spoken.

The Vietnam War

Many have rethought the Vietnam War and, although the war-pitch was in full fervor at the time, more and more of a national consensus questions American involvement. George Romney, father of Massachusetts governor Mitt Romney and former governor of Michigan reflects the sentiments of many today. As a presidential candidate, he, with others, was invited by President Lyndon Johnson to travel to Vietnam on a "fact-finding" mission and came home stating that United States' presence was needed in Vietnam and that the war was a just cause. Not many months later, reconsidering his position and having further information, he said that those who had gone on the trip were "brainwashed" into accepting the pro-war stance. That statement was not popular at the time, but has since become a common view.

The upsurge in American commitment to South Vietnam really began with what is often referred to as the "Gulf of Tonkin Incident." On August 4, 1964, President Lyndon Johnson went on national television to announce that North Vietnamese torpedo boats had made an "unprovoked attack" against an American ship. It had been, President Johnson said, on "routine patrol" in the Gulf of Tonkin two days earlier when it was fired upon. Then, on the day of the president's speech to the nation, he said that the North Vietnamese had launched a further "deliberate attack" on two other U.S. ships. Because of the unprovoked hostility, the nation was told that activities in Vietnam would escalate and that bombing raids would begin to "retaliate" for the aggression.[28]

Unfortunately, the American public was not given the true picture of events. As Jeff Cohen and Norman Solomon wrote in their 1994 article, *30-Year Anniversary: Tonkin Gulf Lie Launched Vietnam War*:

> *Rather than being on a routine patrol Aug. 2, the destroyer Maddox was actually engaged in aggressive intelligence-gathering maneuvers—in sync with coordinated attacks on North Vietnam by the South Vietnamese navy and the Laotian air force.*
>
> *"The day before, two attacks on North Vietnam . . . had taken place," writes scholar Daniel C. Hallin. Those assaults were "part of a campaign of increasing military pressure on the North that the United States had been pursuing since early 1964."*
>
> *On the night of Aug. 4, the Pentagon proclaimed that a second attack by North Vietnamese PT boats had occurred earlier that day in the Tonkin Gulf—a report cited by President Johnson as he went on national TV that evening to announce a momentous escalation in the war: air strikes against North Vietnam.*
>
> *But Johnson ordered U.S. bombers to "retaliate" for a North Vietnamese torpedo attack that never happened.*[29]

Believing that the aggression was real and without cause, the American public lined up behind their commander-in-chief and patriotically prepared for another war. The *New York Times* reported that President Johnson "went to the American people last night with the somber facts;" and the *Los Angeles Times* wrote that we "need to face the fact the Communists by their attack on American vessels in international waters, have themselves escalated the hostilities."[30]

Thirty years after the Vietnam War, now having the gift of hindsight, many have reassessed America's presence in the undeclared war. Tom Wells' chronology of the war and the public reaction to it appeared in *The War Within: America's Battle Over Vietnam.* Published in 1994, this was one of the many voices of reappraisal. In a later interview, Wells

> . . . *described the air strikes that Johnson launched in response as merely 'tit for tat'—when in reality they reflected plans the administration had already drawn up for gradually increasing its overt military pressure against the North.* [31]

When asked why the public was so willing to accept the war and why the media perpetuated the faulty rationale for American presence in Vietnam, Wells said that a chief problem was an

> . . . *almost exclusive reliance on U.S. government officials as sources of information [and] reluctance to question official pronouncements on 'national security issues.'* [32]

Added to the confusion surrounding Vietnam was the fact that the war was undeclared—that even though funded through the U.S. government, it was never officially declared as a war by Congress. More confusion ensued by the actual conduct of the war with apparent actions which assured a "no-win" conflict and tended to harden and demoralize the combatants. Certain vital targets were off limits; "safe havens" were designated for enemy fighters; U.S. tactics were predictable and repetitive; and cease fires were frequently called which allowed the enemy to escape difficult situations and to regroup for further battles.

Why would a "no-win" war be conducted? It definitely further drained the treasury and brought the social ills of warfare to the forefront. It stigmatized an entire generation and made the

United States rethink involvement in far-off wars. Unlike the proclaimed "victories" of previous wars, the effect of Vietnam was to give Americans a distaste for war; particularly one fought in an unknown land against an unknown opponent. It added to the nation's internal unrest while, at the same time, setting a precedent for future world entanglements.

The war in Vietnam lasted from 1964 through 1973 and saw over 58,000 American deaths and Vietnamese, Laotian and Cambodian deaths approaching the millions.

Pre-emptive Warfare

The Iraqi War will be treated at greater length in Part 2, however, it is well to understand that American presence in the Middle East, both in the Persian Gulf War (Desert Shield and Desert Storm) and in the Iraqi war (Shock and Awe, Enduring Freedom) have opened much more blatant warfare than ever before in our nation's history. Again, the public was told that an imminent threat to national security existed—that weapons of mass destruction (WMD) had been developed in Iraq and that they could be poised against the United States. These official reasons were used continuously so that the American people would understand the necessity of engaging in war as an interventionist nation. Intervening in the affairs of another country through preemptive warfare was a new concept that had to be "sold." Added to the threat was Saddam Hussein, a completely evil and unpredictable ruler who would not hesitate to use the WMD.

Why was U.S. intelligence so sure that WMD existed in Iraq? From 1981 through 1988 Iraq used WMD (biological and nuclear warfare) in a war against Iran. Those weapons, for the most part, were not developed in Iraq, however, but in the United States and the West. In other words, the United States furnished the WMD to Iraq. Chris Bury in an ABC article of September 18, 2002, wrote

> *Indeed, even as President Bush castigates Saddam's regime as "a grave and gathering danger," it's important to remember that the United States helped arm Iraq with the very weapons that administration officials are now citing as justification for Saddam's forcible removal from power.*[33]

A news release in the *New York Times* of August 8, 2002 by Patrick E. Tyler offers more detail:

> *A covert American program during the Reagan administration provided Iraq with critical battle planning assistance at a time when American intelligence agencies knew that Iraqi commanders would employ chemical weapons in waging the decisive battles of the Iran-Iraq war, according to senior military officers with direct knowledge of the program.*
>
> *Those officers, most of whom agreed to speak on the condition that they not be identified, spoke in response to a reporter's questions about the nature of gas warfare on both sides of the conflict between Iran and Iraq from 1981 to 1988. Iraq's use of gas in that conflict is repeatedly cited by President Bush and, this week, by his national security advisor, Condoleezza Rice, as justification for regime change in Iraq.*[34]

After supplying Saddam Hussein with WMD, political leaders in the West labeled him as one of the world's worst villains. Most likely, the residue of these WMD were destroyed or sent to Syria or another country with alliance to Iraq and sufficiently hidden so that they were not found by United Nations personnel. Even though supplied by the United States and not found, they were considered ample evidence for "Shock and Awe," the pre-emptive bombing and missile strike against Baghdad, a city of 5 million Iraqis.

This strike was aimed at civilians as well as military—in fact, aiming at civilians was a major part of "Shock and Awe." To a larger extent than any war in which the United States has engaged, the Iraqi War targeted civilians for "terrorist" purposes. What is terrorism? Terrorism is killing and causing civilians to fear, thus forcing government to capitulate by popular demand.

William Van Wagenen, writing of "Shock and Awe" in 2005 asked the question: "Why did the U.S. bother to bomb markets and shopping malls? In war, don't armies kill other armies, and weapons destroy other weapons?"[35] He then answered his questions from authoritative members of the current political administration:

> *Targeting civilians for the sake of achieving political or military goals constitutes terrorism. Rather than denounce the idea that America should engage in state terrorism on a massive scale, President Bush responded enthusiastically to the concept of "Shock and Awe" when it was introduced to him by Secretary of Defense Rumsfeld in the lead up to the war. Several weeks before the invasion, CBS Evening News reported positively about this new strategy, interviewing the main author of Shock and Awe: Achieving Rapid Dominance, Harlan Ullman. CBS also quoted one Pentagon official who had been briefed on the plans as saying, "There will not be a safe place in Baghdad . . . the sheer size of this has never been seen before, never been contemplated before."*[36]

The weapons of Shock and Awe did indeed strike terror in Iraqis. According to an updated study conducted by the Johns Hopkins University Bloomberg School of Public Health, some 654,000 Iraqis have lost their lives as a direct result of the 2003 invasion.[37]

Unfortunately, this followed on the heels of the original Gulf War against Iraq (Desert Shield and Desert Storm) for possession of Kuwait wherein over 56 million tons of warheads were dropped on Iraq within 45 days. Many of the warheads were coated with depleted uranium, an armor-piercing substance that is toxic and highly radioactive. Arthur N. Bernklau, the Executive Director of the Veterans for Constitutional Law Center in New York explained the magnitude of the problem—both for U.S. veterans and for the Iraqi people. In the *Preventive Psychiatry E-Newsletter* of January 24, 2005, he wrote:

> *This malady [from uranium munitions], that thousands of our military have suffered and died from, has finally been identified as the cause of this sickness [Gulf War Syndrome], eliminating the guessing. The terrible truth is now being revealed.*
>
> *. . . Out of the 580,400 soldiers who served in GW1, of them, 11,000 are now dead. By the year 2000, there were 325,000 on Permanent Medical Disability. This astounding number of "Disabled Vets" means that a decade later, 56% of those soldiers who served have some form of permanent medical problems. . . . [The VA Central Office] recently reported (2004) that "Gulf Era Veterans" now on medical disability since 1991, numbers 518,739 veterans."*[38]

Likewise, depleted uranium casualties are numerous among the Iraqis. Official counts of "collateral damage" are mixed; however, the number is apparently escalating at a tremendous pace. Because the effects are sexually transmitted, malformed newborns as well as spouses also suffer.

In 2002, during the media and government build-up to the Iraq War, most Americans evidently didn't understand the circumstances and devastation surrounding the first Gulf War. President George W. Bush's approval rating at that time fluctuated between 70% and 90%; unprecedented in presidential history. Questions and results of the polls were:

> "To the best of your knowledge, do you think Iraq currently possesses weapons of mass destruction, or doesn't it have those?" An overwhelming majority—

80%—said it does have them, while just 11% said it does not. (CBS News, February, 2002)

[In a September, 2002 CBS/*New York Times* poll] among the 80% who believe Iraq has WMD, 78% believe "Iraq is planning to use [them] against the United States." This means that 62% of all respondents believe Iraq has WMD and is planning to hit the U.S. with them. Also, in the August 2002 Gallup question noted above, 83% of those who believe Iraq has developed or is developing such weapons would use them on the U.S.; just 15% of this group felt that Iraq would not use them against the U.S. Thus, more than three-quarters of the total sample (78%) said Iraq would employ weapons of mass destruction against the United States.

It is no surprise, therefore, that nearly 9 in 10 feel Iraq's attempted development of WMD is a critical threat to the U.S. In a mid-2002 poll by the Chicago Council on Foreign Relations, 86% said "Iraq developing weapons of mass destruction" is a "critical threat" to the U.S. . . . In a February 2002 CNN/*USA Today* poll, more than 80% of those who thought Iraq already has or is developing WMD felt that fact does or would constitute a "direct threat" to the United States.

Hindsight has demonstrated an entirely different picture with current polls reflecting distrust of the policy-makers and leaders of the Iraq War. We have more information now—the vital ingredient to free agency. That information allows us to see more clearly and to make wiser decisions. Unfortunately, the added information has come too late for many and the United States has become embroiled in yet another conflict costing millions of lives and billions of dollars. Assumptions were made on incomplete and erroneous information.

Why would we be misled at such a dire cost?

Most of us have great difficulty in understanding why such gross crimes against mankind would be perpetrated as the wars mentioned in this chapter. It is beyond the nature of most to understand the attraction of "power and gain" at the expense of so much devastation and loss of life. Yet, Moroni said that the same secret combination would exist in our generation that had completely destroyed both the Jaradite and Nephite civilizations. Like his generation, he spoke of our "overthrow and destruction" by the same unholy force. Identifying the work of the secret combination is startlingly clear as we view the evidence that it "seeketh to overthrow the freedom of all lands; nations, and countries; and it bringeth to pass the destruction of all people."[39]

The logical question from our study is "Who gains, and why?" As in virtually all things related to conspiracy, time is a critical factor in understanding motives and goals. When time passes and the "big picture" comes into focus, pieces of the conspiratorial puzzle are more obvious. Viewing the world wars, we saw certain ends accomplished that were either allowed or hastened by war. Even at this juncture, the Iraqi War points to some who visibly benefit from the atrocities discussed. In 1991, prophetically, Jacob G. Hornberger of The Future of Freedom Foundation wrote:

> But to be able to serve as the world's policeman—especially in the Middle East—now guarantees total political and bureaucratic control over the lives and fortunes of the American for the indefinite future. Why? Because war and the threat of war always and inevitably entail omnipotent power over the citizenry. Moreover, brutal foreign tyrants against whom such wars can be waged are never in short supply—and especially not in the Middle East! And what better place (from the stand-point of the military-industrial complex) to have the mission of establishing peace and stability than in a part of the world which has never known peace and stability?

> *By becoming the world's policeman whose primary beat is the Middle East, those who are on the military dole have ensured themselves perpetual existence—the perpetual control over the lives and property of the American people.*[40]

Adding to the list of those who benefit—and enlarging the military-industrial complex of which Hornberger wrote, Dr. Jay Gould edited the book, *The Enemy Within* in 1996. Among those poised for gain through the Iraqi invasion are:

> . . . *the British royal family privately owns investments in uranium holdings worth over $6 billion through Rio Tinto Mines in Australia.*
> *The Rothschilds are also profiting enormously from their control of the price and supply of uranium globally.*
> *The ubiquitous Halliburton just recently finished construction of a 1,000-mile railway from the mining area to a port on the north coast of Australia to transport the ore.*
> . . . *Dick Cheney and the Bush family are tied to [British interests] through uranium mining and the shared use of depleted uranium munitions in the Middle East, Central Asia and Kosovo.*[41]

Another view is expressed by Joel Skousen in his highly informative *World Affairs Brief* (www.worldaffairsbrief.com) His feeling is that the United States is intentionally intervening in the Middle East; not to establish democracy but to create an image of America as the bully of the world—much more apparent to foreign nations who are not subject to regulated American media control. Such provoked antagonism towards the U.S. is not accidental but intentional and will be the basis for a justified retaliation against the United States by Russia and China in a third world war. This is intended to force the New World Order upon the entire world. The U.S. is intended to be the target of a preemptive nuclear strike so as to remove the military power of the United States from the world stage, forcing the world to give power to the United Nations to fight World War 3. When one realizes that those in control support all sides that enter wars and can withdraw their support at any time, the magnitude of this observation can be better understood.

Moroni was right!

The engineers, the media, and the political leaders have consistently done their job well. The alleged quotation from Julius Caesar earlier in this chapter seems obviously appropriate: "Beware the leader who bangs the drums of war in order to whip the citizenry into a patriotic fervor." Control of the media that has pushed "patriotic fervor" has engendered an unsuspecting and gullible public who, following national direction, has thought that it was doing the right thing.

However, in the wars that we have reviewed, information—the most precious commodity to free agency—has been lacking. Freedom of choice has been hampered because the public has been given incomplete or incorrect information. What was perceived as agency and freedom of choice has instead amounted to manipulated responses by those in control.

The Lord's direction to his saints about learning is especially instructive to our dispensation. In speaking to the school of the prophets specifically, and to all saints in general, he said to learn

> . . . *things which must shortly come to pass; things which are at home, things which are abroad; the wars and the perplexities of the nations, and the judgments which are on the lands; and a knowledge of countries and kingdoms*—[42]

Making ourselves aware of these things, particularly "the wars and the perplexities of the nations," we will have sufficient information to make righteous decisions and to recognize the pervasive influence of secret combinations.

Chapter 5—Endnotes

1   *Doctrine & Covenants* 98:16

2   as quoted in William Manchester, *American Caesar, Douglas McArthur, 1880-1964*. Little Brown, 1978, p. 692.

3   from the talk "War is a Racket," 1933, by Ret. Major General Smedley Butler, USMC.   www.fas.org/man/smedley .htm.

4   *Ibid.*

5   en.wikiquote.org/wiki/Julius_Caesar

6   Joseph Smith—Matthew 23

7   William Guy Carr, *Pawns in the Game*, 2nd ed., National Federation of Christian Laymen: Toronto. 1956. pp. 67-68.

8   G. Edward Griffin, *The Grand Deception—Part Two: A Second Look at the War on Terrorism*. pp. 2-4.

9   as quoted in Gary Allen, *None Dare Call It Conspiracy*. Rossmore, CA: Concord Press, 1971.

10   Lord Curzon. www.threeworldwars.com/world-war-1/ww1-2 .htm

11   Robert Lekachman, *The Age of Keynes*, Vintage Books: New York, 1968. pp. 32-33.

12   Allen, *Op. Cit.*

13   *Social Justice Magazine*, July 3, 1939, p. 4.

14   *The Tax Exempt Foundations. Hearing before the Special Committee to Investigate Tax-exempt Foundations and Comparable Organizations*. House of Representatives, Eighty-third Congress. Washington, D.C.: May 10— July 9, 1954. pp. 60-61.

15   Interview between Herman Goering and Gustave Gilbert, April 18, 1946. http://buffaloreport.com/030324gilbert.html

16   J. Reuben Clark, Conference Report , April, 1941. pp. 18-19.

17   J. Reuben Clark, 1/24/45 as quoted in Newquist, *Prophets, Principles and National Survival*, pp. 222-223.

18   quoted in Mullins, *The Secret History of the Atomic Bomb*, p. 8, on-line essay at www.whate.to/b/mullins8_q.html

19   Mullins, *Ibid*. p. 8.

20   Mullins, *Ibid*. p. 9.

21   Harry S. Truman, *Off the Record: The Private Papers of Harry S. Truman*, Harper, 1980, p. 304.

22   Kai Bird and Lawrence Lifschultz, eds., *Hiroshima's Shadow*, Pamphleteers Press: Stony Creek, Connecticut, 1998, p. 39.

23   Bird, *Ibid*.

24   J. Reuben Clark, Conference Report, October, 1946. pp. 86-88 as quoted in Newquist, *Prophets, Principles and National Survival*, p. 471.

25   James Madison, 1795, *Works* 4:491-492 as quoted in Newquist, *Prophets, Principles and National Survival*, p. 468.

26   Edward L. Kimball, ed. *Spencer W. Kimball, Teachings of Spencer W. Kimball, Twelfth President of the Church of Jesus Christ of Latter-day Saints*. Salt Lake City: Bookcraft, 1972. pp. 414-418.

27   Mormon 5:4

28   Jeff Cohen and Norman Solomon, "Tonkin Gulf Lie Launched Vietnam War," FAIR (Fairness and accuracy in Reporting), 7-27-94. www.fair.org/index.php?page=2261

29   *Ibid.*.

30   *Ibid.*.

31   *Ibid.*.

32   *Ibid.*.

33   Chris Bury, *A Tortured Relationship*, ABC, September 18,
            2002, quoted in The Future of Freedom Foundation,
            Jacob G. Hornberger, *Players and Pawns: The Persian
            Gulf War*. www.fff.org/freedom/0791a.asp

34   Patrick E. Tyler, New York Times, August 18, 2002. "U.S.
            Aided Iraq in War Despite use of Gas." www.hartford-
            hwp.com/archives/51/220.html

35   William Van Wagenen, "Shock and Awe: Aerial Bombardment
            American Style," Electronic Iraq, July 6, 2005,
            www.electroniciraq.net/news/2035.shtml

36   "Iraq Faces Massive U.S. Missile Barrage," CBS News Online,
            January 24, 2003. www.cbsnews.com/stories/
            2003/01/24/eveningnews/main537928.shtml

37   Johns Hopkins Bloomberg School of Public Health, October
            11, 2006.   www.jhsph.edu/publichealthnews/press_releases
            /2006 /burnham_iraq_2006.html

38   Bob Nichols, "Heads Roll at the Veterans Administration:
            Mushroomong Depleted Uranium (DU) Scandal
            Blamed," January 28, 2005. www.axisoflogic.com/cgi-
            bin/exec/view.pl?archive=137&num=15334

39   Ether 8:25

40   Jacob G. Hornberger, *Players and Pawns: The Persian
            Gulf War*, Freedom Daily, July, 1991. *Op. Cit.*

41   Leuren Moret, "Depleted Uranium Contaminates Europe."
            February 27, 2006. www.countercurrents.org/moret
            270206 .htm

42   *Doctrine and Covenants* 88:79

Chapter 6

TOWARDS A ONE-WORLD GOVERNMENT: THE UNITED NATIONS

The Lord's plan for government

While in Kirtland, Ohio, the Church accepted Section 134 of the *Doctrine and Covenants*. At that time, amidst government oppression for their beliefs, a declaration was made "with regard to earthly governments and laws in general [so that the saints] may not be misinterpreted nor misunderstood." Beginning the revelation, the Lord taught that "governments were instituted by God for the benefit of man." The primary "benefit" to which the Lord had reference was the maintenance of personal freedom.

Without government and a system of laws, "peace and harmony would be supplanted by anarchy and terror."[1] Therefore, a tenet of belief for Latter-day Saints is that "no government can exist in peace, except such laws are framed and held inviolate."[2] To comply with these instructions, members of the Church uphold and sustain the laws of respective countries in which they reside with the caveat that those laws support "that principle of freedom in maintaining rights and privileges."[3]

When discussing the purpose of governmental laws, the Lord clarified his intent that those laws "will secure to each individual the free exercise of conscience, the right and control of property, and the protection of life."[4] By protecting these inherent rights of freedom, the individual could, through his own volition and agency, draw nearer to God through personal choices.

In government there is always a balance between law and anarchy. Too much law destroys freedom, but so also does anarchy. Law has the potential to regulate daily affairs of the person and his property so that personal freedom and control of possessions is restricted. This is the kind of government interference that the American colonists fought against in the Revolutionary War. Anarchy, on the other hand, is the absence of law. Without law, "might makes right" and the individual finds himself without protection in his inherent rights to life, liberty, and property.

It is the job of governments to bring balance between the two extremes. In doing this, the Lord gave several cautions in Section 134—all having to do with preserving individual freedoms.

> verse 4: *[Freedom to exercise religion] unless their religious opinions prompt them to infringe upon the rights and liberties of others; but we do not believe that human law has a right to interfere in prescribing rules of worship to bind the consciences of men.*

> *The civil magistrate should restrain crime, but never control conscience; should punish guilt, but never suppress the freedom of the soul.*

> verse 5: *governments have a right to enact such laws as in their own judgments are best calculated to secure the public interest; at the same time, however, holding sacred the freedom of conscience.*

verse 10: *We believe that men should appeal to the civil law for redress of all wrongs and grievances, where personal abuse is inflicted or the right of property or character infringed.*

We believe that all men are justified in defending themselves, their friends and property, and the government, from unlawful assaults and encroachments of all persons [when government is unable or unwilling.]

Likewise, when this nation was founded, the Lord emphasized that freedom was its foundation. Without individual freedom, agency would be inhibited and accountability would be taken from the person. This, of course, would have frustrated the earthly step of the plan of salvation.

Why national government is effective

In the past, from the time of Nimrod and the Tower of Babel forward, there have been attempts at world government. It has always failed. There are some specific reasons why nations are more poised for governing than a world body. The first, and perhaps the most obvious, is that the nation-system is more direct—the gap between leadership and those governed is much less than it would be toward a set of world leaders. President Ezra Taft Benson taught that "The smallest or lowest level that can possible undertake the task is the one that should do so." He went on to say that

> *This is merely the application to the field of politics of that wise and time-tested principle of never asking a larger group to do that which can be done by a smaller group. And so far as government is concerned, the smaller the unit and the closer it is to the people, the easier it is to guide it, to correct it, to keep it solvent, and to keep our freedom.*[5]

That makes sense. The closer we are to government—particularly at the local level—we are able to be heard and to influence decisions. The further removed that we become, the less our voice counts. Many of us feel helpless to be heard on a state or national level—think of the alienation we would experience on a world level.

Nations engender a sense of togetherness with a common heritage and history. There are identifying characteristics and experiences that belong to one nation and not to another, thus giving us certain commonalities that we are unable to share with those of another nation or culture. We are able to love and feel charity with people of all nations (we especially see this among members of the Church from different lands) but governance is somewhat distinct. Laws are set in place according to national ideals and guidelines. In the case of the United States, for example, John Adams remarked that "Our Constitution was made only for a moral and religious people. It is wholly inadequate for the government of any other." In other words, as correct as it was, it couldn't have been codified into law for all people in all lands. It was specific, as the Lord taught in Section 101 of the *Doctrine and Covenants*, to the United States of America. The nation at its inception had reached a level of spirituality that allowed our Constitution to be set in place.

The Founders' caution to retain sovereignty

A major thrust in taking sovereignty from nations and "overthrowing the freedoms of all lands, nations, and countries," is to consolidate their leadership into a single unit. The most visible attack on the sovereignty of "all lands" throughout the world is the mounting presence of a one-world government—the United Nations. All of the Founding Fathers spoke boldly of maintaining liberty; however, none more succinctly and prophetically than George Washington in his stirring Farewell

Address. Fearing that the cause of freedom would not always burn, he wrote

> *The unity of government which constitutes you one people, is also now dear to you. It is justly so; for it is a main pillar in the edifice of your real independence; the support of your tranquility at home; your peace abroad; of your safety; of your prosperity; of that very liberty which you so highly prize. But as it is easy to foresee that, from different causes and from different quarters much pains will be taken, many artifices employed, to weaken in your minds the conviction of this truth, as this is the point in your political fortress against which the batteries of internal and external enemies will be most constantly and actively (though often covertly and insidiously) directed; it is of infinite moment, that you should properly estimate the immense value of your national union to your collective and individual happiness; that you should cherish a cordial; habitual; and immoveable attachment to it; accustoming yourselves to think and speak of it as the palladium of your political safety and prosperity; watching for its preservation with jealous anxiety; discountenancing whatever may suggest even a suspicion that it can, in any event, be abandoned . . . .*

Patriotism based upon the theme of nationalism was an internal link to maintaining sovereignty. Washington stressed that the inner desire of the patriot would foster vigilance and keep the nation pure against those with lesser motives. A nation of citizens who cherished freedom to the degree that Washington counseled would not only appreciate its benefits, but would recognize encroachments and "watch for its preservation with jealous anxiety." They would do all within their power to insure that it continued from generation to generation. With such feelings, it would be difficult for a secret combination with the goal of "overthrowing" the nation to succeed.

To understand the pervasiveness of the secret combination into world affairs, it is necessary to understand the disintegration of sovereign nations—particularly the United

States of America. President George Washington was especially insightful about the nation's future and warned of the danger of forming permanent alliances with foreign countries and the need to maintain political independence. This was a major theme of his Farewell Address given in 1796.

> *The great rule of conduct for us, in regard to foreign nations is, in extending our commercial relations, to have with them as little political connection with them as possible.*
>
> *Europe has a set of primary interests which to us have none, or a very remote relation. Hence, she must be engaged in frequent controversies, the causes of which are essentially foreign to ourselves. Hence, therefore, it must be unwise in us to implicate ourselves, by artificial ties, in the ordinary vicissitudes of her politics, or the ordinary combinations and collusions of her friendships or enmities.*
>
> *. . . Why quit our own to stand upon foreign ground? Why, by interweaving our destiny with that of any part of Europe, entangle our peace and prosperity in the toils of European ambition, rivalship, interest, humor, or caprice?*
>
> *It is our true policy to steer clear of permanent alliance with any portion of the foreign world . . . .*

With Washington, Thomas Jefferson added:

> *I have ever deemed it fundamental for the United States never to take part in the quarrels of Europe. Their political interests are entirely distinct from ours. Their mutual jealousies, their balance of power, their complicated alliances, their forms and principles of government are all foreign to us.*
>
> *They are nations of eternal war. All their energies are expended in the destruction of the labor, property, and lives of their people.*
>
> *On our part, never had a people so favorable a chance of trying the opposite system of peace and fraternity with mankind, and the direction of all our means and faculties to the purposes of improvement instead of destruction.*[6]

Adherence to the Founders' counsel kept the United States from entering into permanent alliances and treaties with foreign nations until the United Nations Charter was signed in 1945. In fact, when the League of Nations was proposed at the conclusion of WWI, even though it was spearheaded by the President of the United States, it was rejected by the American people on that basis—that the United States should not give up her sovereignty through permanent alliances with foreign countries.

LDS leaders on national sovereignty

President J. Reuben Clark, because of his experience as the U. S. Undersecretary of State and his studies in international law, well understood the consequences of alliances and treaties. He wrote in the *Church News* of February 20, 1952, that

> *Every engagement with a foreign nation which, if met, deprives us of the power to determine our own course at the moment of implementation, impairs our sovereignty.*
>
> *Every treaty of alliance, bipartite or multi-partite (the United Nations Charter is of the latter class,) impairs our sovereignty, because every alliance requires a surrender of rights, since mutual aid in strictly non-sovereign interests is the purpose of the alliance. . . .*

Maintaining sovereignty, then, to a degree is isolationist. The adjective "global" was meant to pertain to commerce and good-will and not to things political and interventionist. Although Washington knew that there might be "*extraordinary emergencies*" when two or more countries would share the same interests against a foreign invading power, he stressed that any alliance should be temporary; and reiterated that permanent unions were never to be forged.

Engagement in treaties, however, has been the primary avenue for American entry into world affairs and, consequently, the door used by the secret combination to acquire a world-wide grasp. While much of the initial mischief was taking place and "peace-keeping treaties" —particularly the United Nations— were fostered following WW2, President Clark explained that there were three major drawbacks. In the same *Church News* article he wrote that all three would reduce the autonomy and sovereignty of the nation, thus placing it at the mercy of decisions beyond the control of America's leaders.

> *(1) . . . under the United Nations Charter, we have lost the right to make the treaties we may wish. All treaties we make must conform to the provisions of the United Nations Charter. Existing treaty provisions that are out of harmony with the Charter, must apparently fall. Having in mind the complicated provisions of the Charter touching international economic and social cooperation, and the intricate international trusteeship system, we may well find that we shall be greatly hampered in the development of our own international trade and commerce.*

> *(2) We have lost the sovereign power to adjust our own international difficulties—a power which has enabled us to live as the most peace-loving nation in the world, and to build up a record of achievement in the peaceful adjustment of international disputes unequalled by any other great nation in the world.*

> *(3) We have surrendered, by the Charter terms at least, those great attributes of sovereignty, upon which the very existence of sovereignty depends: the power to declare war, . . . the power to decide against whom we shall make war, and to determine its terms.*

Relinquishing national sovereignty, key decisions affecting the nation's future were given over to another body with different values and goals. In many cases, the goals of member nations could be in conflict with the distinct goals of the United

States, in which case, the United States would be forced to acquiesce to the dictates of the larger body. Exasperated with the media mindset and public acceptance of the United Nations, President Clark wrote

> *We are entering this with the blind infatuation of a nation of Darius Greens, [a mindless fictional character popular at the time] ignoring all laws, disregarding all experiences, and blindly and blithely moving out with the confidence of a set of ignoramuses. . . .*
>
> *On no account should we have gone forward on the theory that maybe the Charter Organization will work and so let us make a try. Unless we are ready to plumb the depths of sorrow and ill that can come from a failure. . . .*[7]

LDS leaders and the United Nations

Other LDS leaders spoke out with the same vehemence about union with the United Nations and its false promises.

President Stephen L. Richards of the First Presidency in the October, 1947 General Conference said:

> *Have you ever heard of a voice being raised in any of the sessions of the United Nations since its inception more than two years ago protesting the infractions of God's laws or importuning his help in achieving the purposes of that organization? I think you have not, unless perhaps in some innocuous way, because I suspect that it is tacitly agreed that God and religion shall be shut out of the proceedings.*

Likewise, Apostle Albert E. Bowen said in the October General Conference of 1950:

> *We seem to be trying now to rear a government whose proponents and sponsors cannot even invoke divine blessings upon their deliberations or its destiny. What chance do you think it has to heal the wounds of the world?*

President Ezra Taft Benson wrote:

> *Whereas the United States is founded on the concept of limited government, the United Nations concept is one of unlimited government power with virtually no meaningful restraints to protect individual liberty.*
>
> *. . . the U. N. has become a professional politician's paradise. Glancing through the publications of the various U. N. specialized agencies and commissions, one can find daily reports on proposals for setting prices, production quotas, inventories, stockpiles of raw materials, labor standards, wages and monetary policies. Every conceivable sphere of human activity is being analyzed and then planned for so that it will come under the ultimate control of the United Nations. It is becoming a world legislature, world court, world department of education, world welfare agency, world planning center for industry, science and commerce, world finance agency, world police force, and world anything else anyone might want—or may not want.*[8]

Elder Marion G. Romney, later to be a member of the Church's First Presidency, told BYU students in 1955:

> *Frankly now, are we, as rational beings—in the light of history, the signs of the times, and the revelations of the restoration and the Bible—realistically justified in putting our hopes in the United Nations? Doing so, are we not again hoping to "gather grapes of thorns," and "figs of thistles?" I am not here thinking of the fringe benefits admitted by most everyone, but of lasting peace. It seems to me that from the inception of the U. N., we have had nothing but wars and rumors of wars.*

President J. Reuben Clark explained why war—not peace— was an outgrowth of the United Nations:

> *There seems no reason to doubt that such real approval as the Charter has among the people is based upon the belief that if the Charter is put into effect, wars will end. . . . The Charter will not*

certainly end war. Some will ask,—why not? In the first place, there is no provision in the Charter itself that contemplates ending war. It is true the Charter provides for force to bring peace, but such use of force is itself war. . . . The Charter is built to prepare for war, not to promote peace. . . . The Charter is a war document not a peace document. . . .

Not only does the Charter Organization not prevent future wars, but it makes it practically certain that we shall have future wars, and as to such wars it takes from us the power to declare them, to choose the side on which we will fight, to determine what forces and military equipment we shall use in the war, and to control and command our sons who do the fighting.[9]

Clearly, during the formative beginnings of the United Nations, LDS leaders were not only skeptical but were openly opposed to it. As seen, most of the early objections had to do with (1) its propensity for war in the guise of enforcing peace; (2) its Godless nature; and (3) relinquishing elements of national sovereignty. With the passing of time, all of these objections have proven true.

LDS leaders' concerns: the propensity for war

Bearing out President Clark's war concerns, another author has written:

For the past fifty years, as the U.N. lived off the perception that it provided a forum where nations could air their differences off the battlefield, more wars were fought than ever before in human history. Instead of removing the threat to peace, the U.N. has encouraged, even nurtured, regimes that waged violence on their neighbors, and indeed, oppressed and tortured their own people.[10]

Unfortunately, the heritage of war has frequently followed United Nations involvement. Although always proclaiming peace, the modus for achieving it regularly includes the use of military personnel from various nations for enforcement ("peacekeepers"). By this action the United Nations fulfills President Clark's warning that it "makes it practically certain that we shall have future wars."

LDS leaders' concerns: its Godless nature

The response of the U.N. to its "Godlessness" has been that it is dealing with a multitude of nations throughout the world that all have differing approaches to religion. In the interest of not being offensive, religion and references to God are intentionally omitted from U.N. material. On the surface that appears to be a rational response; however, other negative statements made in official U.N. reports about religion and particularly Christianity suggest that the anti-religion attitude of policy-makers may go much deeper. Richard Wilkins, the Managing Director of the World Family Policy Center (a recognized agency dealing with international law and the United Nations) and professor of law at Brigham Young University, has written extensively about his pro-family work with the U.N. Referencing the apparent "deconstruction of the natural family" by the United Nations, Wilkins pointed to a series of steps taken by the world body. The first, he said, is "assertions that religious faith is irrelevant or dangerous."[11]

Much of today's anti-religious stance taken by the United Nations has come under the heading of "families." Because religions have traditionally favored the natural family made up of a father, mother and children, religious views have generally run counter to alternative family lifestyles. Both the women's and the homosexual agendas have particularly singled out religion as a cultural problem. Professor Wilkins, identifying the issue in more detail, offered the following examples:

> *This deconstruction of the natural family commences with attacks upon faith and religion. The CEDAW Committee [Convention on the Elimination of All Forms of Discrimination*

Against Women—an officially convened UN committee], again, is a good example of the approach of some within the modern international community. The committee frequently takes aim at religion and culture, expressing the view that "cultural and religious values cannot be allowed to undermine the universality of women's rights." The committee, in fact, was so bold as to pronounce that "in all countries, [some of] the most significant factors inhibiting women's ability to participate in public life have been the culture framework of values and religious beliefs." The committee concluded that "true gender equality does not allow for varying interpretations of obligations under international legal norms depending on internal religious rules, traditions and customs." The committee, in fact, has gone so far as to instruct Muslim nations that they must read the Holy Qur'an in ways that will better comply with modern social trends.[12]

Imagine being told that the *Book of Mormon* should be rewritten to "better comply with modern social trends!" Imagine being told that passages in the Bible, particularly those dealing with sexual perversions and punishments, must be rewritten or left out! Imagine missionaries not being able to tell about Joseph Smith's first vision because the Lord told him not to join any church for their "creeds were an abomination in [the Lord's] sight" and that the various churches had "a form of godliness but they deny the power thereof."[13]

In that light, parents and others are instructed by the United Nations Convention on the Rights of the Child that they have "freedom to manifest one's religion or beliefs" however, that right (not a God-given right but allowed at the discretion of the United Nations) "may be subject only to such limitations as are prescribed by law" . . . and does not infringe upon "the fundamental rights and freedoms of others." Besides the audacity of granting already inherent rights, the notion of practicing religion within the framework of the "fundamental rights and freedoms of others" is troubling to many. Because of the elasticity and potential magnitude of this phrase, we really aren't sure what to expect. Does a fundamental right include not being exposed to any elements of Christianity—Christmas songs, manger scenes, the Ten Commandments, the mention of God's name—because those symbols may be considered offensive?

In China, for example, a person may be imprisoned for attending Christian meetings, writing favorably about Christianity, or displaying a picture of the Savior—all because these practices are considered offensive. Will the United Nations enforce the same intolerance? To what extent will the U.N. apply the "fundamental rights" of others against the freedom to practice religion? What will that mean to the present missionary program of the Church?

President Stephen L. Richards' observation given just two years following the inception of the United Nations was pointedly prophetic: that God would only be mentioned in "some innocuous way" and that apparently "it [was] tacitly agreed that God and religion shall be shut out of the proceedings."

LDS leaders' concerns: relinquishing elements of national sovereignty.

Because of Latter-day Saints' unique understanding of the divine roots of the United States of America, many Church leaders have warned about losing sovereignty—the right to act independently. The loss of sovereignty necessarily concedes degrees of independence to a "higher" authority: in this case the world government of the United Nations.

In his article, *Globalism and Sovereignty*, Council on Foreign Relations President, Richard N. Haass spoke directly to the issue of sovereignty. He explained that national independence was a detriment to a world congress of nations. Unabashedly, he wrote:

> *Necessity may lead to reducing or even eliminating sovereignty when a government, whether from lack of capacity or conscious policy, is unable to provide for the basic needs of its citizens.*[14]

Of course the immediate problem with this statement is that "basic needs" are undefined. Ultimately, setting basic need standards would be the prerogative of the United Nations. Following Haass' reasoning, the United States could be subject to loss of sovereignty because it "is unable to provide for the basic needs of its citizens." How can that be? Aren't we the wealthiest nation on earth? Why should we fear interference from the United Nations?

In a measure, our nation has already set standards for basic needs called federal poverty guidelines. The income figure set for this year (2006) to determine that a family of four is considered to live in poverty is $20,000 or less. Using statistics from 2004, the National Poverty Center at the Gerald R. Ford Public Policy Center at the University of Michigan determined that 12.7% of all people in the United States lived with less income than established by federal guidelines. With current population statistics at about 300,000,000 people, there are approximately 37,682,000 people in the United States with less income than established by federal poverty guidelines. Unfortunately, if the federal figures were used to determine basic needs for the United States population, under Haass' concept of global government, our country would relinquish sovereignty and the United Nations would assume care for our citizens.

More directly, however, sovereignty is lost through treaties and alliances with foreign governments. In a wartime situation, that means that member nations of the United Nations must be willing to enter foreign countries as "peacekeepers" under the direction of U.N. command. This is done without regard to strife between individual countries and could place any country's military power in conflicts that are wholly outside the interests and concerns of the nations called to do battle. This is what President J. Reuben Clark had reference to when he said that through the United Nations Charter, "we have surrendered . . . those great attributes of sovereignty upon which the very existence of sovereignty depends: the power to declare war. . . . the power to decide against whom we shall make war and to determine its terms."[15]

The question of national sovereignty takes even greater meaning when reviewing our nation's past. Can we imagine the Founding Fathers petitioning their grievances before a world body and having others evaluate those petitions to determine our justification for a war with Great Britain. If granted the right to rebel, the world body would appoint military leaders and raise disinterested volunteers from foreign countries to fight for American independence. As absurd as that sounds, that is the present program encouraged by the United Nations—a direct result of usurped sovereignty.

Another form of treaty is a nation's agreement to a resolution. This is not a military alliance but an agreement to be subject to accords, resolutions, or conventions of the United Nations. Sovereignty is restricted, for once a particular resolution has been ratified, a country is legally bound to fulfill the mandates of the agreement. In 2001, Law professor Richard Wilkins found himself defending his concerns about the United Nations in Melbourne, Australia. A previous talk he had given there had treated the International Criminal Court and had created some attention. Australia's Attorney General took offense to Wilkins' remarks and said:

> It has also been suggested that the ICC [International Criminal Court] will somehow be used as an instrument of social engineering. Conspiracy theorists argue that the Court will try cases based on national policies. These claims are totally false and absurd.

As I have said, the ICC will deal only with serious international crimes. It will not be concerned with domestic social policy. To suggest otherwise is to engage in deliberate scaremongering.[16]

Unfortunately, the Attorney General had the concept that many have had regarding the ICC and other dictums that have originatcd from the United Nations. He saw the U.N. as an abstract body designed to take care of troubling problems with nations other than his own, and considered the sovereignty of his own nation to be sufficient to handle situations within its borders. After Wilkins pointed toward several areas in which Australia's approval of the ICC conceded jurisdiction to U.N. interpretation, he offered an example from the U.N. Declaration on HIV/AIDS. The Declaration included a statement to the effect that all nations would implement its guidelines:

> *Let me tell you what Mary Robinson, the former Irish President, said these guidelines are based upon.*
>
> *According to her, the norms enunciated in these guidelines are 'consistent with fundamental human rights and fundamental freedoms.' . . .*
>
> *What are the fundamental rights that Mary Robinson says that all nations must recognize?*
>
> *One, they include the repeal of all laws condemning homosexual sodomy.*
>
> *Two, the legalization of same-sex marriages.*
>
> *Three, mandatory and graphic sexual training for children. She has three paragraphs on the last of these. She says the training has to include instruction, beginning when the child's at the age of 10, on how to engage in sexual intercourse with members of the same sex. Since this will of necessity be graphic, she says, 'such materials should be exempted from pornography and obscenity laws.'*
>
> *Four, she says that all laws regulating prostitution must be eliminated. Prostitution, in short, must be legalized.*
>
> *Five, she says that the age of consent for all sexual activities should be lowered to 14.*

> *Finally, and most troublingly, she says: 'there must be creation of penalties for anyone who vilifies individuals engaged in same-sex relationships.'   In short, it's not enough simply to normalize, in one fell swoop, all of international law related to homosexuality. We have to provide penalties. . . .*[17]

Would this be enforceable? Where would the penalties come from?   How would they be implemented?   Wilkins continued his example by explaining that Robinson and others said that the judiciary would apply the Declaration's recommendations. Of course, the judiciary is the international judiciary or the ICC. In other words, Australia, as all other nations, would need to have laws in place to carry out the concerns of the world agenda. In the event that those laws were not in place, the International Criminal Court, usurping a nation's sovereignty, would see that the world agenda was implemented.

There can be no question that the above example, if pursued as Robinson directed, would trespass into areas of social policy and social engineering. In fact, should national law run counter to that adopted by the United Nations, "international law established under the ICC and decisions of the ICC take precedence."[18]

The ICC, ratified in April of 2002, is a huge example of loss of sovereignty. Thankfully, the United States was not a signer to the Court approval, but, nevertheless, the ICC is a reality.

U.N. inroads into the traditional family

The traditional position of parents in the natural family has been increasingly belittled by the globalist agenda. Parents are counseled to seek guidance from "experts;" to trust the findings of modern scholarship concerning the family unit; and to allow others to do for their children what they are incapable of doing. Hillary Clinton, in her book *It Takes a Village* outlined recent thought about childrearing:

> *The village itself must act in place of the parents. It accepts those responsibilities in all our names through the authority we vest in government.*

The government, then, assumes the role of parentage with its bevy of experts and unlimited use of time and funds. The role of biological parents, according to this reasoning, besides birthing and supplying temporal comforts, is minimal.

This squares poorly with Latter-day Saint views on the responsibilities of motherhood and fatherhood. As other traditionalists throughout the world, we claim that the responsibilities of childrearing fall directly on parents. The Proclamation on the Family, given to members of the Church in 1995, succinctly stated that "husband and wife have a solemn responsibility to love and care for each other and for their children." That obligation is so strong that "we will be held accountable before God for the discharge of these obligations." Further, the Proclamation reinforces that the family unit is conceived "by divine design" and that, while fathers "preside over their families in love and righteousness and are responsible to provide the necessities of life and protection for their families," that "mothers are primarily responsible for the nurture of their children."

Elder Bruce C. Hafen of the First Quorum of Seventy expressed concern about the apparent assault against the traditional family by the United Nations. In 1989 the U.N. General Assembly adopted the Convention on the Rights of the Child (CRC) that brought alarm to many conservative groups. Six years later, Elder Hafen, a former Provost at Brigham Young University and a specialist in family law, wrote a paper with his son Jonathan, entitled *"Abandoning Children to their Autonomy:*

The United Nations Convention on the Rights of a Child" published in the *Harvard International Law Review.*

The title of Elder Hafen's paper is significant. An overriding theme of the CRC is that children are under too much pressure and need freedom to determine their own destinies. Like education's John Dewey, the CRC opposes the traditional roles of parents and religion. Both, says the CRC, are detriments to healthy children; therefore, children should be released from strictures of parental authority and religion and given autonomy to act for themselves without interference. Elder Hafen correctly identified the impact of the CRC: it would abandon children from any clear direction in their lives at a time when that direction is most needed. In his analysis, Elder Hafen wrote:

> . . . *the parental rights recognized by the CRC apparently extend only to a role in enforcing the rights the CRC grants to the child without recognizing an independent parental right. The CRC's autonomy model tends to view parents as trustees of the state who have only such authority and discretion as the state may grant in order to protect the child's independent rights.*[19]

Coupled with parental restrictions from teaching and providing guidance for children, the CRC also calls for a broad use of media tools to expose children to accepted U.N. standards. Specifically, children would be given the right to "receive and impart information and ideas of all kinds, regardless of frontiers, either orally, in writing or in print, in the form of art, or through any media of the child's choice."[20] Cutting through U.N. rhetoric, Elder Hafen said on Australian national radio:

> *This would include access to information, media information, choices about religion, the choice of whether to be educated, how to express oneself, access to what kind of literature, all of this calls into question the right of parents to direct the upbringing of their children. . . . Are we lowering the threshold so that the State*

can intervene even when parents are not abusive or neglectful but the child makes the argument that the parental conduct is unreasonable or not in the child's interests.[21]

The invasion of the home by other standards than those agreed upon by parents is frightening to most. Into this quagmire, Richard Wilkins adds a further CRC restriction for parents: their "unlawful interference" with a child's "privacy." This further limitation, he states, "could place even the basic ability to discipline and monitor children—activities necessary for effective parenting—into serious doubt."[22] Unfortunately, because of the definition of "family" given by the Committee on the Rights of a Child, this is about what is expected. "The committee views the child as a miniature adult, with rights to privacy, freedom of expression, and freedom to decide what he or she will learn, even against parents' wishes."[23] The actual definition or "concept of 'family' has nothing to do with childbearing or procreation. So understood, any two men or any two women—or any group at all—can claim equal status as a family."[24]

The expressions and dictums of those who create international family policy have prepared us to accept what would have been shocking just a few years ago. In a BYU Devotional Address, Brother Wilkins told about his associate, Kay Balmforth, who attended a 1999 preparatory meeting on the International Conference on Population and Development in New York City.

> *There, Kay watched for three days while the attendees of this important conference debated whether they would even include a reference to "parents" in a document that purportedly created a child's right to sexual freedom, sexual training, and reproductive choice. At this important international meeting, it seemed that the mere mention of parental guidance on sexual matters was anathema.*[25]

Who could have imagined that something so basic to humankind as the role of parents would be an international topic for debate and redefinition?

Other concerns about the United Nations

The internet. In December of 2003, the World Summit on the Information Society (WSIS) was convened with the intent of placing the internet under United Nations control. With the proposed purpose of taking internet services to poorer countries were included issues of content control and government regulation. Unfortunately, any control over the internet would be a move to restrict the flow of information. The Action Plan drafted in 2003 recommended that future internet usage comply with Article 29 of the Universal Declaration of Human Rights: that the "rights and freedoms may in no case be exercised contrary to the purposes and principles of the United Nations." A second summit was conducted in 2005 with others to be scheduled in the future.

World taxes to support the U.N. In January of 2006, the United Nations Development Program met in Switzerland to further its plan to tax world governments for its support. Its plan, outlined in the book *The New Public Finance: Responding to Global Challenges*, published by Oxford University Press, calls for an initial $7 trillion to be disbursed throughout the world by the United Nations. Various proposals to fund the U.N. include transfers of money based on production and natural resources from more developed nations to those less developed; a global tax on foreign currency exchange; and taxes on international travel. In addition to these, there are several other taxes that are proposed to either funnel funds directly to the United Nations or to transfer money from wealthier to less developed nations.

Should U.N. taxes become reality, the United Nations will be an official government. At that time, other nations of the world will stand in the shadow of the conglomerate world government.

> *For it cometh to pass that whosoever buildeth it up seeketh to overthrow the freedom of all lands, nations, and countries; and it bringeth to pass the destruction of all people, for it is built up by the devil, who is the father of all lies.*
>
> *Ether 8:25*

Chapter 6—Endnotes

1   *Doctrine and Covenants* 134:6

2   *Doctrine and Covenants* 134:2

3   *Doctrine and Covenants* 98:5

4   *Doctrine and Covenants* 134:2

5   Ezra Taft Benson, *Teachings of Ezra Taft Benson.* Salt Lake
      City: Bookcraft. 1988. p. 610.

6   Andrew Allison, *The Real Thomas Jefferson*, Washington
      D.C.: National Center for Constitutional Studies: 1983.
      p. 440.

7   J. Reuben Clark, Compiled by Gerald Newquist, *Prophets,
      Principles and National Survival*, p. 454.

8   Ezra Taft Benson, Compiled by Jerreld Newquist, *An
      Enemy Hath Done This*. Parliament Publishers:
      Salt Lake City. 1969. pp. 204-205.

9   J. Reuben Clark, quoted in Newquist, *Prophets, Principles and
      National Survival*, *Op. Cit.* p. 458.

10   Tom DeWeese, "Time to Declare Independence from the
      United Nations." *Capitalism Magazine*, May 5, 2005.
      www.capmag.com/article.asp?ID=4218

11   Richard G. Wilkins, "Rights, Rhetoric, the Family, and
      Social Change," World Family Policy Forum, 2002, p.
      84. www.worldfamilypolicy.org.

12   *Ibid.*

13   Joseph Smith-History 19

14   Richard N. Haass, "Sovereignty and Globalism," February
      17, 2006. www.cfr.org

15   J. Reuben Clark, *Church News*, February 20, 1952

16   Richard G. Wilkins, Speech at Melbourne, Victoria, Australia,
      July 24, 2001. p. 2. www.saltshakers.org.au

17   *Ibid.* p. 8.

18   *Ibid.* p. 3. (*International Criminal Court Manual for the Ratification and Implementation of the Rome Statute.*)

19   Bruce C. Hafen and Jonathan O. Hafen, "Abandoning Children to their rights," First Things, The Journal of Religion, Culture and Public Life. August/ September, 1995, *The Institute of Religion and Public Life.* p. 21.

20   Article 13 of CRC quoted in "Rights Rhetoric, the Family, and Social Change," Richard G. Wilkins, World Family Policy Forum, 2002, p. 86. www.worldfamilypolicy.org

21   The Law Report: "Children's Rights—The Battle of the Submissions." May 12, 1998. www.abc.net.au

22   Wilkins, Speech at Melbourne, Australia, *Op. Cit.* p. 86.

23   *Ibid.* p. 84.

24   *Ibid.*

25   Richard Wilkins, "Defending the Family," BYU Devotional Address, July 6, 1999.

Chapter 7

MEDIA CONTROL: WHY DIDN'T I HEAR THIS ON THE 10:00 NEWS?

Propaganda is to democracy
What the bludgeon is to the totalitarian state.

Noam Chomsky

Freedom of press and speech are indispensable to agency

The first amendment to the Constitution, in addition to affirming personal rights of belief and association, is also a guarantee that we have sufficient information to use our agency. That information might come from associating with others who are free to speak as they desire; and from a free press that is able to publish political or religious beliefs from the entire spectrum. After all, political and religious freedom wouldn't make much sense if we couldn't gather with others to either exchange different points of view or receive strength from hearing our own beliefs reinforced. Likewise, religiously a free press guarantees that we may promulgate our own beliefs so that others might know our doctrines. Without freedom of the press, the entire missionary program of the LDS Church would stagnate. This is why at other times in the world's history when freedoms were stifled by state imposed religious beliefs, that the Church could not thrive nor been taken to "all nations, kindreds, tongues and people."

The Founders recognized that agency must exist in the new nation and that it must necessarily be a hallmark of the government. We have already noted that the Lord said that "the law of the land which is constitutional, supporting that principle of freedom in maintaining rights and privileges, belongs to all mankind."[1] It was intended that "all mankind" had agency—the freedom to make individual decisions. That "principle of freedom," the Framers understood, could only exist in an environment of choices—which, in turn, could only exist with complete freedom of expression. It stands to reason, however, that if any group desired to "overthrow the freedom of all lands, nations, and countries,"[2] a primary way to subvert that freedom would be to curtail expression and the free exchange of information.

Since early colonial times, Americans have touted "freedom of the press" (which has come to mean all forms of media) as a cornerstone of the republic. The Founders believed that given sufficient information, citizens could make informed and good decisions. That information, they assumed, would be balanced because of the very fact that it wasn't restricted—in a free economy there would always be someone who would print or disseminate alternate points of view because there would always be consumers who would want access to those views. It made sense.

Freedom of press and speech: an LDS example

Yet, early in the nation's history, the Lord warned the Saints that this freedom was being encroached. He explained that people could only make decisions based on the information that they had and, unfortunately, that information, as far as the Church was concerned, was not accurate.

At that time there were several publications full of misinformation. In our terminology, we would say that "there were anti-Mormon books everywhere." Because the Saints gathered together and were generally away from large population centers, they could easily be labeled and stories could circulate that may have sounded plausible to those who did not know better. The Lord's answer to maintaining the integrity of information was to "gather up the libelous publications that [were] afloat; and all that [were] in the magazines, and in the encyclopedias, and all the libelous histories that [were] published, and [were] writing."[3]

Once those were gathered together and studied so that the Saints knew what was being said, they could then post corrected information. Freedom of the press could only work if both sides of the issue (in this case, the Church) were represented. Therefore, despite the "diabolical rascality and nefarious and murderous impositions"[4] that members of the Church were facing, the Lord said that they had the responsibility of correcting faulty views about the Church so that "the whole nation may be left without excuse." In other words, so that the nation could exercise free agency in regards to the Church's message, church members were responsible for correcting misrepresentations.

How serious was freedom of the press? As far as religion was concerned, the Lord said that mankind would be "riveted to the creeds of the fathers who have inherited lies" without it.[5] Inheriting lies makes sense when we reread Ether 8:25 and realize that the secret combination "bringeth to pass the destruction of all people, for it is built up by the devil, who is the father of all lies." We shouldn't expect Satan to be forthright and open with his evil plans, but, instead, we must remember that he is a master liar. The most effective lie is incorrect or partial information.

Without information there would be no change for the better because people would be left without the necessary choices for change. The Lord explained that the lack of correct information "filled the world with confusion . . . and [was then] the mainspring of corruption, and the whole earth groans under the weight of its iniquity."[6] Of course, because the Lord's plan was to promote freedom of choice so that "every man may be accountable for his own sins in the day of judgment"[7] and "whatsoever is more or less than this cometh of evil,"[8] it stood to reason that when that plan was frustrated by curtailing information and free agency, "the whole earth groans under the weight of its iniquity."[9]

Not having vital information to make correct decisions, the Lord said, "is an iron yoke, it is a strong band; they are the very handcuffs, and chains, and shackles, and fetters of hell."[10]

Because the consequences of not having information were so severe, the Lord gave a commandment to members of the Church to "spread the good word." He said that people had to understand the message of the restored gospel and to realize that there was another side of Mormonism of which they were unaware. It was the obligation of the Church to "publish to all the world" a true account of the latter-day work. Because of our divine placement in this dispensation, the Lord said this would be "the last effort which is enjoined on us by our Heavenly Father, before we can fully and completely claim that promise."[11]

How important is freedom of information? Most feel that the Lord used descriptive phrases in Section 123 of the *Doctrine and Covenants* that are more powerfully worded than any other scriptures.

> *verse 7: It is an imperative duty that we owe to God, to angels, with whom we shall be brought to stand, and also to ourselves, to our wives and children . . .*

> verse 9: Therefore *it is an imperative duty that we owe, not only to our own wives and children, but to the widows and fatherless, whose husbands and fathers have been murdered under its iron hand . . .*

verse 11: *And also it is an imperative duty that we owe to all the rising generation, and to all the pure in heart . . .*

verse 13: *Therefore that we should waste and wear out our lives in bringing to light all the hidden things of darkness, wherein we know them; and they are truly manifest from heaven . . .*

verse 14: *These things should be attended to with great earnestness . . .*

verse 15: *Let no man count them as small things . . .*

The indispensability of having access to correct information is what the Founders had in mind with the First Amendment to the Constitution. And the Lord bears out the Founders' concerns—just as the lack of correct information "filled the world with confusion" in 1839, the same could happen now.

Freedom of press and speech: a personal example

So as much as we have the responsibility of making correct information known, we also must have the spirit of discernment to know what is correct and what is incorrect. Earlier in this book I mentioned teaching in China and the cultural differences that arise because of infringements on what Americans traditionally define as liberty. An example: in China there is absolute gun control and guns are only owned and used by the military or law enforcement. To bolster the perception of positive affects of gun restriction—especially in comparison with the West—newspapers in China frequently carry articles about wanton shootings and gun-related accidents in the United States. The only information that the Chinese receive about gun use in America is that our country is trigger-happy and that America is a dangerous place to live. On several occasions students voiced their concerns and reiterated how much better they felt living in a place where guns were restricted.

Because the Chinese media continually equated guns and violence, that was the assumed understanding that students had. They were fed one view and never stopped to think of another because it simply never came up. Their freedom of the press— and as far as they were concerned they did have a free press— was truthful, but it failed to give the Chinese people a balanced picture of guns and life in the United States. A truly free press, as envisioned by our nation's Founders, would have allowed all sides of the issue to be presented. There would be those with bias to be sure, but that would be countered with bias on the opposing side of the issue as well as with objective reporting.

Likewise, as far as issues pertaining to The Church of Jesus Christ of Latter-day Saints, there may be bad press and good press. We would never tell someone that they didn't have the right to state or believe anything either against or in favor of the Church; hence the statement—"I may not agree with what you say, but I'll fight to the death your right to say it!" So the issue isn't so much one of what is said but that all views can be aired. That's why the Lord was so concerned about the media in Section 123—not simply that the Church was the object of bad press, but that people couldn't make informed decisions because they didn't have the availability of good press.

Could that happen in America today? Could we find our access to correct information stifled and find that our news source is one-sided, biased information? If so, that would be a tragic blow to our free agency and we would discover that, even with all of our revealed latter-day knowledge, we would be numbered with those "who have inherited lies" because misinformation "filled the world with confusion."[12]

A democracy or a republic?

There is a statement attributed to Benjamin Franklin when asked, "What kind of government do we have?" His reply was "A republic, if you can keep it." Before discussing the difference in governments, however, it would be well for the reader to think about the context of the words "republic" and "democracy." The Constitution guarantees to the states a "Republican form of government" while the term "democracy" is not used in the Constitution. We "pledge allegiance" to the flag and the "republic for which it stands"—not for a democracy. Yet we hear little about a republican form of government today and a great deal about democracy. Politically, at least in many modern textbooks and in the media, our ideal is that of a democracy. The Founding Fathers would have considered this an insult.

To leave no question as to the Founders' feelings toward a democracy, John Marshall, Chief Justice of the Supreme Court, said that, "Between a republic and a democracy, the difference is like that between order and chaos."

Definitions for both words are found in the *Soldiers Training Manual* issued by the United States Government on November 30, 1928. The definitions are:

> *TM 200-25: 118-120. Democracy—A government of the masses. Authority is derived through mass meeting or any other form of direct expression. Results in mobocracy. Attitude toward property is communistic, negating property rights. Attitude toward law is that the will of the people shall regulate, whether it be based upon deliberation, or governed by passion, prejudice, and impulse, without restraint or regard to consequences. Results in demagoguism, license, agitation, discontent, and anarchy.*
>
> *TM 2000-25: 120-121. Republic—Authority is derived through election by the people of public officials best fitted to represent them. Attitude toward property is respect for laws and individual rights, and a sensible economic procedure. Attitude toward law is the administration of justice in accord with fixed*

principles, and established evidence, with a strict regard to consequences. A greater number of citizens and extent of territory may be brought within its compass. Avoids the dangerous extreme of either tyranny or mobocracy. Results in statesmanship, liberty, reason, justice, contentment, and progress.

With the above, two other additions to the definition of a republic should be inserted. (1) A republic is a federation of semi-autonomous states capable of self-government for those affairs not deemed national or interstate in nature; and (2) in a republic, laws limit the majority powers and come to the defense minority rights. According to the words of the Founders and the citations from the above-quoted training manual, the mission of the United States, "to make the world safe for democracy," would be antithetical to good government. The Lord was much more specific in revealing the correct purpose of government in Section 134 of the *Doctrine and Covenants*. He said in verse 2, that the purpose was to "secure to each individual the free exercise of conscience, the right and control of property, and the protection of life."

The problem, of course, in a purely democratic state, is that the majority votes for what it wants. The majority is able to vote itself special privileges from government, or even the assets of another class. We earlier discussed the redistribution of wealth—facilitated by the rule of the majority. In this type of government, politicians quickly learn that catering to the majority is the way toward election and reelection.

The republican form of government, in contrast, states that electing "honest men and wise men" as Section 98 of the *Doctrine and Covenants* prescribes, insures that the best decisions are made based upon law and not upon catering to the wants of the majority. Much of the difference in governments rests in the attitudes of the electorate, although the Constitution builds in many safeguards to promote a republican form of government. Those attitudes, you will recall, were probably best summed up by John Adams who said that our form of government was for a religious people and highly unsuited for any other.

Why discuss the difference between republics and democracies at this juncture of our discussion about media? As you read the following examples of media influence and the restriction of information that flows to an electorate in an unrighteous government, recall the Lord's definition of good government: to "secure to each individual the free exercise of conscience." In other words, good government will see that we have sufficient information for the "free exercise of conscience." To limit and restrict information necessarily means that there is an uninformed electorate that can be manipulated. This is the danger of a democracy—and the danger of making the world "safe for democracy."

World War One and the Creel Commission

The Lord said that world problems during the early history of the Church stemmed from both misinformation and the lack of information resulting in a "world filled with confusion." That description was apt of the United States as the country entered the First World War. Returning again to the Wilson Administration, let's examine the little-known United States Committee on Public Information—often referred to as the Creel Commission. You will recall that the nation at that time was largely pacifist. Wilson had been elected to a second term of office in 1916 using the slogan, "He kept us out of war." The nation had no intent of becoming embroiled in a European conflict that didn't in the least affect United States' interests. George Creel was given the task of changing national opinion.

To add power to the new committee, he brought in two men who would to go on to completely reshape the new field of public relations. The first, Walter Lippman, was a young CFR leader who was close to the Wilson administration and would continue to write and shape public opinion for another half-century. The second, Edward Bernays, the nephew of Sigmund Freud, was an upcoming publicist that would transition democracy into a tool for the elite.

To get an idea of Bernays' abilities, think for a moment about a traditional breakfast. What do you think of? If you are like most, you will come up with bacon and eggs—so what? Prior to 1915, bacon was not part of a traditional breakfast—so Edward Bernays was hired to increase bacon consumption in the United States. He incorporated a new theory of gaining assent from recognized leaders either with their knowing cooperation or without. He conducted a survey among physicians and received their overwhelming recommendation that Americans should eat a hearty breakfast. Coupled with predictive results from the physicians, he began an advertising campaign stressing that a breakfast of bacon and eggs was just that—a hearty breakfast. It may sound simple, but look where we are today because of it.

Bernays' work with the Creel Commission was not as innocuous, in fact it had far-reaching political implications that literally changed the mindset of Americans from pacifist to warlike. The task given to the Creel Commission was to create public opinion from passive demeanor to an overwhelming desire among Americans to enter the "Great War" on the side of England. MIT professor and political philosopher Noam Chomsky writes that Bernays and the Creel Commission "succeeded within six months in turning a pacifist population into a hysterical, warmongering population which wanted to destroy everything German, tear the Germans from limb to limb, go to war, and save the world."[13] Thus began the use of modern political propaganda.

There were a few techniques that were used to create the sudden shift among Americans. The dehumanization of the German people was necessary and the mind-image was implanted that they had inflicted tremendous injustice upon the rest of the world. Americans were fed a steady diet of images portraying cruelty, abuse to children and women, and obnoxious personality traits that made Germans most unlikable. Adding this to the sinking of the Lusitania convinced Americans that it was in the best interest of the world to enter the war and "make the world safe for democracy."

Because propaganda through the media has been on-going since the Creel Commission, it would be well to examine some of Bernays' writing. In his book entitled *Propaganda* written in 1928, he said that

> *The conscious and intelligent manipulation of the organized habits and opinions of the masses is an important element in democratic society. Those who manipulate this unseen mechanism of society constitute an invisible government which is the true ruling power of our country. . . . We are governed, our minds are molded, our tastes formed, our ideas suggested, largely by men we have never heard of. This is a logical result of the way in which our democratic society is organized. Vast numbers of human beings must cooperate in a manner if they are to live together as a smoothly functioning society. . . . In almost every act of our daily lives, whether in the sphere of politics or business, in our social conduct or our ethical thinking, we are dominated by the relatively small number of persons . . . who understand the mental processes and social patterns of the masses. It is they who pull the wires which control the public mind.*[14]

Obviously, Bernays' intent was that thought should be the prerogative of the elite and not the American public. In this, both he and Walter Lippman completely agreed. Lippman often spoke in terms of "the herd" when talking about the public. He felt that the herd "was too ignorant to participate in democracy beyond selecting from what he called the choice between 'tweedledee and tweedledum.'"[15]

Bernays recognized the extent of his work and admitted that what he had begun to implement was a two-edged sword. Years later during the beginning years of the Second World War he wrote that "Goebbels . . . was using my book, *Crystallizing Public Opinion* (1923) as a basis for his destructive campaign against the Jews of Germany."[16] Worldwide, politicians and governments concluded that controlling thoughts of electorates and "the masses" was the key to directing their respective countries towards their preconceived goals. Chomsky's analysis of political "mind shaping" beginning with the Creel Commission is long, but is instructive in understanding modern-day applications of mind and media control. He writes:

> *Among those who participated actively and enthusiastically were the progressive intellectuals, people of the John Dewey circle, who took great pride, as you can see from their own writings at the time, in having shown in what they called the "more intelligent members of the community," namely themselves, were able to drive a reluctant population into war by terrifying them and eliciting jingoist fanaticism. The means that were used were extensive. For example, there was a good deal of fabrication of atrocities by the Huns, Belgian babies with their arms torn off, all sorts of awful things that you still read in history books. They were all invented by the British propaganda ministry, whose own commitment at the time, as they put it in their secret deliberations, was "to control the thought of the world."*
>
> *But more crucially, they wanted to control the thought of the more intelligent members of the community in the U.S. who would then disseminate the propaganda that they were concocting and convert the pacifist country into wartime hysteria. That worked. It worked very well. And it taught a lesson: State propaganda, when supported by the educated classes and when no deviation is permitted from it, can have a big effect. It was a lesson learned by Hitler and many others, and it has been pursued to this day.*[17]

—Which takes us back to democracy. Although the electorate of the country assuaged itself with platitudes of democracy and freedom to choose, in reality, with limited information, there was little freedom of choice. The results were preselected by those manipulating the information given to "the herd." The language reinforced freedom as did the sentiment that what was transpiring was a groundswell movement—but the reality was much different. Freedom had been taken away by secret actions of the power brokers.

Which emphasizes the initial problem that the Lord spoke of in *Doctrine and Covenants* 123, and Moroni spoke of in Ether 8. The Lord was emphatic that for free agency to work and for people to truly be free to make choices, it was necessary that choices *could* be made. The most germane choices were good and evil. In order to make those choices, both spectrums of information had to be available for scrutiny. Because those whom we have studied thus far in this chapter specialized in restricting information, that lack of information became the frame of reference for the majority. Sadly, those accepting the skewed information unwittingly became tools of a satanic force. By blindly following the Pied Piper of German revulsion, millions lost their lives both at home and abroad and our nation began its plummet into bankruptcy.

Moroni's message is also revealing. He gave us ample warning about the secret combination whose intent was to destroy "the freedom of all lands, nations, and countries." It would be difficult to argue that the work of the Creel Commission did anything but that, and that it laid a foundation for subsequent loss of free agency by restricting information. But Moroni also warned against those that "uphold" or "suffer" secret combinations to get above them. That's where we come into the picture.

Although we may be restricted in receiving all pertinent information, the Lord will not fail to let us know what is good or evil . . . if we ask him. Unfortunately, many fail to use the spirit of discernment and allow themselves to be blindly caught up in emotion—and the ploys of media artists aim directly at the emotions. "Upholding" the secret combination and "suffering" that it has power to influence us by restricting our agency is a sin that Moroni told us to repent of.[18]

How do we repent? We trust in the Lord and not in ourselves or in "the arm of flesh."[19] The "arm of flesh" is a good description of misplaced trust. Over and over the Lord has directed the Saints to appeal to him in prayer for guidance while our modern world teaches that various "experts"—academics, military and government leaders, scientists, etc., know so much more than we do; hence, we need to follow their advice. The Lord agrees that their knowledge is good, but with a necessary qualification:

> *O that cunning plan of the evil one! O the vainness, and the frailties, and the foolishness of men! When they are learned they think they are wise, and they hearken not to the counsel of God, for they set it aside, supposing they know of themselves, wherefore, their wisdom is foolishness and it profiteth them not. And they shall perish.*
>
> *But to be learned is good if they hearken to the counsels of God.*[20]

If they are righteous and holy, we ought to listen. Yet, even fulfilling that qualification, we are not absolved from appealing personally to the Lord for direction. The Lord taught in what is frequently called "the Lord's prayer," to pray not to be led into temptation. It is tempting to follow others and to neither stand out nor to be different—but our position is to ask the Lord for the strength to be a "peculiar people," and to be "apart from the world." Repentance is that "thy will and not mine be done."

Repentance also entails seeking information. Paul taught that we should "prove all things and hold fast to that which is true." Section 123 of the *Doctrine and Covenants* begins with the Lord telling the Saints to gather all of the antagonistic publications against the Church—read, be informed, find out what is being said! Once armed with knowledge, it is much easier to stand alone. Recall that Moroni said that he warned modern-day readers about the secret combination of the last days so that we could identify it. Those identifying characteristics were given to us so that we would not be caught upholding Satan's plan to curtail freedom.

The modern Creel apparatus

Media of today has incorporated many of the successful innovations of the Creel Commission. And, to guarantee its effectiveness, much of its ownership has been consolidated into the hands of just a few. When we looked at the events leading to World War One, we found that the twenty-five largest newspapers were controlled by J. P. Morgan. Early, the manipulators of American culture learned the value of the press and learned that ownership ensured that the public could learn of certain events while they could be restricted from knowing about others. As much as any other activity, control of the media gave them power over the larger population.

Understanding this concept, the Counsel on Foreign Relations and Trilateral Commission have made it a point to include media owners and personalities in their memberships. The current roster of the CFR includes eighty-seven people connected directly to media. It might be surprising to know that personalities such as Dan Rather, Richard C. Hottelet, Tom Brokaw, David Brinkley, John Chancellor, Marvin Kalb, Barbara

Walters, Diane Sawyer, Jim Lehrer, and Daniel Schorr are all members of the CFR and that the owners of all major networks are also counted as members.

This is why Noam Chomsky, in defining democracy, said that

> *An alternative conception of democracy is that the public must be barred from managing of their own affairs and the means of information must be kept narrowly and rigidly controlled. That may sound like an odd conception of democracy, but it is important to understand that it is the prevailing conception.*[21]

The goals of the CFR, as we have seen, have included the use of war and other forms of strife to ameliorate the traditional values of Americanism. This has been done for "power and gain," including the loss of national sovereignty and the inclusion of the belief that global management is much more effective than national. To bring us in line with those values, Chomsky says that "information must be kept narrowly and rigidly controlled."

An unsettling aspect of media control is that although it may be immoral, it is not illegal. Those behind the movement to remove sovereignty and to redefine key doctrines in America's freedom platform do not violate law in controlling the media. Money, recognition, and sophistry have been sufficient to this point in tilting the media message away from America's founding premises of liberty. In this regard, the current proposed media uses of the United Nations have been especially alarming. As seen in the chapter, *The United Nations: Towards a One-World Government*, many of the goals of the world body are anathema to the traditional family unit. It is proposed that children be allowed, even encouraged, autonomous decision-making in areas that many parents find objectionable. Further, the same proposals include strictures against parents teaching or enforcing values that run counter to U.N. philosophy. It is in this context that Article 17 of the United Nations Convention on the Rights of the Child stated that:

> *States [Nations] Parties recognize the important function performed by the mass media and shall ensure that the child has access to information and material from a diversity of national and international sources, especially those aimed at the promotion of his or her social, spiritual and moral well-being and physical and mental health.*

The material to be shared with the youth of the world will be for the "social and cultural benefit to the child in accordance with the spirit of Article 29." That article insists that any such material must be in accord with "the principles enshrined in the Charter of the United Nations." This may be better understood in a 1997 recommendation addressed to the nation of Armenia by the UN Convention on the Elimination of All Forms of Discrimination Against Women wherein leaders of the country were directed to "use the education system and the electronic media to combat the traditional stereotype of women 'in the noble role of mother.'"[22]

The control of any information is broken into two separate channels—(1) giving an abundance of information about attitudes that are being fostered, and (2) withholding information that either bears out an opposing point of view or invites criticism of the favored policies of an administration.

The first is akin to Bernays' use of graphic examples of German atrocities to encourage hostile attitudes leading to WW1; or the author's earlier example of Chinese news being heavily skewed toward gun abuse and misuse in America. In more catastrophic situations, the media hype surrounding the Gulf of Tonkin incident to propel the United States into the Vietnam War; or fear of "weapons of mass destruction" held by Iraq; or the continual reference to the graphic annihilation of the Twin

Towers of New York by terrorists—all invoked to solicit a mass national mindset in support of government activities. In all cases, trusted sources of the news media manipulated readers' emotions with controlled information. Knowing the predetermined goals of an administration or controlling power, we are able to see certain areas of emphasis and de-emphasis. What are the apparent goals of those who would "overthrow" our freedom and what are the attitudes that they would foster? Here are a few that we might consider with a short paragraph following each to explain how these views have been implemented and "sold" to the public:

Popular themes in today's media

A global outlook is healthy and will prevent future wars whereas a nationalistic view is unhealthy and leads to limited economic growth and intolerance of others.

A substantial amount of news occupying our television sets is international rather than national. We hear of international leaders, various summits and conferences, and world leaders— particularly of the United Nations—that are spoken of in the highest terms. Generally, our international news shows an interventionist bent such as a war-torn country invaded by aggressors that needs our help; poor third-world countries that need aid and intervention from the United States; or war situations that depict our country liberating others. The premise is that our taxes are being well-spent abroad and that the world needs our manpower. Sometimes anti-war, anti-interventionist, or otherwise nationally-oriented protestors do receive news attention; however, that is almost always shown as detrimental to our true national interests.

Law enforcement is ever-present and police protection is always necessary to shield people from crime. Because of the prevalence of criminals, more sophisticated tracking devices and weaponry are necessary and, should a person attempt escape, it is impossible.

Watching television—either news or primetime entertainment—will always find police battling criminals. No longer, however, do we simply show police in the light of public servants, but we see an inordinate amount of time dedicated to SWAT teams, bomb squads, and highly technical surveillance equipment. Episodes that we would rarely see in a real-life situation, we see enacted two to four times each one-hour segment. Why? Some have postulated that we are vicariously learning that, no matter what may occur, we are to obey and even fear the strength of law enforcement.

Guns are inherently bad. If a person feels that he must have them, they should always be locked and separated from ammunition so that they cannot be readily used.

In the event of a gun-related accident, local—and sometimes national—news makes mention of it. This is especially true when children are involved. Unfortunately, this has been called a "self-fulfilling prophecy" in that children are now infrequently exposed to gun usage and, because guns are continually in the news, have a greater curiosity about them— consequently, this is often a contributing factor to gun-related accidents. Conversely, when personal guns are used to prevent crime, the situations rarely come to our attention through the media.

Public education is the future of our society. Any who would advocate alternative forms of education rob their children of necessary social interaction and allow them to receive inferior training.

Public education generally receives a great deal of local coverage—both good and bad. On a national level in the event of multiple murders and heinous crimes on the schoolyard, the need for social interventionist programs is highlighted along with the need for stricter gun control. Because of their prevalence, drugs are often mentioned and the partnership of the school with law enforcement is stressed. In all cases, when there is disturbance, the media reports that it is firmly under control and that the schools are now safe. This brings to mind President Boyd K. Packer's statement to the BYU College of Education: "In many places it is literally not safe physically for youngsters to go to school. And in many schools—and it is almost becoming generally true—it is spiritually unsafe to attend public schools."[23] With all of the negative press given to public schools, it is interesting that parents who withdraw their children are often asked about their concern for the social needs of their children. Although alternate forms of education do come to the attention of the news media, they are treated as curiosities and outside the pale of the normal.

We must love all and be accepting of any lifestyle choices a person desires to make. Any negative attitudes toward homosexuality or other perceived sins are the fault of the person holding those attitudes and should be corrected to demonstrate complete acceptance.

Forcing anyone's friendship or acceptance on another definitely infringes on that person's right of association. Although that may be true, there has been a concerted effort through media to reinforce certain values, among which is homosexuality. Other accepted values are premarital sex and sexual relations out of marriage; lack of church attendance or reference to scriptures (except derogatorily;) immodest clothing; frequent offensive language; and defiance of parental authority on the grounds that parents are incompetent to raise children. Of all of these, because homosexuality is the most out of the norm of accepted behavior, it has received the most favorable attention of the media. Generally, anyone opposed is labeled intolerant or naïve. To reinforce this attitude, the media has unabashedly promoted "hate-crime" legislation in an attempt to promote accepted attitudes.

Those who tout the U.S. Constitution and use descriptive words such as "unconstitutional," "tyranny," or "God-given rights" are generally radical and out of touch with reality.

Over the years, language usage changes and what was in vogue at one time falls into disuse at another. Those who read the words of the Founding Fathers will be familiar with a different vocabulary than everyday American speech, just as will those who accustom themselves to reading scriptures. Because that language is not promoted through the media, it is generally perceived as archaic and unusual. Likewise a constitutional setting is generally at odds with modern media, hence flag-waving and red, white and blue lapel pins do receive media promotion while substance does not. Likewise, candidates from the two major political parties always receive media time while third-party candidates and those sharing a constitutional message do not.

Mainstream religion is acceptable; however, belief systems that we do not understand are suspect and people who follow them are somewhat odd and on the edge of acceptable society.

Although the First Amendment to the Constitution guarantees that we have the right to worship—or not to worship—as we choose, there are somewhat stringent guides in place for acceptable beliefs. Religious activity outside those guides is suspect and promoted through the media as aberrant or peculiar. As members of the LDS Church, we need to imagine how our Church would have been portrayed had the media been as pervasive in the days of Joseph Smith and Brigham Young. Unconformity of thought and belief is discouraged by the media while mainstreaming is encouraged.

Military service is the highest form of love that a person can have for his or her country. All military service is a form of protecting our country from evil and those who would do harm to the United States.

Military news and movies based on military themes are always popular with the media. Generally, in all news reports of military activities the phrasing is incorporated: "fighting for our freedoms," "fighting for democracy," or "fighting to keep America safe." Patriotism and military are joined as synonymous. The antithesis of this is the anti-military protest in which the media often allows time but shows the protest in an un-American light manned by people on the periphery of acceptability. Frequently, a government "expert" is brought in to explain that demonstrations of this nature damage the stature of the military and injure the cause of democracy.

People who demonstrate against government policies are generally misguided and on society's fringes. Level-headed and upstanding people conform to government policies.

There are many kinds of demonstrations—some soliciting more negative play from the media than others. Anti-abortion demonstrations protesting the Roe v Wade Supreme Court decision have more recently been deemed acceptable, as are current pro-gay rallies. On the other hand, demonstrations against government policies such as the war in Iraq, U.S. immigration policy, or political leaders such as the President or

Vice-President receive virtually no coverage in the media. In the event that any demonstrations are reported with contrary views to government policy, they are shown to be poorly led, disorganized, and made up of scruffy, unemployed followers.

An aside: a specific warning to Latter-day Saints

We have looked at the media as it applies to free agency. Our concern has been that news reports and other programming are balanced giving consumers access to all available information. It is only through an uncontrolled media—real freedom of the press—that people can truly choose right from wrong. Of all of the concerns that we ought to have in maintaining freedom—according to both the words of Jesus Christ and Moroni—our interest should be the correct dissemination of information. As consumers of information, our responsibility is to weigh and discern if it is correct and complete. Because this is often difficult given media control that exists in our country, we must appeal to the Lord for guidance in the decisions that we make. In voting, supporting issues, and giving assent to both local and national policies, we have the obligation to make righteous decisions and to be wary of allowing ourselves to be found upholding the directions of unholy combinations.

Indirectly, but in a very real way, we have this obligation. In a very direct sense, though, members of the Church are affected by the media. For many years, The Church of Jesus Christ of Latter-day Saints was the recipient of bad press. The Word of Wisdom was misunderstood and nonmembers of the Church often felt a "we're better than you are" attitude from church members because of it. Likewise, the past doctrine of polygamy has been misunderstood by members of the Church as well as nonmembers and been a subject that has spawned poor media. Periodically, this still surfaces with groups that claim doctrinal purity from the teachings of early LDS leaders. From time to time other misunderstood doctrines such as the Blacks and the priesthood, the temple endowment ceremony, and even temple work for the dead have found their way into the media and have become issues of public discussion.

Because of the awkward doctrines (awkward because they are difficult to explain without foundations of both faith and knowledge) that have come to the attention of the press and the discomfort that many have experienced in attempting to explain Mormon doctrine in a nonMormon environment, church members have taken great delight in some of the more favorable press releases. All said and done, members of the Church would rather be stars in a mainstream environment than individuals in a defensive position.

President Gordon B. Hinckley has provided the Church with very favorable press; new temples throughout the world have opened doors for positive relations; Brigham Young University has been nationally acclaimed in many areas; the Tabernacle Choir continues to be the subject of positive media reports; and the personal leadership of various Latter-day Saints in national and world affairs continues to give the Church a media-friendly image. These media images, however, are byproducts of Mormonism—not given because good press was the Church's main concern. In fact, we live at a time, unlike our Mormon forefathers, when the Church is generally seen from the outside as a good institution building strong Americans. Which reminds one of a statement attributed to President George Albert Smith, the eighth president of the Church: "What's wrong? Has the Lord forsaken us that everyone is saying good things about us?"

So despite how good it may feel to be the subject of good press, and despite the missionary advantages of accolades about the fulfillment of Mormon life, perhaps we would be better off in an environment of bad press. Mosiah Hancock, an early member of the First Quorum of Seventy reflected in his journal:

> *Brigham Young conversed freely on the situation of the Saints in the mountains, and said that he dreaded the time when the saints would become popular with the world: for he had seen in sorrow, in a dream, or in dreams, this people clothed in the fashions of Babylon and drinking in the spirit of Babylon until one could hardly tell a saint from a black-leg.*[24]

In fact, if Satan were to have his way, the press would always be favorable to the Church. So the issue again is not one of positive press but of complete access to information. Why would Satan want the Church to enjoy good press?

> *[Because] others will he pacify, and lull them away into carnal security, that they will say; All is well in Zion; yea, Zion prospereth, all is well—and thus the devil cheateth their souls, and leadeth them away carefully down into hell.*[25]

Good press makes us self-content and reinforces pride— the greatest red flag to the Nephite prophets. Pride is the "carnal security" that Nephi warned our generation about. Brigham Young knew the saints—he knew that their Achilles Heel was popularity. We know today that popularity is gauged more by the media than any other single factor. Television, radio, magazines, newspapers, and movies are all ways that popularity is determined. Brigham Young once more:

> *I look at this and I am satisfied that it will not do for the Lord to make this people popular. . . . What is the reason for this? Christ and Baal cannot become friends. When I see this people grow and spread and prosper, I feel that there is more danger than when they are in poverty. Being driven from city to city and into the*

mountains is nothing compared to the danger of our becoming rich and being hailed by outsiders as a first-class community.[26]

Unfortunately, President Young's words describe the current situation of the saints. There is wealth, we generally live well, we live in first-class communities, and we are the recipients of positive press. That really isn't a bad thing, but, as the early church leader said, there is a danger that "Christ and Baal" will attempt to become friendly. Cultivating that friendship, especially through the use of media, may ultimately do more harm and be more difficult to overcome in the long run because the Church is placed at the behest of the media. As we have seen, those who control the media are the real masters of our popularity—we are not. Consequently, we may not always ride the wave of popularity and instead may find ourselves in an unpopular position. That's not necessarily bad, in fact, that has always been the history of the true church.

In all *Book of Mormon* situations, when the Church was popular, it was ripe for a fall. The more popular that it was, the harder it fell. Remember, Mormon and Moroni were the editors of the book and prepared it for readers today because there were situations which paralleled what they knew about us. Mormon wrote in 4 Nephi:

> *And now I, Mormon, would that ye should know that the people had multiplied, insomuch that they were spread upon all the face of the land, and that they had become exceedingly rich, because of their prosperity in Christ.*
>
> *And now, in this two hundred and first year there began to be among them those who were lifted up in pride, such as the wearing of costly apparel, and all manner of fine pearls, and of the fine things of the world.*
>
> *And from that time forth they did have their goods and their substance no more common among them.*

> *And they began to be divided into classes; and they began to build up churches unto themselves to get gain, and began to deny the true church of Christ.*[27]

Later on, in his own book, Mormon tells us that he saw our day and describes many of our latter-day sins. He knew that although he was describing members of the Church two hundred years following the visit of the Savior to the Nephites, he was also describing perils that would confront church members in our dispensation. Doesn't Mormon's description parallel the fears that Brigham Young voiced about popularity? The above description of the Nephites lets us know that they continued talking about church and doctrine and simply became more and more popular because they had welded the "form of Godliness" into what people wanted. They knew how to master good press.

Because of favorable press the Church grew at a phenomenal rate. The problem, of course, was that when times became rocky (as they had been throughout the books of Helaman, 3 Nephi, and now 4 Nephi) the church population frequently faltered. The summer saints left and only those with real relationships with the Savior weathered the storms.

So again, favorable press has never been the Lord's concern. Popularity, according to the *Book of Mormon,* has continually been a tool that Satan has been able to ply to meet his ends. With his control of the mass media through secret combinations, this is even more evident. (Actually, when one looks at many of those who have achieved popularity through the media, one wonders if the Church desires to be in that grouping anyway.)

Avoiding the media control trap
Media control is effective when only the accepted or establishment sources are available to the general public. Fortunately, through the years, there have been those who have

labored to seek information beyond the accepted news sources and, in turn, have written to disseminate their information. Books and newsletters have, in the past, been the primary sources for "behind the scenes" and in-depth reporting. Although many of these sources have been excellent vehicles in bringing greater understanding to us, we are fortunate to live at a time when alternative news sources are flourishing via the internet.

Although the use of the internet to acquire unlimited information is under some jeopardy through the United Nation's World Summit on the Information Society (2003, 2005), it is still available to search out key and invaluable information. The advent of the internet has brought heretofore hard-to-find information within reach of the general public and has made information restriction much more difficult. There are still trusted writings available in book and newsletter form; however, the internet is kept current and offers the advantage of multiple links to research various topics. In other words, should a person desire to follow a particular event or subject, there are several links or websites which can be compared

As with all sources, the student needs to be aware that disinformation (intentionally misleading information) and misinformation are often found side-by-side with good, solid research. Through abundant information—beyond that received through controlled media—we are able to exercise real freedom of choice and decision-making. Thus we are able to exercise Brigham Young's sentiment that "The greatest and most important labor we have to perform is to cultivate ourselves;"[28] and John's instruction that "Ye shall know the truth and the truth shall make you free."[29]

Chapter 7—Endnotes

1   *Doctrine & Covenants* 98:5

2   Ether 8:25

3   *Doctrine & Covenants* 123:4-5

4   *Ibid.*

5   *Doctrine & Covenants* 123:7

6   *Ibid.*

7   *Doctrine & Covenants* 101:78

8   *Doctrine & Covenants* 98:7

9   *Doctrine & Covenants* 123:7

10   *Doctrine & Covenants* 123:8

11   *Doctrine & Covenants* 123:6

12   *Doctrine & Covenants* 123:7

13   Noam Chomsky, Talk at MIT, March 17, 1991. *Alternative Press Review*, Fall, 1993. www.evans-experimentalism.freewebspace.com /chomsky03.htm

14   Edward P. Bernays, *Propaganda*. New York: Horace Liveright. 1928.

15   Stephen Bender, "Karl Rove and the Spectre of Freud's Nephew," February 4, 2005. www.americanidealism.com

16   http//wikipedia.org/wiki/Edward_Bernays

17   Chomsky, Ibid.

18   Ether 9:23

19   2 Nephi 4:34

20   2 Nephi 9:28-29

21   Chomsky, Ibid.

22   Richard G. Wilkins, "Rights Rhetoric, the Family, and Social Change." World Policy Forum, 2002. p. 84.

23   Boyd K. Packer, David O. McKay Symposium, Brigham Young University. October 9, 1996.

24   *Life Story of Mosiah Lyman Hancock, 1834-1907*. Salt Lake City: Private Printing. p. 73.

25   2 Nephi 28:21

26   Brigham Young, *Journal of Discourses* 12:270-271, August 16, 1868

27   4 Nephi 1:23-36

28   Brigham Young, *Journal of Discourses* 17:141, July 19, 1874.

29   John 8:32

Chapter 8

EDUCATION:
WHAT IS A PARENT TO DO?

The philosophy of the school room in one generation, will be the philosophy of government in the next generation.

Abraham Lincoln

The rise of tax-exempt foundations

The twin approaches of media control and government sponsored education are the primary means of controlling a nation's thought. By monitoring the components that go into a person's thinking process, the end result is more or less predetermined for the majority—those who fail to search further and engage in original thought. It was with this in mind that, when all was coming to a head in the Wilson Administration, the tax-exempt foundation was born.

The sixteenth amendment to the Constitution was (dubiously) accepted by voters and the graduated income tax furnished means to: (1) redistribute the wealth of the country; (2) support government programs, wars, etc., and repay the Federal Reserve Corporation for loans (with interest); and (3) ensure that few others would reach the levels of wealth that a few bankers and industrialists then possessed.

The last item is not generally understood; after all, the graduated income tax was meant to be a tax on the rich—wasn't it? The redistribution of wealth seemed to indicate a "Robin Hood" approach—to take from the rich and give to the poor. Instead, however, the organization of tax-exempt foundations had another affect—to perpetuate the influence of certain families while allowing them to maintain control of their wealth. Others, without the status of the tax-exempt foundation, would necessarily become a part of the graduated income tax ladder and share their wealth.

Throughout this chapter we will explore certain tax-exempt education foundations. It is not the intent of this book to forward the presumption that all foundations have a hidden agenda for there are many well-meaning families and corporations that have promoted beneficial programs and positive education. For our purposes, however, we will look at a few of the largest foundations—most in the area of education—that were begun at the turn of the twentieth century. When the sixteenth amendment was ratified in 1913, the existing foundations became tax-exempt. The primary foundations were under the direction of the Carnegie, Rockefeller and Ford families.

The goals of the international bankers remained the same in the classroom as they were in the media and other aspects of American daily life. As in so much of our history, hindsight allows us to focus today on both the comprehensiveness and effectiveness of the educational programming that was done. Before treating specific educational policies, though, the power of these particular tax-exempt foundations must be understood. Much of the information about foundation influence has come through a Congressional investigation conducted by the 83rd Congress in 1954. W. Cleon Skousen wrote:

> *Generally speaking, the Rockefeller Foundation, the Carnegie Foundation, the Ford Foundation and a host of other Wall Street philanthropies have always been looked upon as generous, capitalistic santa clauses. Let us repeat a previous quotation in*

which Dr. Quigley admits the development of an explosive situation back in the early 1950s when the use of tax-exempt foundations for U.S. subversion almost spilled out in public view. In fact, public hearings were heard, but the Establishment's choke-hold on the press was sufficient to keep the public from becoming aware of the scandalous proportions of the facts which were discovered.[1]

Congress looks at foundations and education

The Congressional hearings were under the direction of U.S. Representative Carroll Reece of Tennessee and were known as the Reece Committee Hearings. The investigation took several months and filled over 2,000 pages of transcripts that documented the goals, pervasive influence, and tactics of these particular "interlocking" foundations. "Interlocking" was the word agreed upon by the Committee because of the concerted thrust of the foundations to achieve their ends. Far from the "Santa Claus" image, the Committee warned of foundation control exercised over formal education and its direction against traditional American values. The Committee's findings were that:

The power of the individual large foundation is enormous. It can exercise various forms of patronage which carry with them elements of thought control. It can exert immense influence on educational institutions, upon the educational processes, and upon educators. It is capable of invisible coercion through the power of its purse. It can materially predetermine the development of social and political concepts and courses of action through the process of granting and withholding foundation awards upon a selective basis, and by designing and promulgating projects which propel researchers in selected directions. It can play a powerful part in the determination of academic opinion, and, through this thought leadership, materially influence public opinion.

This power to influence national policy is amplified tremendously when foundations act in concert. There is such a concentration of foundation power in the United States, operating in

the social sciences and education. It consists basically of a group of
major foundations, representing a gigantic aggregate of capital and
income. . . . It has ramifications in almost every phase of research
and education, in communications and even in government. Such a
concentration of power is highly undesirable . . .[2]

What an indictment of Foundations! According to the
Reece Committee, the influence of tax-exempt foundations
permeated—in a negative way—virtually every facet of
American life. The terminology of the Committee is disturbing:
"thought control," "invisible coercion," "predetermine the
development of social and political concepts," "thought
leadership," "materially influence public opinion," "power to
influence national policy," and "ramifications in almost every
phase of research and education." When these features of the
foundation arm of the international bankers are held up next to
Moroni's warning, there is a chilling realization that freedom of
thought has been severely compromised. Information, either by
its withholding or its embellishment, has been corrupted for at
least three generations.

Even though the Committee came to these conclusions, it
is important to understand that there was nothing blatantly illegal
in the approaches that were initiated by the foundations. They
may have been unAmerican and immoral in the view of many,
but not illegal. As in so many areas, our system of laws makes
certain assumptions that all people hold the same basic values.
Opposing values and beliefs are condoned in our thought and,
therefore, laws do not legislate against our personal opinions and
values. The Committee hearings were not directed so much at
illegal activities as they were at what was the accepted best
education for American children.

Conclusions of the Reece Committee centered on school
control by educational foundations and their apparent influence
against traditional curriculum. Throughout the hearings,

members of the Committee expressed surprise and alarm at foundation agenda and its schoolroom application.

> . . . *The aggregate thought-control power of this foundation and foundation-supported bureaucracy can hardly be exaggerated. A system has thus arisen . . . which gives enormous power to a relatively small group of individuals, having at their virtual command, huge sums in public trust funds. It is a system which is antithetical to American principles.*
>   . . . *The impact of foundation money upon education has been very heavy, largely tending to promote uniformity in approach and method, tending to induce the educator to become an agent for social change and a propagandist for the development of our society in the direction of some sort of collectivism. Foundations have supported text books (and books intended for inclusion in collateral lists) which are destructive of our basic governmental and social principles and highly critical of some of our cherished institutions.*
>   *In the international field, foundations, and an interlock among some of them and certainly intermediary organizations, have exercised a strong effect upon our foreign policy and upon public education in things international. This has been accomplished by vast propaganda . . . through the power of the purse. The net result of these combined efforts has been to promote "internationalism" in a particular sense—a form directed toward "world government" and a derogation of history, propagandized blindly for the United Nations as the hope of the world, supported that organization's agencies to an extent beyond general public acceptance, and leaned toward a generally "leftist" approach to international problems.[3]*

Throughout the Committee Report, foundations were evaluated as detrimental to education and blamed for limiting information. As the above excerpt from the final Committee Report stated, much of the curricular and text work sponsored in the public schools addressed internationalism. The intent of the curriculum was to foster the mindset that a "higher order" of thought included a world perspective while a nationalist approach to education was outdated and only contributed to further world problems and misunderstandings.

The dramatic curriculum shift

To illustrate Reece Committee concerns, a memorandum by a congressional attorney was presented on the subject of the National Education Association (NEA) and the "world-minded American." In 1948, with grants from the Rockefeller and Carnegie Foundations, the NEA published the book *Education for International Understanding in American Schools— Suggestions and Recommendations.* According to the Committee's research director, the book encouraged teachers "to foster two things in this country: a development of an understanding of international affairs, and, at the same time, the teacher must lead the way to a breakdown, so to speak, of our allegiance to a local or nationalistic viewpoint."[4]

The book asked, "What schools and what teachers have the responsibility for educating children and youth for international understanding?" and answered, "all elementary and secondary schools have that responsibility; and every administrator and supervisor as well as every teacher of every subject on every grade level shares a part of it."[5] Then, quoting extensively from the text, the congressional attorney summarized its major points:

> . . . [to] *"cultivate a sense of public responsibility for the success of the United Nations."*

> *"They must understand why it is impossible for any group of people to survive long in modern society isolated from others."*

> *"It means, for example, that peoples and nations must learn to act cooperatively on such essential matters as employment, expansion of agriculture, health, and trade. Solution of economic*

problems on a purely national basis without regard to the effect of their conduct on other peoples and nations breeds economic war."[6]

This and several other foundation-sponsored books were studied by the committee—all generally directed toward the same end. Most came with teachers' guides to help implement the text material. The teacher's guide to the above text gave the following instructions:

> . . . *the firm establishment of a world organization and the achievement of a world order will be a slow and gradual process, the children in our schools will be called upon to sustain, and strengthen, this movement and to lend their efforts to its advancement. Teachers thus carry a larger responsibility than most of their fellow citizens for contributing to the maintenance of enduring peace. . . . As citizens, teachers must try to give children and youth a chance of survival; as teachers, they must equip children and youth to make use of that chance.*[7]

> *This will certainly involve curriculum revision and the recasting of many time-honored educational policies and practices. This report summons the teaching profession of the United States to unite in planning and executing an educational program for a peaceful world.*[8]

> . . . *[give students] "an ability to think and act as Americans who see beyond the confines of their own Nation and its own problems.*[9]

> *The world-minded American knows that unlimited national sovereignty is a threat to world peace and that nations must cooperate to achieve peace and human progress.*[10]

> *The nation-state system has not been able to the present time to abolish wars. Many persons believe that enduring peace cannot be achieved so long as the nation-state system continues as at present constituted. It is a system of international anarchy—a species of*

jungle warfare. Enduring peace cannot be obtained until the nation-states surrender to a world organization the exercise of jurisdiction over those problems with which they have found themselves unable to deal singly in the past.[11]

More recently, the idea has become established that the preservation of international peace and order may require that force be used to compel a nation to conduct its affairs within the framework of an established world system.[12]

Education for international understanding involves the use of education as a force for conditioning the will of a people, and it comprises the home, the church, the school, and the community.[13]

. . . the failure of the League of Nations makes even more clear the fact that it is in the area of 'political' organization where failure seems to be consistent. This suggests that the difficulty may be traceable to the dogma of unlimited sovereignty—that nothing must be allowed to restrict the complete independence of the state. It suggests also that the dogma of sovereignty has a high emotional content [and should it continue] international cooperation of a political nature will at best be tenuous."[14]

These were new ideas for both teachers and students. As an above-cited quotation reads, there would be "curriculum revision and the recasting of many time-honored educational policies and practices." Teachers who had directed classes toward the Founding Fathers, nationalism, and the providential placement of the United States in world history, were now instructed to change their outlook from national to global. This view often encroached on personal and family values and included significant adjustments.

To add substance to the transition to globalism, the new educational approach was dressed with science and facts. Generally, facts and science are placed on an immutable plane— they are thought of as apparently stable and free of manipulation.

Thus, much of the data and evidence which promoted foundation agenda was both "scientific" and "factual." In the scientific arena, the social sciences came into prominence and, more frequently, adopted the mandate of "social engineer" to "prepare" students for their shift from national goals and values. The term "social engineer" was used throughout the Congressional Report of the Reece Committee.

Rewriting the old history

Likewise, "facts," being the stuff of academia that they are, were vital to convince a new generation of the validity of foundation direction. Those facts were most prevalent in the realm of national history and spurred an historical approach now generally known as "revisionist" history. Revisionism looks at ulterior motives for causes of historical events and downplays any altruism on the part of historical leaders. Thus revisionism would have the Founding Fathers of the Constitution as a group of self-interested men designing laws to protect their material wealth against the masses of early American colonists. Revisionism touts both apparent and unapparent idiosyncrasies while often ignoring tradition and time-honored interpretations of history. Thus, revisionist history rewrites events in a country's history to emphasize self-interest and de-emphasize nationalism. Hence the young schoolboy who knows that Washington had wooden teeth but lacks understanding of the events or divine influence at Valley Forge.

Latter-day scriptures do not sanction the revisionist approach to American history. To the contrary, we learn that God "established the Constitution of this land by the hands of wise men whom [he] raised up unto this very purpose."

Jerome Horowitz, the author of *The Elders of Israel and the Constitution*—one of the great texts written for Latter-day Saints describing the relationship of church members to the

United States Constitution—summarized a few of the Reece Committee findings. In particular, he was concerned about the influence of foundations and their attempts to discredit the Founding Fathers and the righteous influence that pervaded the formative councils of early America. Quoting from the Reece Committee's findings, he wrote

> *They had in mind the discrediting of the American founders and the demeaning of the nation's Constitutional structure of government. So they approached several of the most prominent historians of that day with this proposition but they were turned down flatly.*
>
> *[They] then decided that it was necessary for them to build their own stable of historians. They therefore approached the Guggenheim Foundation which specializes in the awarding of fellowships and said, "When we discover a likely young person who is studying and looking forward to becoming a teacher of history, we will take him to London to pursue his studies." So they took 20 or so to London and there were briefed in what was expected of them. This group then returned and eventually became the most active influence in the American Historical Society.*
>
> *This coincides with the appearance . . . of book after book, the contents of which cast aspersion on the early leaders of the country and relegated their ideas to the realm of myth.*[15]

The revisionist message has prompted many to ask, "Why has history changed?" President Ezra Taft Benson wrote, "The real story of America is one that shows the hand of God in our nation's beginning. Why is it that this view of our history is almost lost in classrooms in America? Why is it that one must turn to the writers of the eighteenth and nineteenth centuries to find this view inferred or stated?"[16] The change, most historians attribute to the educational dominance of tax-exempt foundations.

Elaborating further, President Benson said that "Their purpose has been and is to create a 'new history.' By their own admission they are more influenced by their own training and other humanistic and scientific disciplines than any religious conviction." Therefore, to prove their predetermined point, "facts" and circumstances have been brought forward to the exclusion of the admitted motives of those who made the history. An example of revisionism that was particularly odious to President Benson was that the Revolutionary War was won because British generals were inept; that France came to the aid of the fledgling patriots; and that the Americans were "just very lucky." Rather than looking for secular answers, President Benson suggested a better source was to look toward those who lived and sacrificed their lives through the experience. To him, and to most Latter-day Saints, George Washington's appraisal was more accurate: "The success, which has hitherto attended our united efforts, we owe to the gracious interposition of heaven; and to that interposition let us gratefully ascribe the praise of victory and the blessings of peace."[17]

Revisionism was at the core of American history taught under foundation funding. That history, as well as the very direction of foundation-sponsored education, was found to be both "un-American" and unworthy of tax-exempt status. Although this recommendation was given by the Committee, the influence of the foundations was sufficient to defeat its proposal. Even more fearful than losing tax-exempt status, however, was concern of foundation leaders that the findings and research of the Reece Committee would be publicized and that the general citizenry would be made aware of their semi-clandestine practices. Quoting Dr. Carroll Quigley in *The Naked Capitalist*, Dr. Skousen referred to the Congressional hearings and their potential to draw attention to the bankers influence in public education. Quigley wrote:

> *The Eighty-third Congress in July 1953 set up a Special Committee to Investigate Tax-Exempt Foundations with Representative B. Carroll Reece, of Tennessee, as chairman. It soon became clear that people of immense wealth would be unhappy if the investigation went too far and that the 'most respected' newspapers in the country, closely allied to these men of wealth, would not get excited enough about any revelations to make the publicity worth while, in terms of votes or campaign contributions.[18]*

As we have seen, the power of the controlled media has generally sifted information that people receive; consequently, few people heard about the Reece Committee and its findings. The Ford Foundation allotted $15 million to control the dissemination of the hearing's results, thus ensuring that the Committee would soon be a forgotten chapter in educational influence. Commenting on the above statement by Quigley, Dr. Skousen pointed to the clandestine tactics used by the hidden powers.

> *Note how this last sentence reveals the Achilles Heel in the secret society's operations. The whole concern of the globalist conspiracy is to do their work in such a way that the public will not become sufficiently aroused to use their "votes and campaign contributions" to knock the agents of the Establishment out of political power in Washington.[19]*

The Reece Committee submitted its report on December 16, 1954. Some discussion of its findings carried into Congress and a few speeches entered the Congressional Record about abuse of the tax-exempt status and the negative impact on education. Generally, however, nothing was done to stem the influence of the tax-exempt foundations. In 1958, Rene Wormser of the Committee wrote a comprehensive book about information uncovered by the Reece Committee entitled *Foundations: Their Power and Influence*. This was an eye-opening book (again reprinted in 1993) that lays an excellent foundation for today's educational researcher. Dr. Skousen summarized a few of Wormser's key points:

> *Political maneuvering to prevent the hearings from being effective.*
>
> *How rich banking and industrial families give their money to foundations without losing control of their funds.*
>
> *Who actually runs the tax-exempt foundations?*
>
> *How the major foundations are all interlocked into a monolithic monopoly of power to carry out globalist policies.*
>
> *Policy of continually emphasizing pathological aspects of American society to discredit its culture.*
>
> *Foundations use their funds to subvert and control American education.*
>
> *Financing and promoting socialist textbooks.*
>
> *Helplessness of the average citizen.*
>
> *Foundations finance the betrayal of America's best interest to achieve collectivist internationalism.*
>
> *Rhodes scholars fed into Government service by foundations.*
>
> *The Carnegie Endowment for International Peace caught promulgating war.*
>
> *History books which keep Americans from learning the truth.*[20]

Educational foundations today

Unfortunately, the dangers of foundation influence in American education did not die with the Reece Committee. The Carnegie Foundation for the Advancement of Teaching (CFAT) continued to dominate most educational direction and, on a national level, recommended a Task Force on Education during the John F. Kennedy Administration. Included in the Task Force were Francis Keppel, John Gardner and Ralph Tyler—all former presidents of CFAT. In 1962, less than a decade following the Reece Committee, Francis Keppel became the United States Commissioner of Education.

Under Keppel's direction the Elementary and Secondary Education Act (ESEA) became law in 1965 and pushed the globalist agenda further. Ethnic heritage and bilingual education became standard curricula; social workers and child psychologists entered the schools; and more extensive childhood education was promoted. Further legislation was added to the ESEA in 1994 entrenching it even deeper into the school system. Offering federal money to implement "innovations" in teaching, the ESEA spawned the various "titles" which officially brought behavioral programming to the public schools. Title I gave special provisions for disadvantaged children; Title II initially began with school libraries and textbooks but evolved into educational technology and "basic skills improvement." Title III brought more psychological input such as guidance, testing, counseling, and thirteen special programs among which are health education, population education and global education. Title IV added more guidance and counseling using social workers, psychologists and psychiatrists; it promoted added emphasis to early childhood education; and it increased funding for approved learning resources. Title V became one of the most intrusive additions to the act with grants and resources for state education agencies to collect and exchange both academic and affective data on each student enrolled in state education systems. For further discussion concerning the impact of the ESEA (an act that allows for indefinite expansion) and other similar legislation, the reader is directed to B. K. Eakman's insightful book,

Educating for the 'New World Order', from Halcyon House, Portland, Oregon.

The triumvirate of Keppel, Gardner and Tyler was extremely effective in promoting foundation agenda. Ralph Tyler, then the director of the Center for Advanced Study of the Behavioral Sciences at Stanford, chaired the Committee on Assessing the Progress of Education and began national assessment testing. Although testing students is often viewed as a necessary factor to determine if teaching has been successful, national testing formally introduced the federal government into public education. Whereas states and local school boards, following constitutional mandates, had heretofore determined curriculum, federal testing forced local curriculum to adjust to the national assessment. It has long been known in education that testing determines curriculum—"If the question is going to be asked, I'd better teach my students how to answer it! And if the question is an attitudinal or affective question about beliefs and values, I'd best teach the correct responses!"

Frankly, the initial assessments were fairly objective and covered learning in both reading and mathematics. At the time, concerns were related more to the entry of the federal government into the classroom than the objectivity of the tests. Proving those concerns valid, once the federal door was opened, testing veered toward the affective domain and results were given to the various school social workers and psychologists (provided for by Title IV of ESEA.) These concerns came to fruition in the Goals 2000 and No Child Left Behind programs.

Setting the stage for later developments, the Carnegie Foundation entrenched itself as *the* decision-making body for American education. Eakman wrote:

> *President Nixon appointed Alan Pifer, president of Carnegie Corporation in New York, to head a special education group. President Ford continued to rely on the foundation's advice and*

> *proposals. This allowed the Carnegie Foundation to settle in, as it were, at the federal level and begin setting educational priorities from that vantage point. President Carter handed the organization a cabinet-level agency, the U.S. Department of Education, replacing the old Office of Education. President Reagan, apparently not recognizing the extent of foundation control or the existence of 1960s-era policy blueprints, unwittingly launched his decentralization policy, which permitted . . . mandates emanating from Washington as mere local and state initiatives, through "decentralized" state agencies. . . .[21]*

Then, under the direction of foundation leadership in key positions, public schools *officially* reflected foundation ideals. Schools were *officially* transformed (although they really had been many years earlier) from academic emphasis to emphasis on social beliefs and cooperation. Eakman continues:

> *Moreover, the groundwork laid some twenty-five years ago has been implemented with barely a hitch. CFAT has been, through successive administrations, liberal and conservative, the primary mouthpiece for government policy on education. Its edicts, in the form of official reports, are nearly always carried out; its "findings" are consistently taken as gospel; its members head the most prestigious review boards, committees, and task forces on education matters.[22]*

Today, CFAT and their proxies in federal and state governments co-control educational research, including three computer banks of test result data including personal, non-academic information, opinions, and attitudes which in 1988-1989 were integrated into a supercomputer: the Elementary and Secondary Integrated Data System. . . . As a result, curriculum and testing research now has a mandated psychological emphasis which was first outlined in a 1973 federal publication entitled *Handbook on Performance Objectives.* This is the same publication that defines "cognitive learning" as a "belief system."[23]

Thus the emphasis of education shifted from academic achievement to stress upon attitudes and beliefs. Quite obviously, in the process of school redirection some academic excellence was lost. Reading levels typically dropped as did math and general knowledge skills. The academic decline of America's students became (and is) a major concern. Unfortunately, though, as low achievement is publicized, the immediate response encouraged by both government and professional educators is that more money is needed.

More dollars for education

In 2002, Herbert J. Walberg compiled a study of public school costs for the Hoover Institution. Using 1998 figures, he calculated that the average graduating student received $108,730 of taxpayer money for his K-12 education. Some students received considerably more support, for example Cleveland, Ohio, spent $297,282; Milwaukee, Wisconsin, spent $243,886; Columbus, Ohio, spent $197,886; and Washington, D.C. spent $181,851. Obviously, with inflation, those figures are substantially higher today. Sadly, however, increased spending has little bearing on student performance. In fact, North Dakota spent $75,542 per student and South Dakota spent $77,818— among the lowest of educational spenders. Walberg wrote, "The Dakotas are also efficient in another way; their students typically score in the highest range on national examinations."[24] Evidently, money spent on education is not the chief predictor of learning— in fact, there is little correlation

Reading, writing, arithmetic . . . and values

Perhaps more troubling than academic decline and soaring educational cost, is the entry of schools into the

subjective area of values and belief systems. These for many—
and necessarily for Latter-day Saints—are sacred parental
responsibilities that cannot be delegated. Generally the belief
systems encouraged by the NEA and other educational policy-
making groups incorporate humanist ideals which are antithetical
to LDS theology—thus working counter to the Lord's definition
of education.

Reviewing humanist influence in government sponsored
schools and the apparent manipulation that can occur, one can
more easily understand Karl Marx's rationale to incorporate
public education into Communist philosophy. In a general
conference address, President Ezra Taft Benson told the saints:

> *The tenth plank of Karl Marx's Manifesto for destroying our
> kind of civilization advocated the establishment of "free education for
> all children in public schools." There were several reasons why
> Marx wanted government to run the schools. . . . one of them [was
> that] "it is capable of exact demonstration that if every party in the
> State has the right of excluding from public schools what-ever he
> does not believe to be true, then he that believes most must give way
> to him that believes least, and then he that believes least must give
> way to him that believes absolutely nothing, no matter in how small a
> minority the atheists and agnostics may be."*[25]

By controlling the input of the curriculum and
discouraging Christian belief systems, it is not difficult to follow
the above reasoning. Erasing and challenging traditional
approaches to religion, in a somewhat short period of time, many
of us have witnessed the ban from schools of Christ-oriented
Christmas themes and music; Christmas and Easter vacations
now renamed winter and spring breaks; and all prayers. Virtually
all things connected to Christianity are critically reviewed and
secularized. On the other hand, we have also witnessed the rise
of clubs, studies and other information directly in contrast to

Christian ideals. President Benson continued his conference comments:

> *It is self-evident that on this scheme, if it is consistently and persistently carried out in all parts of the country, the United States system of popular education will be the most efficient and widespread instrument for the propagation of atheism which the world has ever seen.*[26]

Using the vantage of hindsight, we are able to look at President Benson's comments today and realize their prophetic nature. Much of the influence to which he alluded was ushered into the schools by John Dewey—the guru of public education promoted by the various education foundations. Beginning with Rockefeller support during the fledgling years of the foundations, Dewey's educational ideals became standard during the Progressive Education era of the 1930s and 1940s and are carried substantially into today's classrooms. Dewey was as much a philosopher as an educator, his philosophy forming the basis for his educational direction. A sizable part of that philosophy was humanism: the belief than man, rather than a supernatural being, can best determine his needs and values. The ideal of humanism, in fact, was central to Dewey's belief about learning. Dewey, a chief architect of the Humanist Manifesto, taught that constructive thought could only happen if a person was unhampered by religious concepts and definite values of right and wrong. Those preconceived conclusions were, in his philosophy, detrimental to a person's freedom to think and act for himself.

In Dewey's well-read essay, "How We Think" published in 1910, he taught that there were two main inhibitors to thought and problem solving: (1) a belief in God, and (2) parents who taught values. Both, he said, restricted thought and precluded the acceptance of ideas which ran counter to their teachings.

To place his philosophy in perspective, a familiar scripture from section 68 of the *Doctrine and Covenants* reads:

> *(25) And again, inasmuch as parents have children in Zion, or in any of her stakes which are organized, that teach them not to understand the doctrine of repentance, faith in Christ the Son of the living God, and of baptism and the gift of the Holy Ghost by the laying on of hands, when eight years old, the sin be upon the heads of the parents.*
>
> *(26) And this shall be a law unto the inhabitants of Zion, or in any of her stakes that are organized.*
>
> *(28) And they shall also teach their children to pray, and to walk uprightly before the Lord*

Note that verse 25 uses the word "understand." Parents do not simply take care of having children's ordinances performed, but they teach children in such a way that the children know and understand the doctrines of the Church. Clearly, this directly contradicts Dewey's educational philosophy—that which is supported by foundations and most professional educational organizations.

Not only are parental and religious values challenged in today's classrooms, but equally troubling to some is the documenting of personal beliefs through testing and assessment. These, evidently, are both maintained and retained, and are a part of a student's identity—thus juxtaposed to much of what we call a "right to privacy." This, of course, is contrary to the American ideal that our thoughts, values and religious ideas are personal to ourselves and not a part of public knowledge.

More affective means less academic

With the decline of academics and the definite bent toward foundation objectives, information has been both restricted and somewhat manipulated. The public schoolroom, instead of being a place where young adults receive information liberally, has often become a source of biased and limited information—sometimes at odds with eternal goals and beliefs. In many cases, then, schooling restricts agency because of insufficient or wrong information.

Perhaps an apocryphal story, but years ago the president of Harvard University was asked why Harvard graduates continually were at the top of the country in academia. They produced more scientific papers, had more academic award winners, and placed more high-level university positions than any other institution. The president answered that the reason for Harvard's success was that it demanded the highest qualifications for entrance into the university. Because it took only the "crème" into its student body, the success of its students was somewhat predetermined. He then went on to say that in most cases input determined output and summarized his view with the statement: "Garbage in—garbage out."

This is another way of saying that excellence is based not only on individual merit but also on both the quality and the quantity of information received. Generally, but not in all cases, if a person has limited or restricted access to facts, his ability to think and make informed decisions will be impaired. Given sufficient access to information, a student—or anyone—has a greater opportunity to excel. When the conduit to information is stifled or restricted, that person's information is curtailed thus limiting his opportunity for excellence as well as free agency.

Like the public media, education may be either broadening or limiting. Complete freedom to think and act is dependent upon access to information; the more accurate information that we have, the better equipped we are to make correct and righteous decisions. According to Joseph Smith, once possessing knowledge of correct principles we are capable of governing ourselves. Were there no access to those principles, our ability to govern ourselves—to righteously exercise our agency—would be severely restricted for most.

Similarly, we have noted that the information offered through public schooling is limited to its curriculum. The provenance of that curriculum has created concern for many. Curriculum is limited by those who determine the curriculum—which is geared to testing—which is determined by those who draft national and standardized tests—who are aligned with the tax-exempt foundations—which are controlled by the international banking establishment.

Moroni's concern for freedom and the lack of it that would prevail in our dispensation was accurate. All of our traditional and institutional methods of acquiring information have come under establishment control. Public education, frequently sold as a bastion of information dissemination to foster progression, often appears to have the opposite effect. Although seemingly benign and offered at the expense of much philanthropy, some have seen modern education as a "wolf in lamb's clothing." An excellent book documenting counter-productivity in public schooling is Samuel Blumenthal's *NEA: Trojan Horse in American Education*. As the title denotes, what we are led to believe about formal schooling may be something entirely different.

The Latter-day Saint educational ideal

John's concise statement, "Ye shall know the truth and the truth shall set you free,"[27] should be the object of all education. As Latter-day Saints, we have a broad definition of truth given to us in section 93 of the *Doctrine and Covenants*:

> *(24) And truth is knowledge of things as they are, and as they were, and as they are to come;*
>
> *(25) And whatsoever is more or less than this is the spirit of that wicked one who was a liar from the beginning.*

Truth, then, is not a matter of pragmatism (Dewey's ideal) or education for a short-sighted goal. Instead, as Brigham Young taught, real education is all-encompassing. The broad education that includes all truth is education that will allow us to more perfectly incorporate our agency and make decisions that will draw us nearer to a complete mastery of our own decision-making. President Young taught:

> It is the duty of the Latter-day Saints, according to the revelations, to give their children the best education than can be procured, both from the books of the world and the revelations of the Lord.[28]

> The idea that the religion of Christ is one thing and science is another is a mistaken idea for there is no true religion without true science and, consequently, there is no true science without true religion.[29]

> We differ very much from Christendom in regard to the sciences and religion. Our religion embraces all truth and every fact in existence, no matter whether in heaven, earth or hell. A fact is a fact, all truth issues forth from the Fountain of truth, and the sciences are facts as far as men have proved them. . . . every truth which you and all men have acquired a knowledge of through study and research, has come from [the Lord]—he is the Fountain whence all truth and wisdom flow.[30]

This is the kind of education that Wilford Woodruff had reference to when he inaugurated the private school system of the Church in 1888. Rather than dividing secular from spiritual as other schools did, he instructed the Saints that the Gospel of Jesus Christ should act as a thread running through the entire curriculum. Issuing a proclamation to the Latter-day Saints, he wrote:

> *Religious training is practically excluded from the [public]*
> *schools. The perusal of books that we value as divine records is*
> *forbidden. Our children, if left to the training they receive in these*
> *schools, will grow up entirely ignorant of those principles of*
> *salvation for which the Latter-day Saints have made so many*
> *sacrifices. To permit this condition of things to exist among us would*
> *be criminal. The desire is universally expressed by all thinking*
> *people in the Church that we should have schools where the Bible,*
> *the Book of Mormon and the Book of Doctrine and Covenants can be*
> *used as text books, and where the principles of our religion may form*
> *a part of the teaching of the schools.*[31]

Latter-day Saint education was meant to be a complete exposure to truth; a much different approach than that offered through state sponsorship. The vital aspect of its approach was learning, to be sure, but also thought and analysis. This, in a framework of truth and revelation, provided the foundation for true education. Although truth-teaching in its entire realm is a parental obligation, that does not necessarily mean that parents do the actual teaching of their children—although many LDS parents do and have enjoyed paramount success. Instead, it means they assume the responsibility of overseeing education and ensuring that it complies with truth and correct principles. For a further review of the singular importance of education to Latter-day Saints, the reader is encouraged to read the author's book *Revealed Educational Principles & the Public Schools*, and Neil J. Flinders ground-breaking work, *Teach the Children: An Agency Approach to Education.*

Unfortunately, given the fact that most children attend public or government schools we must concede that many of the ideal values that LDS parents would like taught cannot be part of the public curriculum. Because public schools are geared to and reflect the values of the majority, they will never be representative of religious thought. This is why Brigham Young and the early prophets spoke out in favor of a church-controlled private school system. It is with this same idea in mind that the Communist Manifesto targeted government-sponsored education for all.

Summary

The consortium of international bankers and industrialists who have controlled other large-scale events and popular opinion, have also unduly influenced public education. Through developing and then controlling tax-exempt foundations, school curriculum has frequently been modified to reflect goals and attitudes at odds with mainstream America. This has been accomplished through control of educational organizations, textbook publishing, establishing criteria for teacher education, and writing educational law. Of late, the primary influential foundation has been the Carnegie Foundation. This group has been aided substantially through both the Ford and Rockefeller Foundations.

The apparent purpose of educational control is to restrict freedom through both the lack of sufficient information and the use of misinformation. A particularly disturbing aspect of foundation control is de-emphasis of academic information at the expense of probing for beliefs and other subjective and personal data.

While government-sponsored education delves into humanism, history reconstruction, and globalist-oriented curricula, we as Latter-day Saints must not lose the vision of our own heavenly mandate as parents. Education for our children must incorporate broad knowledge and must demonstrate the constant and consistent intertwining of scriptural and spiritual teachings with traditional subject material. Just as importantly, education must reinforce its own ultimate purposes: to provide the necessary information for children to exercise their agency correctly, to make righteous and informed decisions, and to heed the Lord's educational directives in section 130 of the *Doctrine and Covenants*—

>   *(18) Whatever principle of intelligence we attain unto in this life, it will rise with us in the resurrection.*
>   *(19) And if a person gains more knowledge and intelligence in this life through his diligence and obedience than another, he will have so much the advantage in the world to come.*

And section 131—

>   *(6) It is impossible for a man to be saved in ignorance.*

Chapter 8—Endnotes

1   W. Cleon Skousen, *The Naked Capitalist*. Private
         printing: 1970. p. 57.

2   *Tax-Exempt Foundations. Report of the Special
         Committee to Investigate Tax-exempt Foundations and
         Comparable Organizations*. House of Representatives,
         Eighty-third Congress.
         December 16, 1954. United States Government
         Printing Office. Washington: 1954. p. 17. (An
         unabridged copy of the Reece Committee
         Hearings may be found at
         www.americandeception.com

3   *Ibid*. pp. 18-19.

4   *Tax-exempt Foundations. Hearings before the Special
         Committee to Investigate Tax-exempt Foundations
         and Comparable Organizations*. House of
         Representatives. Eighty-third Congress.
         Washington, D.C.: May 10—July 9, 1954. p. 64.

5   *Ibid*. p. 65.

6   *Ibid*.

7   *Ibid*. p. 7.

8   *Ibid*. p. 8.

9   *Ibid*.

10   *Ibid*.

11   *Ibid*. p. 70.

12   *Ibid*. p. 69.

13   *Ibid*.

14   *Ibid*. p. 71.

15   Jerome Horowitz, *The Constitution of the Founding
         Fathers*, Archive Publishers. 1996: Grantsville,
         UT., p. ii.

16   Ezra Taft Benson, *This Nation Shall Endure*, Deseret
        Book Company. Salt Lake City: 1977. p. 14.

17   *Ibid*. p. 15.

18   Skousen, *Op. Cit*. p. 58.

19   *Ibid*.

20   *Ibid*. pp. 59-61.

21   B. K. Eakman, *Educating for the 'New World Order.'*
        Halcyon House. Portland, OR: 1992. p. 126.

22   *Ibid*. p. 127.

23   *Ibid*.

24   Herbert J. Walberg, "Hold Schools Accountable for Cost
        Of Finished Graduate", Hoover Institution
        Weekly Essay, June 10, 2002. www.hoover.org

25   EzraTaft Benson, *Improvement Era*, December, 1970.

26   *Ibid*.

27   John 8:32

28   Brigham Young, *Journal of Discourses* 17:45. April 18,
        1874.

29   Brigham Young, *Journal of Discourses* 17:52. May 3,
        1874.

30   Brigham Young, *Journal of Discourses* 14:117. May 14,
        1871.

31   Wilford Woodruff, Circular Letter to Stake Presidents,
        June 8, 1888, in Jack Monnett, *Revealed
        Educational Principles & the Public Schools*,
        Archive Publishers. Grantsville, Utah: 1998. p.
        244.

Chapter 9

GADIANTONS IN REAL TIME: APPLICATIONS IN TODAY'S WORLD

Today's challenge in reading the scriptures

A danger in reading scriptures is the mindset of "that was then but things are different now." Although we often draw parallels and verbalize principles, we find it easy to view our lives as being much different than the lives of our *Book of Mormon* counterparts. After all, they didn't have the media challenges that we face today—televisions weren't in every household, the internet wasn't a temptation, nor were "R" and "X" rated movies. Although there was some drunkenness mentioned in the scriptures, there weren't bars, packaged liquor stores, and six-packs of beer for sale at every convenience store. The world was much tighter and extended family members could generally be found close to the same places they were born— unlike our situation with automobiles, highways and airplanes that allow us to easily escape the watchful eyes of home. In short, many read scriptures but find it difficult to genuinely relate to scriptural situations.

Nephi lamented: "O wretched man that I am! Yea, my heart sorroweth because of my flesh; my soul grieveth because of mine iniquities. I am encompassed about because of the temptations and the sins which do so easily beset me."[1] Although we understand the grief that sin brings, we most likely say in our minds, "Nephi, if you only knew!" And perhaps our mind dialog continues: "Nephi, you didn't pick up magazines and see sex on every page or turn on the television and see and hear suggestive clothing and language on every channel. You weren't confronted with drugs and word of wisdom temptations constantly. And when you were alive, Wal-Mart wasn't open on Sunday."

Although all of these differences are true today, we must remember that they have always been true. In all ages scriptures have been written by past prophets and read by "modern" readers. Nephi faced the same challenge when he read and interpreted the writings of Isaiah for his brothers. Laman and Lemuel probably thought that Isaiah's writings didn't apply to them because their circumstances were entirely different; after all, how could a family of nomadic wanderers identify with a palace prophet. Like many scripture readers today, they said "We're different! We don't relate!"

Even though circumstances might be different, Nephi explained, "I did liken all scriptures unto us, that it might be for our profit and learning."[2] Our reading challenge today is similar. We don't read simply to meet goals or to study *Biblical* or *Book of Mormon* history; but we read to liken and to apply their direction to our daily lives.

Often in teaching children we ask, "What would Jesus do?" Likewise as we read from prophets and come across principles which parallel dilemmas that we face, we might ask, "What would Nephi do in my situation?" In asking the question, we shouldn't try to remove ourselves to his circumstances, but instead liken his principles to our circumstances. If Nephi, Alma, Moroni, or any of our scriptural heroes were alive today, how would they act and react to our world?

Fortunately, unlike Christendom in general, we have living prophets and apostles as guides. For Latter-day Saints, picturing ancient prophets is more easily accomplished.

In relating scriptures to ourselves, however, sometimes it is not only the principles that must be understood in today's arena, but we also must transpose scriptural warnings and situations. In other words, not only visualizing what Nephi would do but also asking what Korihor, Kishkumen, or Gadianton would do given all of the modern devices and technology that lend themselves to temptation and sin.

The pattern of secret combinations

When Mormon and Moroni wrote to latter-day readers of the *Book of Mormon* about events leading to the second coming of the Savior, they spoke of one international conspiracy—a massive secret combination that will have power over all "nations, lands and countries." From research, it appears evident that there is indeed a single, Satanic force that permeates nations and governments leading toward the goal of destroying the freedoms of all people. Satan's temporal implementation of this attack is more complex, however, including multiple and oft times competing predator nations that conspire for world power. Satan often sacrifices one or more of his antagonists in order to allow another to achieve total supremacy in the end.

The object of this book is to demonstrate the concerted effort of the great secret combination of our day to bring about its stated purposes and its powerful influence upon people in the 21st century.

The tactics of secret combinations are so successful, however, that it would only be wishful-thinking to suppose that there were no other secret combinations. Although a master plan is in place to "overthrow" the agency of all lands through the great latter-day secret combination, other secret groups have formed using the same methods and promises. Thus a living Gadianton or Kishkumen today would incorporate the principles that were applied in overthrowing ancient civilizations while adapting them to current conditions. *Book of Mormon* scripture relates that the major principles that brought success to Gadiantanism were:

(1) To successfully recruit members into secret combinations they should be offered power, gain, and freedom from prosecution.

(2) To escape prosecution, the government, particularly the "judgment seat," must be controlled by the secret combination. In this way, favorable judgments will be delivered to those who are part of the combination while those opposing its actions will receive harsh treatment.

(3) To expedite the goals of the combination and insure that the majority of people are not aware of its activities, the secret combination will commit many "secret murders."

Helaman explained that secret combinations were so powerful and prevalent during his administration of the Church that many, even among those considered righteous, did "partake of their spoils and join with them in their secret murders and combinations."[3] By the assent of so many who were most likely not directly involved in murders and plotting the activities of the secret combinations but who, nevertheless, shared complicity through silence and ultimately condoning illegal behavior through their inaction, the pervasiveness of secret societies spread. In this way, the secret organizations captured "the sole management of the government insomuch that they did trample under their feet" the rights of others.[4]

The prophet Nephi, following his father Helaman as the church spokesman, made a similar observation: that the "Gadianton robbers fill[ed] the judgment seats—having usurped the power and authority of the land."[5]   That power and authority allowed "the guilty and the wicked to go unpunished because of their money; and moreover to be held in office . . . that they might the more easily commit adultery, and steal, and kill, and do according to their own wills—"[6]

To many, the writings of Helaman and Nephi seem distant. It is difficult in our generation to identify with complete misuse of the judgment seat and authority figures that would "trample under their feet and smite and rend and turn their backs upon the poor . . . ."[7] Worse, because we assume today that "crime does not pay" and that eventually those who sin— especially to the point of taking the lives of others—will always be caught, it is hard to imagine a culture where such things went unpunished.   Although plausible, it is difficult to visualize Helaman's explanation that those involved in secret combinations "would protect and preserve one another in whatsoever difficult circumstances they should be placed, that they should not suffer for their murders, and their plunderings, and their stealings."[8] Thus, government officials and those empowered through secular authority—even though their activities were "contrary to the laws of their country and also to the laws of their God," could "murder, and plunder, and steal, and commit whoredoms and all manner of wickedness."[9]

However, as appalling and as far from the parameters of today's conventional society as these scriptural observations seem, Moroni reminded us that "it hath been made known unto me that they are had among all people."[10]   In other words, the wickedness and methods of accomplishing "power and gain" found in the *Book of Mormon* also parallel conspiracies in today's world.

To more completely understand the relevance of Gadianton principles and techniques to present living, we will use the bulk of this chapter to examine their application to one of Satan's more powerful tools in this generation—illicit drugs.

The nature of illicit and recreational drugs

Illegal drugs are extremely conducive to the principles of Gadiantanism. To users, the illegality of their usage holds the seeds of rebellion, glamour, and daring. The drug substance adds various ploys: some may be simply for escape while others may produce a "high" or temporary physical thrill. They may cause a lowering of inhibitions, psychedelic experiences, increased energy, or perceived sharpness of thought. Almost all create physical or emotional dependency. Packaged in an attractive way with ready availability and peer influence, many succumb to their usage.

In all aspects of illicit drugs, Satan is a winner. The user loses his agency both by a drug's influence and its addictive qualities; the seller has "dug a pit for his neighbor"[11] and has damaged if not destroyed another life; and the grower, processor, and transporter have all become complicit. Huge amounts of money are channeled from individuals into the hands of those who will use it to perpetuate further control and abuse.

The Lord explained that the nature of addictive substances lends itself to Gadianton techniques. In fact, the word of wisdom was revealed in 1833 as a forewarning to the Saints "in consequence of the evils and designs which do and will exist in the hearts of conspiring men in the last days."[12] In other words, evil and conspiring men—conspiracies—would rise up based on the ability that certain drugs would possess to enslave others.

But if the Gadianton principles found in the *Book of Mormon* are applied to drug usage, we should expect to not only see people buying and selling drugs. Secret combinations encourage and take advantage of addictions to be sure, but other characteristics are evident also. They are manifested by power, gain, freedom from prosecution, government prominence, judiciary control, and secret murders.

An example: the Iran-Contra Affair

The Iran-Contra affair received a great deal of media attention during the 1980s. Ostensibly, the issue was presented to the American public as the sale of unlawful munitions to Iran and Central America in exchange for American hostages taken in Lebanon and illegal arms sold to Nicaragua. Although generally unknown to the nation until the mid-1980s, the transactions had begun several years earlier. Both sets of arms dealings were against U.S. law and were forbidden by Congress.

During the various CNN hearings that several of us watched, it was implied that the United States felt a deep obligation to aid the freedom-fighters of Nicaragua, known as the Contras, in their struggle against the Communist-inspired Sandanistas. The television hero of the publicized hearings was Lt. Colonel Oliver North—a humanitarian patriot who organized many of the necessary arms deliveries to the oppressed Contras. Because of the establishment media shield surrounding the hearings and the press, most Americans, although hearing "Iran-Contra" continuously for several months, only knew this much about the affair.

In reality, the relationships developed by the United States with Lebanon, Iran, the Sandanistas and the Contras were not that benign. Arms were not "given" to the Contras—they were either sold or traded for cocaine. And, in order to prevent an overbalance of arms going to the Contras and to prolong the civil war, the United States also provided weaponry to the Sandanistas. Munitions were also sold to Iran. Testimony claimed that the money from these sales was used to free

American hostages who had been captured in Lebanon. For our purposes in this introductory example of modern-day Gadiantonism, we will limit our information to United States' activities in Central and South America—primarily Nicaragua, Honduras, Panama and El Salvador—during this period.

Until 1986, very few knew of U.S. involvement in Central America until a plane was shot down over Nicaragua. Of the crew members, only Eugene Hasenfus survived. He was paraded on Nicaraguan national television and admitted that he was working for the Central Intelligence Agency (CIA). Eventually, the publicity engendered by this event coupled with knowledge of Iranian dealings that surfaced, found their way into the U.S. media. Although in reality, the two situations were only vaguely related, U.S. Attorney General Edwin Meese lumped them together and they became known as "Iran-Contra." Following a perfunctory investigation, Congress asked the Attorney General to appoint an Independent Counsel to investigate American activity.

Lawrence Walsh was appointed but not authorized to delve into the entire scope of U.S. involvement. Instead, he was given specific parameters focusing on White House personnel, the CIA, and the National Security Council. Although limited in his investigation, Walsh was able to demonstrate that many top-ranking leaders in the Reagan Administration were involved in illegal activities. The penalties were in most cases minimal with pardons following; nevertheless, their complicity was obvious.

> *Walsh eventually filed charges against many of them. Casper Weinberger [Secretary of Defense] was indicted on June 16, 1992, on charges of obstruction of justice and of Congress, perjury, and false statements to Iran-Contra investigators. Duane Clarridge [senior CIA official] was indicted on November 26, 1991, on charges of perjury and making false statements to Congress. Oliver North [White House aide, National Security Agency] was found guilty on*

May 4, 1989, for altering and destroying government documents, aiding and abetting, and was immune against prosecution on the basis of testimony given to Congress.

Claire George [senior CIA official] was indicted and found guilty on December 9, 1992, of making false statements and perjury before Congress. Elliott Abrams [Assistant Secretary of State] was indicted and pled guilty on October 7, 1991, to withholding information from Congress. Alan Fiers, Jr., [Chief of CIA Central American Task Force] pleaded guilty on June 9, 1991, to withholding information from Congress. Robert McFarlane [National Security Advisor] was indicted and pled guilty on March 11, 1988, to withholding information from Congress. Thomas Clines [CIA] was charged and found guilty on September 18, 1990, of tax-related crimes and sent to prison.

Richard Secord [Major General USAF] was charged and pled guilty on November 8, 1989, to making false statements to Congress. Albert Hakim was charged and pled guilty on November 21, 1989, to supplementing the salary of Oliver North. Carl Channell [fundraiser with White House connections] pled guilty on April 29, 1987, to conspiracy to defraud the United States. Richard Miller [fundraiser with White House connections] pled guilty on May 8, 1987, to conspiracy to defraud the United States. John Poindexter [Vice-Admiral and National Security Advisor] was found guilty on April 7, 1990, of conspiracy, obstruction of justice, and making false statements to Congress. . . .[13]

Although Independent Prosecutor Lawrence Walsh secured the above indictments, many felt that his six years of investigation should have gone beyond the lesser issues of who knew about the arms for hostages activities and who withheld information from Congress. True, that information was certainly revealing and demonstrated a substantial degree of dishonesty within government; however, the investigation ignored or swept aside the greater issues of drug trafficking and involvement of higher-level officials. Summarizing the view of many who were aware of drug activities in South America, in August of 1996,

Gary Webb became a Pulitzer Prize winning journalist for his series entitled *Dark Alliance* in the *San Jose Mercury News*. He wrote that the "Contra war was not a real war at all. It was a charade, a smoke screen . . . to provide cover for a massive drug operation by criminal CIA agents and others."[14]

Generally, reaction to government complicity in drug smuggling is a "cold shoulder" or disbelief. It seems preposterous that it might even be considered. Even if there were individuals who would attempt to take advantage of the illicit drug market, they would most likely be a very small minority and, we would assume, would be readily apprehended and submitted to the wheels of justice. Drug trafficking in any magnitude, it seems, could not exist. Despite this popular opinion, though,

> One of the many bizarre aspects of this massive drug trafficking, involving key government agencies and branches of government, including the White House, is the illiteracy and indifference of the American public when so many highly documented books have been written about the activities.
>
> Hundreds of witnesses have testified before Congress about their direct knowledge and/or participation in this drug trafficking. Many television shows have addressed this fact, with witnesses who were a part of it. The criminal elements are aware of it. Those connected with the intelligence agencies are aware of it. Numerous articles appear in newsletters pertaining to these agencies describing the drug trafficking. The media, with its awareness of these facts, certainly knew about it.[15]

And yet, mention of government complicity in bringing huge quantities of drugs into the United States normally brings cries of disbelief. To the contrary, we see billboards and public broadcasting spots highlighting the "war on drugs;" schools tout the D.A.R.E. program; and the federal government sponsors a Drug Enforcement Administration (DEA). It seems preposterous to even consider that anyone connected with government could align themselves with illegal drugs. But that is exactly what a *Book of Mormon* Gadianton would have done.

The Iran-Contra chapter in American foreign policy must include the ugliness of drug involvement—an issue not readily accepted but extremely well documented. The documentation comes directly from those who were part of it. Many military personnel, pilots, CIA, government officials, and others found themselves in the middle of transporting illegal drugs from Central American stations to points throughout the United States. Some knowingly participated while several others only became aware of their activities as circumstances surfaced. Many, believing that they were patriotically following their lines of duty, were shocked at their unknowing complicity in bringing illicit drugs into the United States. Once discovering their unwitting participation, several became "whistleblowers," both writing and testifying of things that they had seen and heard.

One whistleblower, Celerino Castillo was a supervising agent for the DEA—in fact, he was at different times the lead agent in both Guatemala and El Salvador. In his book, *Powderburns: Cocaine, Contras & and Drug War*, he painfully explained the conflicts of believing in the anti-drug policy while watching it flaunted. In a written statement delivered on April 27, 1996, to The House Permanent Select Committee on Intelligence, he wrote:

> *For several years I fought in the trenches of the front lines of Reagan's "Drug War," trying to stamp out what I considered America's greatest foreign threat. But, when I was posted in Central and South America from 1984 through 1990, I knew we were playing the "Drug War Follies." While our government shouted "Just Say No!" entire Central and South American nations fell into what are now known as "Cocaine democracies."* . . . .

I became so frustrated that I forced myself to respond to the Intelligence Oversight Board report citing case file numbers, dates, and names of people who were murdered. In one case several Columbians and Mexicans were raped, tortured and murdered by CIA and DEA assets, with the approval of the CIA. Among those victims identified were Jose Ramon Parra-Iniguez and his two daughters. . . . Also included among the dead were several Columbian nationals: Adolfo Leon Morales-Arcilia, Carlos Alberto Ramirez, and Jiro Gilardo-Ocampo. Both a DEA and a CIA agent were present when these individuals were being interrogated (tortured). The main target of that case was a Guatemalan Congressman (Carlos Ramiro Garcia de Paz) who took delivery of 2,404 kilos of cocaine in Guatemala just before the interrogation. This case clearly implicated the Guatemalan government in drug trafficking. (The Guatemalan Congressman still has his U.S. visa and continues to travel at his pleasure into the U.S.) . . . .

When the Boland Amendments cut the Contras off from a continued US government subsidy, George Bush [Sr.], his national security advisor Don Gregg, and Ollie North, turned to certain foreign governments, and to private contributions, to replace government dollars. Criminal sources of contributions were not excluded. By the end of 1981, through a series of Executive Orders and National Security Decision Directives, many of which have been declassified, Vice President Bush was placed in charge of all Reagan administration intelligence operations. All of the covert operations carried out by officers of the CIA, the Pentagon, and every other federal agency, along with a rogue army of former intelligence operatives and foreign agents, were commanded by George Bush.

The 2,404 kilos of cocaine referred in his statement equates to 5,289 lbs.! Following his several-page testimony to the Committee, Castillo concluded by asking, "Why am I doing this?" He answered that the war had shifted from drugs to "a war against the criminals within my own government." That war, he wrote, must be won first.

If not, we will continue to have groups of individuals who will be beyond any investigation, who will manipulate the press, judges and members of our Congress, and still be known in our government as those who are above the law.[16]

Castillo reported that he was concerned about the large amount of cocaine taken into Florida, Texas, and California, that was orchestrated by Lt. Colonel. Oliver North of the National Security Agency (NSA). Interviewing with *The Texas Observer* in 1994, he discussed the drug transfers; his reporting to the U.S. Ambassador of El Salvador; and his visit with President George Bush, Sr. at a cocktail party in Guatemala City in 1986. It was there that he spoke directly with the Vice President about his concerns but, he said, Vice President Bush "just smiled and walked away from me."[17]

Castillo hardly stands alone for there are many such witnesses. For a more detailed look at this aspect of Gadiantonism, the reader is encouraged to read *Defrauding America: Encyclopedia of Secret Operations by the CIA, DEA, and other Covert Agencies* by Rodney Stich; *Compromised: Clinton, Bush and the CIA* by Terry Reed and John Cummings; and *The Big White Lie: The CIA and the Cocaine/Crack Epidemic* by Michael Levine.

Michael Levine, for example, worked for 25 years with the Drug Enforcement Administration (DEA) and other government drug-related agencies. He wrote that "the so-called war on drugs is the 'biggest, whitest, and deadliest lie ever perpetrated on U.S. citizens by their government.'"[18] While acting as a DEA agent, Levine continually found links from the CIA to drugs imported into the United States. His findings were that several federal judges and administrators of the U.S. Justice Department apparently were active participants in the covert dealings, and that penalties and sentences (when government officials were found enmeshed in the Central American drug trade) were consistently reduced or eliminated and were kept from general knowledge. Levine, like others with similar experiences, sought to expose the corruption through his first-hand information—only to be targeted by the Justice Department with fabricated charges and threatened prison.

The Cutolo affidavit. Col. Edward P. Cutolo of the U.S. Army was assigned through the CIA to supervise Operation Watchtower—a drug-trafficking operation specializing in placement and control of radio beacons to guide pilots from Columbia to Panama without detection. Learning the specifics of the operation's purposes, Cutolo conducted an investigation that uncovered high-level involvement. Knowing the sensitive nature of his information, he was fearful for his life and decided to write a detailed affidavit of the investigation describing CIA and military drug activity. Fortunately, the affidavit was distributed among several close friends because "Cutolo was killed, as were several other people working with him to expose the drug trafficking operations. Their deaths, as with dozens of others, protected high U.S. officials . . . ."[19]

Because the Cutolo affidavit was circulated prior to his murder, the results of his investigation are known. CIA operatives are named along with Col. Manual Noriega—then Panama's Defense Force Officer assigned to Customs—and his link to drugs and the CIA.

One of Col. Cutolo's informants was CIA operative Edwin Wilson who he quoted extensively in his affidavit. Having had dealings worldwide with the CIA in the areas of drugs and arms sales, and eventually testifying of his CIA dealings through his experience in the private sector, Wilson was later silenced with a lengthy federal prison sentence. Most of the information referring to him in Cutolo's affidavit mentioned him in conjunction with Robert M. Gates (Deputy Director of the CIA under William J. Casey, Director of the CIA from 1991 to 1993, and current president of Texas A & M University) and William J. Casey (Director of the CIA from 1981 to 1987).

> *Edwin Wilson explained that Operation Watchtower had to remain secret . . . . There are similar operations being implemented elsewhere in the world. Wilson named the "Golden Triangle" of Southeast Asia and Pakistan . . . . Wilson named several recognized officials of Pakistan, Afghanistan, Burma, Korea, Thailand and Cambodia as being aware and consenting to these arrangements, similar to the ones in Panama.*
>
> *Edwin Wilson explained that the profit from the sale of narcotics was laundered through a series of banks. Wilson stated that over 70% of the profits were laundered through the banks in Panama. The remaining percentage was funneled through Swiss banks with a small remainder being handled through banks in the United States.*[20]

Emphasizing the gravity of Cutolo's information, his affidavit told of Elaine Tyree, an Army servicewoman who discovered the nature of Operation Watchtower and wrote about it in her diary. She was killed because of her knowledge. To direct the focus away from her killer and the reason for her death, the military court charged her husband, Private William Tyree, with her murder. Word of potential impropriety escaped and Senator Jake Garn's office requested a full investigation. Although the first trial found no evidence of her husband's guilt, some concerned military leaders placed pressure on the court with the intent on demonstrating that he was culpable—thus removing suspicion from the real cause. Cutolo wrote in his affidavit: "On 29 February 1980, Pvt. Tyree was convicted of murder and will spend the duration of his life incarcerated."[21]

Prior to his incarceration, Tyree made many details public that his wife had found. Following her death "Tyree had repeatedly contacted members of Congress about his findings of drug trafficking from Central America; of the drugs and arms trafficking at Fort Devens, and the threats to him and his wife."[22] In a later affidavit, Tyree explained that his wife began receiving telephone calls and notes on her parked car threatening her "to stop writing and reporting secret activities . . . ."[23] Another affidavit by Sergeant Kenneth Garcy explained that "Elaine Tyree was keeping a record of what she learned about the drug operation and that she intended to turn the diary-style book over to the Criminal Investigation Division. (CID)[24]

Paul Neri of the National Security Agency (NSA) was one of the individuals Col. Cutolo entrusted with his affidavit. Following Cutolo's death, Neri distributed the affidavit to members of Congress and to the media. In his cover letter explaining the affidavit, he wrote of certain individuals with interest in Cutolo's revelations:

> *Both Col. Rowe and Mr. Pearce agreed to go public, after the meeting with [Congressman] Larkin Smith, to call for a full investigation into the events described in Col. Cutolo's affidavit. But both men died prior to the meeting with Smith.*
> *. . . The men who died so far . . . were good men. They attempted to let the public know what really occurred in Latin America, and in the never ending drug flow.*[25]

Most likely, the meeting was scheduled with Congressman Smith because of his recent legislation calling for stronger federal drug enforcement. Then, in the strangest of coincidences, Larkin Smith was killed in a plane crash. Shortly following the crash, Paul Neri also died.

These deaths followed a pattern that was exposed in Cutolo's affidavit: "I have seen other men involved in Operation Watchtower meet accidental deaths after they were also threatened."[26] Discussing the accidental deaths, Rodney Stich added:

Sgt. John Newby received threatening phone calls and then died in a parachuting accident when his chute failed to open. Col. Robert Bayard was murdered in Atlanta, Georgia in 1977 . . . . Col. Cutolo died in a one-car accident near Skullthorpe, England, in 1980, while on a military exercise near the Royal Air Force base at Skullthorpe. Cutolo's death was under strange circumstances . . . .

Colonel Baker died . . . . Colonel James Rowe was assassinated on April 21, 1989 [while investigating links to] Cutolo's murder and to CIA operatives Edwin Wilson and Thomas Clines. Pearce was killed in a helicopter accident in June 1989 under mysterious circumstances. Congressman Larkin Smith died in an airplane accident on August 13, 1989.[27]

The Arkansas drug connection. Much of the drug activity discussed in this chapter both precedes and overlaps the Iran-Contra period when the United States was covertly sending weapons to Nicaragua in exchange for cash and drugs. Although some attached heroic names to America's on-going relationship with Nicaragua, Panama, and other Central American countries ("freedom-fighters," anti-Communists, etc.) those who saw the covert workings of the CIA and other government involvement were more objective and less flattering. Rather than simply arming anti-Communists (the Contras) so that they could oppose tyranny (the Sandanistas) and bring freedom to Nicaragua, the United States found itself on both sides of the conflict. Rodney Stich wrote:

The CIA sought support from Congress for its Contra operation by reporting that the Sandanistas were trafficking in drugs and claimed that the Contras were not doing the same. Actually, U.S. intelligence agencies were selling arms to both the Contras and the Sandanistas and taking drugs as part payment. The drugs were then shipped back to the United States in the same aircraft used for shipping arms.[28]

A place where much of the Contra-Sandanista activity came together was Arkansas. As unlikely as it might seem, the state of Arkansas offered similar terrain and weather features that were found in Nicaragua to train army leaders. Eventually the covert flight training center at Nella, Arkansas, graduated over 40 Nicaraguan nationals who could begin to assume responsibilities from the illegal and unfunded Americans involved in the Contra-Sandanista war. It was felt that this was vital because if an American were to be captured or shot down, the publicity of actively participating in a war that Congress had voted against could be devastating (as it eventually proved to be.)

Another feature that Arkansas offered was a business climate that could accommodate the "laundering" of cash in large amounts. Much of this was due to a usury provision in state law that set a ceiling of 10% interest. Because businesses sought higher rates of return, bond companies were formed that took Arkansas money and invested it in other states. Not only did this allow higher rates to be earned but because of lax requirements in reporting, the bond businesses avoided the usual paper trail of money and offered laundered or clean money in return.

Another feature that was vital to the success of the covert operation in Arkansas was government protection and "cover-up" of suspicious activity. As will be seen, state leaders were only too anxious for large cash infusions that could be gained from this operation. Some of the money indeed went to economic development; a large portion, however, was siphoned by political and industrial leaders. True to the needs of those sponsoring U.S. involvement in the Contra War, the state offered protection and the ability to carry out its plans.

One of the best and most complete first-hand accounts of Arkansas activity prior to and during the Contra period is that of former CIA asset Terry Reed. With John Cummings, he co-authored *Compromised: Clinton, Bush and the CIA*—an incredibly detailed book recounting his experiences with political and hand-picked leaders of the Central American paramilitary involvement. As the title denotes, his activities in Arkansas brought him into contact with powerful political figures that were destined to soon occupy the White House and serve in key administrative positions.

Terry Reed unfolds a story of intrigue, spies, aliases, and "handlers," and of danger as operatives learned too much. Initially, many of the figures involved in the U.S. dealings with the Contras did so with altruistic motives. Although declared illegal by the Boland Amendment, they, with White House approval under the Reagan Administration, sought to "level the playing field" by supplying arms and weaponry to fight Communist aggression in Central America—particularly in Nicaragua. Because of the illegality of American entrance into the war and the restriction of Congressional funding, a "black budget" source was necessary to carry on the proposed CIA work. According to William Casey, the Director of the Central Intelligence Agency, the clandestine funding was necessary to continue the agenda of the CIA even though Congress declared that agenda to be outside of the law.

Improvising without a true money source, small planes were stolen in the United States for CIA service. Then, in order to supply arms, flawed weapons were taken from national guard warehouses and tooling was created to replace defective munitions parts. The tooling took place in Russellville, Arkansas, about 100 miles northeast of a small rural airstrip in Mena—the Arkansas base for the arms transfers. Sometimes other countries acted as "go-betweens" in these transfers; however, the majority of exchanges were made directly with CIA planning and transportation. Upon delivering arms shipments, planes returned with large sums of cash and frequently a partial payment of cocaine.

Similar to other documented military ventures referred to in this chapter, there were several witnesses to illicit activity who became whistleblowers. The events at Mena were somewhat contained because of (1) the central direction of the program; (2) the wide national publicity given to the Iran-Contra activities; (3) the prominence of the characters involved; and (4) the small, manageable number of participants.

Reed, a talented pilot with military experience in Vietnam, was somewhat familiar with U.S. covert operations. At age 21 he had excelled in military training, had received top secret security clearance, and performed as a target selector and photography analyst during the war. At that time, part of his assignment was to select targets in Laos, a country that was considered outside of the war. In summarizing his Vietnam experiences he wrote: "The CIA was 'on the ground' in Laos despite Richard Nixon's public denial. He conveniently misled the public by making statements shrouded in deceit such as, 'There are no American troops in Laos,' the operative word being 'troops.'"[29] Reed knew better.

With this background, and convinced that he was above-all a patriot, it was not surprising that when he was contacted by Oliver North to be a part of a covert CIA activity in Central America, he readily agreed. He was immediately directed to another CIA asset in Arkansas who became a close friend—Barry Seal. Seal, with a group of hand-picked pilots flew missions from a little-known airfield in Mena, Arkansas; a site that Seal had used to set up his company, Rich Mountain Aviation. Reed, although a close friend of Seal's who spent quite a bit of flying time with him, spent the majority of his time in Nella, Arkansas, where he acted as a flight instructor training future Nicaraguan pilots.

Barry Seal and his group used the Mena Airport as their home base generally delivering arms shipments to Honduras or

El Salvador and returning through Panama to Mena with both cocaine and money. How much cocaine? Seal testified before a government select committee that the two years prior to 1982 (the year he moved his operation to Mena) that he had made approximately 60 trips to Central America and had brought back roughly 18,000 kilos—almost 20 tons![30] There is no reason to think that the quantity of his cocaine deliveries were any less after moving to Mena. How much money? Although estimates were about $40 million monthly, Reed was sure that there was "a great deal more."[31]

Not wanting to have the cash aboard the aircraft, large duffle bags of money, usually containing about $3 million with each trip, were dropped at a prearranged spot before landing at Mena. In most cases the drops were made just out of Little Rock at the Triple-S Ranch owned by Seth Ward—a coincidence because Reed had originally been business partners with Ward when he had first arrived in Arkansas. The money was picked up by Finus T. Shellnet, Ward's son-in-law.[32]

Upon discovering the drop-off point, Reed wrote, "Ain't Arkansas a nice, cozy, small world." Why? Reed continued: "Shellnut worked for Dan Lasater, Bill Clinton's personal friend and the man who employed Clinton's brother, Roger . . . ."[33] And Dan Lasater of Lasater & Co. was the primary bond dealer that the state of Arkansas and other notables used. Seth Ward, the owner of the Triple-S Ranch had another son-in-law with higher name-recognition—Webb Hubbell. Webb was a former mayor of Little Rock and a partner in the prestigious Rose Law Firm where Hillary Rodam Clinton was also employed. During the Clinton presidency, he would become the U.S. Deputy Attorney General.

Because of the large sums of money entering into Arkansas, DEA agents who were unaware of CIA and state connections began researching. They quickly found Barry Seal and Rich Mountain Aviation but, not knowing Seal's CIA background, were perplexed that the federal prosecutor refused to follow through with a case against him. Then, through a series of apparent "double-crosses," Seal was given a $29 million bill from the IRS because he had earlier given testimony before the Presidential Commission on Organized Crime about profits he had made while working undercover for the U.S. Government. He was stripped of most of his assets and sentenced to spend nights in a halfway house. It was while entering that building that he was ambushed and assassinated by two men who fired fifteen shots at him.[34]

It was about that time that Roger Clinton was arrested and serving time for drug trafficking. Although he would later be pardoned by his brother, there was fear that he would implicate others. Because of those problems and a significant concern of the operation's directors that the state of Arkansas was taking more money from the Mena operation than originally agreed upon, a meeting was held among the major players in the spring of 1986. Pseudonyms were used for several of the attendees; however, Reed identified some of those present. They were: William Barr (Attorney General of the United States under President George H. W. Bush), Lt. Colonel Oliver North, Governor Bill Clinton, and Bob Nash (soon to be appointed president of the Arkansas Development Finance Authority—where much of the Mena money was shuffled—and eventually Assistant to the President and Director of Presidential Personnel during the Clinton presidential administration). At the meeting mention was also made of two others with authority in the operation: William J. Casey (Director of Central Intelligence) and Clark Clifford (former Secretary of Defense).

At the meeting, the investigating DEA agents were discussed. When asked how much they had learned, North replied, "Oh . . . right to Ed Meese's personal bank account as well as to several FBI, DEA, FAA and Customs officials."[35] At that time, Ed Meese was serving as the United States Attorney General.   It was immediately determined that Col. Tommy Goodwin, the Director of the Arkansas State Police, should be notified and that the two agents should be reassigned.

Bill Clinton was chastised and, following a verbal exchange with William Barr, the money problem was brought to the table. Summarizing, the local CIA lead agent said:

> *And this could cause long-term problems for our other operations in Arkansas. This state has a terrible budgetary shortfall . . . . Governor Clinton has real problems on his hands. Our operations transfused over $250 million into his economy in less than two years . . . and his people stole . . . er, diverted . . . from us another $75 to $100 million. . . .*
>
> *The state's "habit" now required "fixes" totaling hundreds of millions of dollars annually to support the economic growth package Clinton had promised his electorate . . . .*[36]

When it is realized that the state of Arkansas was to receive only 10% of the profits from the arms/drugs/money transfers, the reader can get a better picture of the amount of money that was involved. Reed goes on to relate:

> *Johnson [Barr] quickly grasped the political implications with the gubernatorial election just eight months away. "Is he in danger of not being reelected over this money issue?" Johnson asked.*[37]

Then Felix Rodriguez, another outside attendee offered: "I can talk to my people in Panama. I'm sure they would love to . . . become Arkansas sugar daddy. They're always looking for good 'Third World' investment opportunities."

To this, Oliver North added, "I'll go with you to see Noriega's people. If we're successful, you can brief Nash that there'll be a new 'investor' for Arkansas . . . .[38]

Although Reed, to his knowledge, did not bring drugs into the United States, a subsequent assignment in Mexico made his participation more obvious. Sent to Mexico to lay the groundwork for transferring much of the Mena operation, he became more involved with the total picture. As part of his relocation he set up a CIA front organization dealing with machinery and manufacturing. Because some of his machinery had accidentally been diverted to the wrong location in a previous shipment

> . . . . *To avoid another cargo mix-up, both Terry and Desko [a former friend who was also working in Mexico] decided it was necessary to open the two conex containers stored in the warehouse to determine which one to ship. . . .*
>
> *After breaking the metal band attached to the handle of the container nearest the hangar door, Terry, to his horror, unexpectedly found the "hard evidence . . . ."*
>
> *The two men were looking in disbelief at a load of cocaine that measured at least 10 feet by 20 feet and 5 feet deep.*[39]

Having had prior suspicions, Reed "now knew for a certainty that the CIA was in the drug business . . . in a big way."[40] He estimated that the load had to weigh several tons. Fearing for his own life as well as those of his wife, Janis, and their three children, the Reeds were able to escape to Mexico. With his insider knowledge he felt that finding the right government leaders, his testimony might curtail some of the illicit drug trade entering the United States. Rather than welcoming his information, however, he was stonewalled and Reed and his family have been in and out of hiding for over a decade. At some peril, Reed meticulously documented people and events in his

500+ page work—all of which corresponds and is consistent with other known evidence.

What happened to the drugs?

The tonnage of cocaine that entered the United States from Central America during the time period studied was gigantic. It was estimated during the 1980s, for example, that 150 tons of cocaine entered the country each year from Latin America worth approximately $29 billion annually.[41] It hasn't stopped and we have every reason to believe that the same conduits for disseminating drugs are still in use today.

The record of whistleblowers who have come forward after drugs have entered the country has been minimal. In 1998, CIA Inspector General Frederick Hitz completed a two-volume investigation into allegations of drug trafficking by the CIA during its dealings with the Contras. Upon release of the declassified version—particularly volume two—there was no longer a question of government complicity in bringing drugs into the United States.

But although many of the whistleblowers quoted in this chapter were exonerated from earlier ridicule, the issue of names and culpability remain. So even though there was an apparent admission that there was CIA and FBI involvement, there is still a large gap in who did what, and where and how they did it.

A particularly telling revelation that was found in the report had to do with SETCO, a CIA front air freight company that had shipped several tons of cocaine. The investigation showed that they were paid by accounts established by Oliver North. The money paid to SETCO was laundered drug money that most likely had been channeled through a CIA asset. The most obvious individual fitting that category was Albert Vincent Carone who had a history of dealing with the Gotti mafia family and other organized crime kingpins. By acting as a "bagman" (a go-between who collects money and gives it to higher level operators,) North's exposure was reduced and another tier was added to the paper trail.

Jim Huck in his insightful book *Silent Repression: the CIA's Covert Operations*, explains that the CIA was, in many cases, not only the importer but was directly responsible for drug distribution. Using investigative reporter Gary Webb as one source, combined with his own research, he wrote:

> *[Webb] described the role of Blandon [operating with CIA approval] and Meneses [a mafia figure from Nicaragua who was known as "the king of drugs" and employed CIA operants] in the circulating of crack cocaine in the neighborhoods of Los Angeles and New York City. [He} . . . ran a series of stories which alleged that the Contras provided millions of dollars in crack cocaine to the Crips and Bloods street gangs of Los Angeles. In turn millions of dollars in drug profits were funneled back to the Contra army in Central America.*
>
> *Webb showed how Contra leaders and CIA operants allegedly sold drugs in Los Angeles, delivering cut-rate cocaine to the gangs through a young South-Central crack dealer named "Freeway Ricky" Ross. Unaware of the origin of the shipments, Ross turned the powder into crack and wholesaled it to gangs across the country. . . . The story alleged that Ross moved about $100 million worth of crack a year in the 1980s. He bragged that he sometimes moved $2 million worth in a single day.*
>
> *Ross purchased crack cocaine from Blandon who was the conduit for thousands of kilos of coke which flowed through Ross and other big middlemen to Los Angeles street gangs such as the Crips and the Bloods from 1982 to 1986. Ross had maintained a monopoly on the Los Angeles market, paying Blandon approximately $50,000 per kilo which was about $10,000 below market value. Ross was selling over 100 kilos of crack cocaine a week . . . .*[42]

Ricky Ross was convicted in 1996. He will be eligible for probation in 2008. Neither Juan Norwin Meneses (now living in the United States) nor Danilo Blandon have been convicted of any crime.

Obviously, with the amount of cocaine and other drugs entering the United States, the examples cited account for only a small fraction of the total. There are apparently many distributors and methods of distribution. It certainly makes one wonder about the "war on drugs." With knowledge of much that has been discussed in this chapter and personal experience, Michael Levine, a former DEA agent, told a group of students:

> *"The drug war's a sham . . . .*
> *"I threw my life to the winds believing in the war against drugs. If I died, I believed I was dying for a just cause.*
> *"I realized the reality of what I was doing never quite matched what the public was seeing.*
> *"It's all a show. We need more money. We're going to get these guys," Levine said mimicking the politicians. "The drug war is the laughing stock of South America."*[43]

Other government drug involvement—Southeast Asia

Central America was definitely a major stage for importing drugs into the United States. The modern history of using drugs for profit and manipulation, however, probably began with the opium trade in China from the 1840s through the 1860s when Great Britain dramatically increased the amount of opium entering China. This had the effect of sapping a great deal of China's strength and money, and provoked a rebellion stemming from Chinese royalty. The reaction to British drug-pushing is historically known as the Opium Wars—the first ending with the Treaty of Nanking in 1842 wherein Hong Kong was ceded to England with $21 million in silver; and the second ending in 1860 with England firmly entrenched in both Shanghai and Hong Kong including control of Chinese manufacturing and banking.

In recent history, the world-wide production and sale of drugs has had a great deal of involvement by elements of the United States government. Although there have been staggering profits for those participating in the drug trade, the rationale for promoting it has generally been to use the income from the sale of drugs to equip local armies to keep presumed enemies of the U.S. in check. This is because Congress has normally vetoed funding for miscellaneous wars throughout the world causing the CIA and other agencies to resort to "black budget" financing from the sale of drugs.

Because of internal warring in Burma, Jim Huck reported that "from the end of World War II to the 1960s [the] CIA subsidized army increased opium production by nearly 500 percent from 80 tons to 500 tons annually. During the Vietnam War with the U.S. military presence in Southeast Asia, drug production soared to even higher levels. Then, after 1975 with the military withdrawal and a series of droughts in the area, production sharply dwindled. At that time Khun Sa was the primary "drug lord."

> Khun Sa stated that Richard Armitage, at that time an envoy in the American Embassy, financed drug smuggling in Vietnam and Bangkok from 1975 to 1979. CIA agents Daniel Arnold and Jerry Daniel trafficked weapons and drugs with Khun Sa. The operation was believed to be at its peak in 1975 and 1976 under George Bush. In a letter to George Bush, [Bo} Gritz maintained that Khun Sa claimed that he had once engaged in narcotics transactions with Richard Armitage, who later became the Assistant Secretary of Defense, Shackley, as well as other American officials. Bush was head of the CIA in 1976 when Khun Sa said that he was selling drugs to top CIA officials.[44]

Eventually, Khun Sa strengthened his position even greater by taking over rival drug producers, hiring more chemists, and establishing more refineries. He became the largest opium producer in the world and controlled over 60% of the world heroin market. Then, in 1986, the following exchange took place when Lt. Colonel Bo Gritz, having White House approval, met with Khun Sa about information that might lead to American troops still missing from the Vietnam War (MIAs). At that time

> *Khun Sa said that he wanted to end the opium and heroin traffic in his territory and to expose American officials involved in the drug smuggling. Gritz claimed that he took this message to the United States government and was told by Tom Harvey of the National Security Council that "there is no interest here" in the Khun Sa overture. Gritz had in his possession 40 hours of video tape of Khun Sa who "charged American officials, both past and present, with being the chief buyers of drugs produced in that part of the world." He also claimed that he wanted to stop drug trafficking, but that the United States government would not let him. Khun Sa said that the CIA were some of his best customers. He offered support to the DEA to alert them of drug movements, but this was rejected at the headquarters level.[45]*

Laos was another area of CIA activity. As early as 1959 the CIA began using men from the Hmong tribes to patrol the Chinese border and to enter into China. After installing a puppet leader in Laos and encouraging the Hmong to follow him, the CIA settled in on the primary cash crop—opium.

> *To gain support from the Hmong, the CIA supplied the tribesmen with rice. This enabled them to concentrate on growing the main cash crop of opium. The Hmong relied on support from Air America for their rice supplies. Thus, air power became the essential factor which allowed the CIA to keep Vang Pao in power. After Vang Pao was able to consolidate his power, the CIA helped him to sustain an army of 30,000 men from a tribe of only 250,000 people. The CIA relied on the villagers to supply the manpower to continue to replace the wounded and killed. By the early 1970s, 30% of the Hmong*

recruits were 14 years old; another 30% were 15 and 16; and the remaining 40% were over 45.

In return for providing recruits, the Hmong opium growers received CIA support and their economy flourished. . . . Thus, the CIA relied on Vang Pao to supply soldiers in its secret war, and the CIA supplied his tribesmen with rice while opium was grown and frequently flown on CIA planes.[46]

Remember, all of this was happening when the President and others were telling the American people that the United States was containing the war in Vietnam—that there was no military activity in Laos!

There have been many "leaks" about the prevalence of drugs in Vietnam and the complicity of high level government and military officials. The results of spurred drug production at that time couldn't help but increase the numbers of individuals, many of them U.S. servicemen, who were dependent upon heroin. In 1970, a year that saw the production of over a thousand tons of heroin, there were 750,000 heroin addicts in the United States. The figures are equally staggering for other nations throughout the world.

In one operation which was conducted repeatedly during the Vietnam War, a highly intricate method of importing heroin was developed using the cadavers of dead military personnel. Retired Chief Master Sergeant Bob Kirkconnell who was an Air Transportation Supervisor, reported that while stationed in Okinawa, Japan, during the Vietnam War, that an Air Force C-5 landed. Although supposedly in for minor servicing, it became apparent that a broken part was needed before the plane could continue with its cargo of human remains of men killed in action to Travis Air Force Base in California. This would take more than the allotted 24 hours that it could stay on the base without undergoing inspection by Japanese Customs.

The Customs officials soon came to Sgt. Kirkconnell to tell him that all of the bodies in the body transfer cases had their internal organs removed and that they had been instead "stuffed with bags of pure heroin." Shortly thereafter, Kirkconnell was visited by representatives of the Air Force Office of Special Investigations (OSI) and an Army Investigator from the Criminal Investigations Division (CID). He was told to turn over all documentation of the flight and its circumstances. He submitted the various pieces of evidence assured that they would become court documents. Although a court was convened, his evidence was "lost" and never presented. He later wrote:

> *All of us who knew the enormity of this case were flabbergasted. The forged documentation was flawless and had to have been done by experts in the air transportation field. Also, our people who saw the two imposters [those accompanying the dead remains] said that their uniforms and ID cards were perfect.*
>
> *Further, when we talked about this, we were astounded with the enormity of the operation. The mortuary in Vietnam had to have put the heroin in the bodies, and the one at Travis Air Force Base had to remove the heroin, and it had to be distributed. ID cards had to be obtained and orders had to be made, etc. This was no smalltime operation.*[47]

Although this does sound very professional, this method of transportation could not possibly account for the thousands of tons of drugs imported into the United States. It does demonstrate, however, the commitment and the ends that those charged with the responsibility were willing to exact.

An estimate of opium production from Burma alone as of 1992 was 300,000 tons—all under the knowledge and complicity of the United States Central Intelligence Agency.

Too many coincidental deaths

Although murder is one of the most heinous of crimes, our society finds satisfaction in knowing that it is rarely undiscovered and unpunished. Because of growing numbers of visible law enforcement patrols; various publicized "manhunts;" and recent publicity given to "cold case" files wherein murderers are often caught and convicted years after crimes were committed—there is cultural security in knowing that murderers are brought to justice.

Apparently, this is a truism as far as local matters are concerned; however, many deaths appear to have more far-reaching implications. Where political and corporate intrigue are involved—particularly as they pertain to "whistleblowing"—causes of deaths are frequently misdiagnosed and responsible parties are allowed to remain aloof from legal persecution. Whistleblowers are those primarily targeted because they have incriminating information about secret plans or the guilt of certain individuals that could lead to both the discovery of a conspiracy and the prosecution of key individuals. A common saying goes: "dead men tell no tales."

The correlation of suicides and mysterious deaths with those about to reveal critical information is amazingly high. A case in point that is rarely disputed is the murder of Lee Harvey Oswald as the "lone assassin" in the slaying of President John F. Kennedy. A plethora of evidence has surfaced indicating that many others were involved in President Kennedy's death. The immediate murder of Oswald following the assassination precluded any testimony he might have given that would have implicated others—thus protecting the identity of others who may have been involved.

Not only was Oswald killed but Rodney Stich wrote in his well-documented book *Defrauding America*, that:

It has been reported that over 100 key witnesses to the JFK assassination died within a few years of the killing. The London Sunday Times estimated that the odds of sudden deaths among approximately three dozen witnesses over such a short time span would be 100,000 trillion to one. Despite the pattern of killings and mysterious deaths of informants under these unusual conditions, the Warren Commission held that they did not establish any relationship with the Kennedy assassination or constitute a conspiracy to silence opposition to the Warren Commission findings.[48]

In our current study, in addition to Barry Seal, at least four other pilots lost their lives under questionable circumstances. One was checked out with sufficient fuel for three hours, yet ran out of fuel in mid-air after two hours of flight. Foreign intelligence determined that three were killed in a mock crash—not a real crash—one with his throat slit.

Perhaps the most shocking deaths to occur were those of Kevin Ives, seventeen years of age, and his friend Don Henry who, most evidence corroborates, must have stumbled upon one of the dropped duffle bags of money in the Mena Arkansas area. Their bodies were laid in identical positions across train tracks where they were run over by a train in August of 1987. The coroner, Dr. Fahmy Malak, concluded that the boys had smoked twenty marihuana cigarettes, and had passed out on the tracks.

Malak's autopsies and determinations of previous deaths that he had made as a medical examiner had been questioned in twenty other cases. His explanations of "natural causes" and "suicides" were so notorious that questions were raised by both the *Los Angeles Times* and *Dateline NBC*. No wonder then, that the Ives family requested a second autopsy and the bodies of the boys were exhumed.

The second autopsies performed by Dr. Joseph Burton, an Atlanta medical examiner, were very different. His findings indicated that Don Henry had been stabbed and Kevin Ives' face had marks of a blow to the head delivered by the butt of a gun which conformed to a gun that had been carried by Don Henry. A grand jury was then convened and determined that indeed, the deaths of the two young men were murders. Even so, then-Governor Clinton halted the investigation into the deaths.

Jean Duffey was in charge of the Arkansas Seventh District Drug Task Force at the time. As her task force looked at Mena and possible connections to the murders, they found that many leads took them to public officials. Perhaps this was why the task force was shut down as was the federal grand jury. Working with the unit and ultimately on her own, she remarked that, "Witnesses tend to turn up dead. Many witnesses have turned up dead in the case primarily talking about the murders of Kevin and Don."[49]

Duffey had reference to the following individuals who most likely "knew too much" about the murders:

Jeff Rhodes—His body was found shot, mutilated, burned, and stuffed in a trash dump in April of 1989.

Keith McKaskel—The former bar bouncer was found stabbed to death (with 113 stab wounds) in November, 1988. He had warned his friends that he would be killed for what he knew.

Keith Koney—He died in a motorcycle accident after an unconfirmed high-speed chase.

Gregory Collins—He was shot in the face in January of 1989.

Jordan Kettleson—Another who may have had information on the Ives and Henry deaths. Kettleson was shot dead in the front seat of his pickup truck.

James Milam—A possible source of more information. His body was found decapitated and ruled that he died of natural causes by Dr. Fahmy Malak.

Richard Winters—He was a suspect in the original deaths of the two boys. He was killed in a set-up robbery in July of 1989.[50]

Another coincidental death was related by Terry Reed following his departure from the CIA. He had filed a suit against Raymond "Buddy" Young for the "fabrication of false evidence." Young had been Governor Clinton's Chief of Security and at the time of the action in 1995, had been appointed by President Bill Clinton to be a Regional FEMA Director. In an interview with Marvin Lee on May 8, 1995, for the *Washington Weekly*, the following dialog appeared:

> *MR. LEE: Are you suffering any threats and intimidations because of your suit?*
>
> *MR. REED: Certainly. I am operating right now under a written death threat that is not only aimed at me but at my wife and children as well. And it is not aimed at my book Compromised . . . it is aimed at staying out of federal court. So it is a direct threat to "stay out of court or I die" as the threat says.*
>
> *MR. LEE: You said on the Chuck Harder show a few weeks ago that one of your witnesses had died. Can you elaborate on that?*
>
> *MR. REED: Yes, we had a witness I had developed. His name was Robert Bates. Bates was a mechanic at the Mena Airport. A 39-year old mechanic, and a person who had come forward voluntarily to assist me in some of our investigative efforts as we put together our evidence and witness list for the trial.*
>
> *It's been about, I assume it's about five weeks ago Mr. Bates turned up very mysteriously dead, having allegedly drunk himself to death on mouthwash, which I find very strange behavior. I have talked to other people in the Mena area. Mr. Bates is from a very affluent family and this was very unusual behavior. I still don't buy*

off on the results from the autopsy. His body was shipped to Little Rock to have an autopsy performed, and of course they found evidence of this fluid in his stomach which they claim led to his untimely death.[51]

Michael Levine, a former DEA agent, spoke to a student group about the war on drugs. The reporter, Paul Kirk, in the student newspaper wrote:

> *Levine hinted that those in the DEA who come too close to the political reality of the drug war sometimes mysteriously lose their lives.*
> *Levine recalled the time a former agent, Sandy Barrio, was accused by the DEA of drug smuggling. He died of strychnine poisoning while awaiting trial.*
> *But Barrio's death certificate was fixed to read that he died of asphyxiation on a peanut butter sandwich, Levine said.*[52]

Added to the mysterious deaths listed above can be another ten pages of names and information regarding each individual tabulated by Rodney Stich in *Defrauding America*. Under a chapter entitled *Silencing Whistleblowers*, the following are included on pages 466 through 475:

> *Barbara Wegler. She died from unknown causes on March 5, 1995. Several weeks earlier I was in touch with her concerning her investigation of covert activities based upon information given to her by Bill Tyree. She was to provide me with information about what she found, but died before she could do this.*

> *FBI agent Diane Novinger. Novinger said to me that she discovered during an FBI investigation that Vice President George Bush and two of his sons were using drugs and prostitutes in a Florida hotel while Bush was Vice President. [This is the same information given by Barry Seal who claimed to also have tape recordings and a surveillance video (*Compromised*, pp. 212-213)] She said that when she reported these findings to her FBI supervisors they warned her not to reveal what she had discovered. Novinger had been requested to infiltrate drug trafficking operations in South America and the*

United States. She was pressured to quit her FBI position; her husband was beaten to death; and four hours after she appeared on a July 1993 talk show describing her findings (after she was warned not to appear), her father mysteriously died. A dead white canary was left on his grave as a warning to her. After receiving death threats she went into hiding from where she occasionally appeared as a guest on talk shows . . . .

Wife of DEA pilot Basil Abbott. She was killed in Europe in 1982 after talking to European reporters about the DEA drug trafficking operation into the United States. She sought publicity to obtain the release of her husband who had outlived his usefulness to the DEA.

William Casey, Director of the CIA. He was a key participant in the October Surprise operation and its related Iran-Contra arms and drugs activities. He experienced seizures on the morning that he was to testify before the Senate Intelligence Committee and underwent brain surgery. He died several months later on May 6, 1987. Friends believe that Casey would have told the truth if he had testified, thereby implicating people in high positions. CIA operatives have told me that the rumor within the CIA is that Casey's medical condition was induced by drugs.

There were a number of strangely occurring deaths surrounding Bill Clinton—both as governor and as president. The intent of this chapter has been to isolate those deaths that appear to be related to the drug trade and government complicity. That said, in divergence to the general theme, one of the most bizarre statistics surrounding Mr. Clinton relates to his bodyguards. The job of a bodyguard, of course, is to follow and to be with the person to be protected at all times. In such a position, a bodyguard is privy to information unknown by most others. The following Clinton bodyguards are dead:[53]

Major William S. Barkley, Jr.
Captain Scott J. Reynolds
Sgt. Brian Hanley
Sgt. Tim Sabel
Major General William Robertson

Col. William Densberger
Col. Robert Kelly
Spec. Gary Rhodes
Steve Willis
Robert Williams
Conway LeBleu
Todd McKeehan

It is difficult to imagine that so many deaths among key people are coincidental. The only answer that does not defy preposterous odds is that found within the *Book of Mormon*. Helaman, describing the followers of Kishkumen and Gadianton, wrote that "they began to set their hearts upon their riches; yea, they began to seek to get gain that they might be lifted up one above another; therefore they began to commit secret murders, and to rob and to plunder, that they might get gain."[54]

Defining the Gadianton connection

Power and gain. At the outset of this chapter, we looked at Gadianton principles found in the *Book of Mormon* and said that the use and promotion of illicit drugs offered a modern-day study in the application of those principles.

The fundamental goal since Cain's acceptance of Satan's compact and found throughout the pages of the *Book of Mormon* is to achieve power and gain. There is no question that both of these are hallmarks of drug involvement. Normally, money equates with power and gain and certainly, no one could deny the huge profits found in drug dealing. Barry Seal, perhaps the primary drug trafficker in the Mena, Arkansas, phase of the Contra episode stands out as an example. His estate at the time of his assassination was estimated at $50 million. In fact, he bragged that he earned $750 thousand from one single delivery. Then, like a multitude of other examples, there is the case of Ricky Ross who, with a corner on the Los Angeles crack cocaine market, sold up to $2 million in drugs daily.

Escaping the consequences of sin. The Gadiantons were also promised freedom from prosecution for their sins. As they grouped together in their crimes, Helaman's account reads that "they would protect and preserve one another in whatsoever difficult circumstances they should be placed, that they should not suffer for their murders, and their plunderings, and their stealings."[55]

Throughout our examples, we have seen that "plunderings and stealings" have continued unabated. Rarely have those involved suffered for their misdeeds unless they either "knew too much" or stepped outside of the closely knit drug pushing community. As far as suffering legal ramifications, there have been only minimal consequences. Whereas today's violators of laws against the use of marihuana and cocaine for personal use are given felony convictions amounting to several years imprisonment, those perpetrating the crimes through smuggling and distribution are generally held harmless. The exceptions to this rule are those operating outside of the closed drug cartels and those protected by government.

Government connections. Helaman further related that the Gadiantons of his day were enmeshed with government. This, in spite of the republican form of government under which the Nephites operated. Mosiah had counseled his people prior to his death: ". . . choose you by the voice of this people, judges, that ye may be judged according to the laws which have been given you by our fathers, which are correct, and which were given them by the hand of the Lord."[56] Today, we could make a similar statement. We know that the laws of our nation were inspired by God and given to righteous men. Likewise, then, it is our duty to select judges and political leaders to carry out those laws.

Mosiah explained the reason that the Nephite government system should be based on the "voice of the people." He said that ". . . it is not common that the voice of the people desireth anything contrary to that which is right."[57] Although it was not common for the majority to make wrong decisions, he indicated that it certainly was possible. Given our use of media and disinformation today, we can probably understand this principle better than the Nephites who first heard Mosiah discuss the role of the "voice of the people;"—hence our Latter-day responsibility to search for truth.

Mosiah, however, did not teach that the will of the people would always be accurate. He said that it would generally be right but "if the time comes that the voice of the people doth choose iniquity, then is the time that the judgments of God will come upon you."[58] Helaman's book explains that is exactly what happened. Approaching his discussion of Gadianton power during his lifetime, he first told readers that ". . . the people began to grow exceedingly wicked again. For behold, the Lord had blessed them so long with the riches of the world that they had not been stirred up to anger, to wars, nor to bloodshed, therefore they began to set their hearts upon their riches."[59] In other words, their primary concerns centered around themselves: "What's in it for me? How can I get more? How can I have more *things* and *control* than others?

Understandably, with a selfish mindset, our concerns shift from what is best for society to what is best for *me*. In a democratic environment, this is a dangerous motivation. The politician pandering to ego and selfish desires only needs to make promises of lower taxes with more benefits. An impossibility but a popular vote-getting ploy. It worked in Helaman's time—and it works in modern-day America. It was so successful during his administration of the Church that he lamented that the Gadiantons ". . . did obtain the sole management of the government, insomuch that they did trample under their feet and smite and rend and turn their backs upon the poor and the meek, and the humble followers of God."[60]

This is exactly what we have seen in our study of drugs. We have been cajoled and pacified with dialog about a war on drugs emanating from our government. With escalating drug abuses, it sounded both good and necessary and fit well into a politician's arsenal of rhetoric. As it turned out, those who proposed the solution were, in fact, the problem.

Our study is not a critique of all elected officials. Obviously, there are those who are dedicated, prayerful, and committed to making decisions that contribute to unleashing agency and making America great. There are those, however, who have become self-serving and have placed personal interests above those of the nation's citizenry.

In such a situation, we have seen how government leaders in the highest echelons have "trampled under their feet" the lives of others to serve their own ends. Politicians have done favors; have taken advantage of their positions by manipulating situations to serve themselves; and have aggressively snuffed competition and those who have challenged them. Appointments have been made, regardless of moral fiber, to like-minded individuals in accord with their plans and who are willing to further the interests of certain kingpins. Through studying government involvement in drugs we have witnessed a terrible self-indictment showing utter disregard for the lives and well-being of others while further emphasizing the power and gain of elected and appointed leaders. Thus, as quoted at the outset of this chapter, our nation shares a common bond with the observance of Helaman's son, Nephi, about the

> . . . *Gadianton robbers filling the judgment seats—having usurped the power and authority of the land; laying aside the*

> *commandments of God, and not in the least aright before him; doing no justice unto the children of men;*
>
> > *Condemning the righteous because of their righteousness; letting the guilty and the wicked go unpunished because of their money; and moreover to be held in office at the head of government, to rule and do according to their wills, that they might get gain and glory of the world, and, moreover, that they might the more easily commit adultery, and steal, and kill, and do according to their own wills.*[61]

Committing secret murders. Obtaining most of our news from the media, we hear little of suspicious murders that might relate to government or power-broker cover-up. Most who become aware of the many cases of apparent foul play and murder to silence a person who "knows too much," are incredulous. It seems with all that we read and hear, that murderers are brought to justice and pay for their crimes. Helaman told us that in his day, however, that was not true. Likewise, as we have seen, it is not true today either.

In *Compromised: Clinton, Bush and the CIA*, Terry Reed continually referred to the 42 people who were close to Bill Clinton and were in positions to know incriminating things about him who mysteriously died. For him, that was an intimidating statistic that reflected upon his attitude when he found himself with knowledge that was also damaging to the leader. Incredible odds, and yet none have been indicted or convicted of those deaths.

Dead men tell no tales.

Chapter 9—Endnotes

1   2 Nephi 4:17-18

2   1 Nephi 19:23

3   Helaman 6:38

4   Helaman 6:39

5   Helaman 7:4

6   Helaman 7:5

7   Helaman 6:39

8   Helaman 6:21

9   Helaman 6:23

10   Ether 8:20

11   2 Nephi 28:8

12   *Doctrine & Covenants* 89:4

13   Rodney Stich, *Defrauding America: Encyclopedia of Secret Operations by the CIA, DEA, and other Covert Agencies*, 3rd Edition. n.d. Diablo Western Press: Alamo, California. pp. 205-206.

14   *Ibid.* p. 463

15   *Ibid.* p. 433

16   Permission to reprint from Celerino Castillo & Michael C. Ruppert, *From the Wilderness.* www.copvica.com

17   Stich, *Op. Cit.* p. 247

18   *Ibid.* p. 345

19   *Ibid.* p. 351

20   *Ibid.* pp. 354-355

21   *Ibid.* p. 353

22   *Ibid.* p. 360

23   *Ibid.* p. 359

24   *Ibid.* p. 360

25   *Ibid.* p. 355

26   *Ibid.* p. 353

27   *Ibid.* pp. 353-354

28   *Ibid.* p. 349

29   Terry Reed and John Cummings, *Compromised: Clinton, Bush and the CIA.* S.P.I. Books: New York. 1994. p. 18.

30   Mara Leveritt, "The Mena Airport," August 25, 1995. *Arkansas Times Online*, onlinenewspapers.com/usstate /usarkans.htm

31   Reed and Cummings, *Op. Cit.* p. 149

32   *Ibid.* pp. 138-139

33   *Ibid.* p. 139

34   *Ibid.* pp. 220-221

35   *Ibid.* p. 240

36   *Ibid.* p. 244

37   *Ibid.*

38   *Ibid.*

39   *Ibid.* p. 343

40   *Ibid.*

41   Jim Huck, *Silent Repression: The CIA's Covert Operations.* Chapter 5, The CIA: "Cocaine Importing Agency." www.angelfire.com/ca3/jphuck, p. 13

42   *Ibid.* p. 29

43   Tom Donahue: Interview with Terry Reed and John Cummings Hour 2, *America's Town Forum*, p. 21 www.theconspiracy.us/9409/0031.html

44   Huck, *Op. Cit.* P. 7

45   *Ibid.*

46   *Ibid.* p. 8

47   Bob Kirkconnell, www.wanttoknow.info/
         militarysmuggleheroin

48   Stich, *Op. Cit.* p. 466

49   Gary Lane, July 29, 1998. "Mena Murders in Arkansas."
         www.daveshultz.com/clinton/mena.html

50   *Ibid.* and www.povn.com/sandlent/clinton

51   Interview with Terry Reed by Marvin Lee, May 8, 1995.
         Washington Weekly http://dolphin.gulf.net

52   Donahue, *Op. Cit.* p. 21

53   www.povn.com/sandlent/clinton

54   Helaman 6:17

55   Helaman 6:21

56   Mosiah 29:25

57   Mosiah 29:26

58   Mosiah 29:27

59   Helaman 6:16-17

60   Helaman 6:39

61   Helaman 7:4-5

Chapter 10

WHEN FREEDOMS ARE LOST

The move to take the capital the citizens have saved will be disguised as a means of alleviating the needs of the poor, or equalizing the burdens of government, of sharing the wealth. When that comes, the conquest of the citizens will be complete; tyranny will be enthroned till liberty is again brought back across many bloody fields of battle. Thus will history again repeat itself.

President J. Reuben Clark[1]

Some freedoms are lost

Because of the nature of freedom and our lack of vigilance, freedoms are often lost to "conspiring men"[2] and secret combinations that "seeketh to overthrow the freedom of all lands, nations, and countries."[3] The Lord's plan dictates that in addition to our responsibility of wisely using our agency, we must assume the added duty of safeguarding our right to use that agency.

As Latter-day Saints we understand that our experience on the earth would be fruitless if we were unable to exercise free agency. The conflict in the premortal existence would have been for naught and, as Lehi so eloquently taught, "men are free according to the flesh; and all things are given them which are expedient unto man. And they are free to choose liberty and eternal life . . . ."[4] Our choice to choose liberty is vital. Imagine not having that freedom! The compilers of the *Book of Mormon* condensed a thousand years of Nephite history which emphasized the importance of liberty and the ease in which it could be lost.

Our generation, has learned that information can be manipulated by both media and formal education. Sometimes, believing that we have had correct information, we have made decisions. Unfortunately, at times we have found that our information was incorrect and that our decisions were wrong. We have learned the value of good sources of truth, and we have found that media and public education can be methods used to curtail freedom.

In this sense, knowledge is power. Knowing things as they really are empowers an individual to exercise his agency. Lacking that knowledge, he, at best, *believes* that he is exercising true agency. How powerful is a knowledge of information? Supposing that pollsters had asked an informed group of citizens about Iraq preceding the 2003 Shock and Awe military invasion. Having knowledge, citizens would have known that there were no weapons of mass destruction in Iraq; that Iraq was not involved in the destruction of the Twin Towers on September 11, 2001; that depleted uranium weaponry would be used; that hundreds of thousands of innocent Iraqis would be killed; and that a "war on terrorism" by definition is never-ending. Assuming that knowledge, supposing that rather than 80% of Americans being committed to following administration leaders, that number were inverted and only 20% agreed with their political leadership . . . would the Iraq War have happened? Probably not. A consensus that is informed and armed with proper information has the power to control events.

Tragically, the information to make informed decisions was available—it simply was not touted by the establishment news media. Because the large majority of Americans felt they were hearing truth, they saw no need to search further. At this juncture we must return to the Lord's constant admonition to refrain from placing our trust in "the arm of flesh." Decisions of the magnitude which we have recently witnessed transcend party loyalty and blind followership. Instead, these are decisions which must first be studied, then prayed over, and then acted upon.

Unfortunately, because we are sometimes negligent in fulfilling responsibilities and because we lack the power to control the ballot box, losses to our agency and freedoms that we take for granted are frequently lost. The inalienable rights of "life, liberty, and the pursuit of happiness," many of which are clearly defined in the Bill of Rights, have been abrogated. Is there any way to get them back?

Freedom's price: Two examples of Nephite prophets and military leaders

Moroni, 74BC to 64BC. The price of liberty and freedom come at great cost—no one understood this better than the first Moroni mentioned of the *Book of Mormon.* Appointed commander of the Nephite armies at the age of twenty-five, he led the Nephites into battles with Lamanites for the cause of liberty. Alma wrote that under Moroni's direction, the Nephites "were inspired by a better cause, for they were not fighting for monarchy nor power but they were fighting for their homes and their liberties, their wives and their children, and their all, yea for their rites of worship and their church. And they were doing that which they felt was the duty which they owed to their God."[5] As Moroni inspired his troops to battle, he did it "with these thoughts—yea, the thoughts of their lands, their liberty, yea, their freedom from bondage." Coming against their enemies, then, the Nephite armies "cried with one voice unto the Lord their God, for their liberty and freedom from bondage."[6]

Victorious, the armies of the Nephites went back to their homes and families, only to once again stray—failing to recognize that their blessings came through the hand of God. The wordsmith, Amalickiah, now desired the kingship and members of the Church as well as others, boosted by their pride, offered their support to him. Moroni was again distressed at how quickly the Nephites would give away their freedoms

> . . . *and he rent his coat; and he took a piece thereof, and wrote upon it—In memory of our God, our religion, and freedom, and our peace, our wives, and our children—and he fastened it upon the end of a pole.*
>
> *And he fastened on his head-plate and his breastplate, and his shields, and girded on his armor about his loins; and he took the pole, which had on the end thereof his rent coat (and he called it the title of liberty) and he bowed himself to the earth, and he prayed mightily unto his God for the blessings of liberty to rest upon his brethren, so long as there should a band of Christians remain to possess the land—*[7]

Moroni was loved by his people, they listened, and many soon recognized the far-reaching consequences of their misplaced support. Moroni taught them that "whosoever will maintain this title upon the land, let them come forth in the strength of the Lord, and enter into a covenant that they will maintain their rights, and their religion, that the Lord God may bless them."[8]

Again the Nephites were victorious, this time over the Amalickiahites, because they "were inspired by a better cause." Moroni, though, understanding the vacillation of the Nephites—their propensity toward pride and their reluctance to safeguard their freedom—mandated that the Title of Liberty be attached to "every tower which was in all the land." Going to the defeated Amalickiahites, he offered the choice to either "enter into a covenant to support the cause of freedom, that they might maintain a free government" or "be put to death." Obviously, "there were but few who denied the covenant of freedom."[9]

Learning of this option in today's world, most readers are shocked. True, it must be understood that this covenant was put forth by a prophet of God and is only invoked on a case by case basis—but it does emphasize the vitality and necessity of freedom. Yet, on further pondering, blood has always been the price of freedom. No lesson in the *Book of Mormon* is so pronounced and graphic as the sacrifice paid for liberty. Could the Lord really expect us to have the same dedication and need as the ancient Nephites?

Lachoneus and Gidgiddoni, 17AD to 26AD. Shortly before the visit of Jesus Christ to the New World, the Gadianton Robbers, the chief secret combination among Lehi's descendants, had a great deal of power. The primary reason for their increased power was the iniquity of the people—both Lamanites and Nephites—who saw that they could monetarily gain by union with the combination. Those that did not join them became fearful of their power and felt compelled to fight them "to maintain their rights, and the privileges of their church and their worship, and their freedom and their liberty."[10] After battling back-and-forth, Lachoneus, the Nephite governor, received a letter from Giddianhi, the leader of the Gadianton Robbers. In it, readers readily see the gift of flattery and wordsmithing often employed by Satan:

> *Lachoneus, most noble and chief governor . . . .*
> *[I] do give unto you exceedingly great praise because of your firmness and the firmness of your people, in maintaining that which ye suppose to be your right and liberty; yea, ye do stand well, as if ye were supported by the hand of a god, in the defense of your liberty, and your property, and your country . . . .*
> *. . . feeling for your welfare, because of your firmness in that which ye believe to be right, and your noble spirit in the field of battle.*[11]

Not unlike condescension and flattery used in political circles today, Giddianhi appealed to Lachoneus' through pride and artificial friendship. Following his build-up, because of his false admiration toward Lachoneus, he offered to allow the governor and his followers to "unite with us and become acquainted with our secret works, and become our brethren that ye may be like unto us—not our slaves but our brethren and partners in all our substance." Should Lachoneus say "No," however, he was bluntly told that "ye shall become extinct."[12]

Lachoneus appointed Gidgiddoni, a man with the spirit of revelation, a great prophet, and the chief judge, to lead the forces against the secret combination. Battles ensued and "there never was known so great a slaughter among all the people of Lehi since he left Jerusalem."[13] As warfare progressed, "the Nephites were continually marching out by day and by night, and falling upon their armies, and cutting them off by thousands and tens of thousands."[14]

This is one of the major wars in the Book of Mormon leaving a substantial part of the population dead. It didn't need to be a war—Giddianhi had offered peace and brotherhood and the protection of human life. Preserving life, however, was meaningless to Lachoneus without freedom. Culminating the final victory, the righteous Nephites cried

> *May the Lord preserve his people in righteousness and in holiness of heart, that they may caused to be felled to the earth all who shall seek to slay them because of power and secret combinations . . . .*[15]

The righteous Nephites offered their lives and all that they had to be free of secret combinations. It was a costly war taking time, property, resources, and lives—yet they felt that their sacrifice was well worth the price. What can we learn from them?

Freedom's price: the Founding Fathers

Patrick Henry offered one of the most quoted speeches precipitating the American Revolution. He reiterated what many felt but hadn't expressed as eloquently and he is generally credited with moving the Continental Congress from a position of debate to commitment in pursuing the war with England. On March 23, 1775 he spoke to the congressional body saying:

> *Should I keep back my opinions at such a time, through fear of giving offense, I should consider myself as guilty of treason towards my country, and of an act of disloyalty toward the Majesty of Heaven, which I revere above all earthly kings . . . .*
>
> *Is life so dear, or peace so sweet, as to be purchased at the price of chains and slavery? Forbid it, Almighty God! I know not what course others may take; but as for me, give me liberty or give me death.*

Patrick Henry was representative of the sentiments toward freedom held by the nation's founders. These were not ordinary men but "wise men who [the Lord] raised up" to accomplish freedom's task—to spearhead (1) the redemption of America by the shedding of blood, and (2) the formation of a "Constitution of the people which [the Lord] suffered to be established . . . for the rights and protection of all flesh according to just and holy principles."[16]

The Founding Fathers and those separatists of their generation in America were committed to the ideal of liberty. Their commitment far exceeded their oratory to the point of declaring open treason—punishable by death—in their execution of the Declaration of Independence. In it, they declared their complete allegiance to liberty; to "mutually pledge to each other our lives, our fortunes and our sacred honor." With them, thousands of patriots fought for freedom; many offering the ultimate sacrifice—hence, the Lord would say that they "redeemed the land by the shedding of blood."

We easily recognize many of the names surrounding our history, but the Lord raised up many others to set in motion freedom's cause. There were fifty-six signers of the Declaration of Independence, a document so loaded with treason that the names of the signers were kept secret for six months following their signing. Of the august body, nine died during the war; five were captured by the British; eighteen had their homes looted and/or burnt; two were wounded in battle; and two lost sons during the war.

Jeff Jacoby wrote in the *Boston Globe* on July 4, 2000, about some of the personal sacrifices made by the founders— names of signers to the Declaration of Independence that most are unfamiliar with:

> *Thomas Nelson Jr. of Virginia raised $2 million for the patriots' cause on his own personal credit. The government never reimbursed him, and repaying the loans wiped out his entire estate. During the Battle of Yorktown, his house, which had been seized by the British, was occupied by General Cornwallis. Nelson quietly urged the gunners to fire on his own home. They did so, destroying it. He was never again a man of wealth. He died bankrupt and was buried in an unmarked grave.*

> *Richard Stockton, a judge on New Jersey's supreme court, was betrayed by loyalist neighbors. He was dragged from his bed and thrown in prison, where he was brutally beaten and starved. His lands were devastated, his horses stolen, his library burnt. He was freed in 1777, but his health had so deteriorated that he died within five years. His family lived on charity the rest of their lives.*

> *In the British assault on New York, Francis Lewis's home and property were pillaged. His wife was captured and imprisoned; so harshly was she treated that she died soon after her release. Lewis spent the remainder of his days in relative poverty.*

John Hart, the Speaker of the New Jersey Assembly, was forced to flee in the winter of 1776, at the age of 65, from his wife's bedside. While he hid in forests and caves, his home was demolished, his fields and mill laid waste, and his 13 children put to flight. When it was finally safe for him to return, he found his wife dead, his children missing, and his property decimated. He never saw any of his family again and died, a shattered man, in 1779.

What price freedom? Although the Lord "raised up" these people to usher freedom's standard, there were no promises of glory and safety. They gave themselves because of a higher commitment or, in Moroni's words, they "were inspired by a better cause." Their lives were secondary to that cause.

The price of freedom: modern prophets

President David O. McKay told the saints that "there are things that are worse than death—one is to be deprived of our liberty."[17] Likewise President Ezra Taft Benson understood the growing sacrifices that would be paid for freedom. He said, "The longer we wait, the heavier the chains, the deeper the blood . . ."[18] Warning of impending troubled times because of diminishing freedoms, President Benson further warned that:

To all who have discerning eyes, it is apparent that the republican form of government established by our noble forefathers cannot long endure once fundamental principles are abandoned. Momentum is gathering for another conflict—a repetition of the crisis of 200 years ago. This collision of ideas is worldwide.[19]

Adding to President Benson's understanding of freedom's price, is the counsel of President J. Reuben Clark, who was recognized as a constitutional scholar throughout the country and was engaged in notable government service. In addition to his recognized legal background, he served as a counselor to three church presidents. In an article for Latter-day Saints about the vitality of the Constitution, he wrote:

> . . . *I say to you that the price of liberty is and always has been blood, human blood, and if your liberties are lost, we shall never regain them except at the price of blood. They must not be lost!*[20]

President Clark's caution was valid. Throughout the history of civilization freedom has only come with the shedding of blood. Even with the continuing lessons of history and the scriptures, however, the thought of pledging our lives, our fortunes and our sacred honor seems distant and foreign. Many feel that we live in an enlightened age, that we are citizens of a free country, and that, frankly, "all is well in Zion." Oh, certainly there are things going on around us that are not good, but as long as we live our own lives properly and raise our children to do the same, everything will be all right. Unfortunately, this is the same doctrine that has produced many of our latter-day troubles.

President Ezra Taft Benson once observed that

> *Our civilization and our people are seemingly afraid to be revolutionary. We are too "broadminded" to challenge what we do not believe in. We are afraid of being intolerant—uncouth— ungentlemanly. We have become lukewarm in our beliefs . . . .*
>
> *This is a sad commentary on a civilization which has given to mankind the greatest achievements and progress ever known. But it is even a sadder commentary on those of us who call ourselves Christians, who thus betray the ideals given to us by the Son of God himself.*[21]

This is another way of saying that Latter-day Saints are "nice" people. We offend as few as possible and avoid making controversial statements that might label us as "extremist" or politically-charged. In our efforts to be neutral, however, we inevitably take sides with those who would allow our freedoms to dissipate. This is not an area for tight-rope walking or being "nice." Rather than shirking from controversy, the Lord's counsel has always been one of boldness. He has commanded us to (1) "be anxiously engaged in a good cause and do many things of [our] own free will;" (2) speak up, for "with some [He] is not well pleased, for they will not open their mouths" and "if they are not more faithful unto me, it shall be taken away, even that which they have;" and (3) to "waste and wear out our lives in bringing to light the hidden things of darkness." Understanding the commission given to the Saints in the Latter-days, President John Taylor taught that members of the Church should be definite and not conciliatory to constitutional abuse. Whether others might allow freedoms to be given away and might be "so blind and infatuated as to trample under foot the Constitution and other safeguards provided for the liberties of man," Latter-day Saints will ". . . stand up for our rights and protect ourselves in every proper way, legally and constitutionally, and dispute inch by inch every step that is taken to deprive us of our rights and liberties."[22]

Today's sacrifices

Fortunately, the time for extreme sacrifices that we read about in scriptural and historical accounts has still not arrived. The sacrifices that we are called upon to make today are not life-threatening; but they do take us away from our worldly pursuits and certainly from comfort and convenience. Anxious engagement in a righteous cause will always draw us away from ways that we would rather spend our time. "Anxious" indicates a strong desire while "engagement" is literally a personal encounter—both are qualities the Lord demands as we exercise our free will in furthering a righteous cause.

The Lord further explains what is required to know a righteous cause. Section 84 of the *Doctrine and Covenants* is a profound call to listen to the "voice of the spirit." Listening to the Lord's voice is so important that he told the saints:

> *And whoso receiveth not my voice is not acquainted with my voice and is not of me.*
> *And by this you may know the righteous from the wicked . . .*
> *Doctrine and Covenants 84:52-53*

What a terrible thing—not to be acquainted with the Lord's voice! It is so terrible that the Lord categorized those not hearing his spiritual promptings as being "wicked." That is because those not living close to his spirit have made a conscious choice to be numb to his voice. On the other hand, we are given to understand that living close to the Lord's spirit, we will know the things we should do and that he will tell us how we should be "anxiously engaged." In this scripture, he explained that not all of us hear his voice—why? The following verse relates that "[our] minds in times past have been darkened because of unbelief and because [we] have treated lightly the things [we] have received."

To unclutter our minds and allow the Lord's voice to give us direction, we must overcome unbelief by faith and treat with respect and sincerity "the things [we] have received." To be perfectly clear, the Lord defined exactly the things members of the Church treat lightly that preclude hearing his voice. Those things have a great bearing upon our current discussion and the warnings from the Nephite prophets to our generation. The Lord admonished us to "remember the new covenant, even the *Book of Mormon* and the former commandments which I have given them, not only to say, but to do according to that which I have written."[23]

He taught us to remember all of his commandments, and then specifically said not only to talk about the *Book of Mormon*, but to do and incorporate its principles into our lives. We must never forget the doctrinal messages nor the wonderful display of God's power throughout its pages; but likewise, we must not forget the specific warnings for us. The warnings are explicit and the identifiers impossible to overlook. Hence the Lord's command to our dispensation: "not only to say, but to do according to that which I have written."

A latter-day example: anxious engagement

The Lord expects his saints to be people of action. One of the most frequently quoted scriptures in the *Doctrine and Covenants* is:

> *Verily I say, men should be anxiously engaged in a good cause, and do many things of their own free will, and bring to pass much righteousness.*
>
> Doctrine and Covenants 58:27

Fortunately, we usually don't need to spend a great deal of time wondering how to be involved. As we attune ourselves, the Lord fulfills his promise that "the Spirit giveth light to every man that cometh into the world; and the Spirit enlighteneth every man through the world, that hearkeneth to the voice of the Spirit."[24] "Every man" must certainly include you and me.

In a former chapter that highlighted today's concerns of a one-world government, we read several writings from Richard G. Wilkins. Brother Wilkins is a former bishop and a law professor at the J. Reuben Clark School of Law at Brigham Young University. His personal story of involvement is instructive for Latter-day Saints:

> *In June 1996, about nine months after the Proclamation [on the Family] was issued, contrary to personal plans and what seemed to be simple common sense, I attended my first UN negotiation, the Second United Nations Conference on Human Settlements (or*

"Habitat II") in Istanbul, Turkey. I had been urged to attend by several scholars from Catholic universities I had met over the years, as well as members of various nongovernmental organizations. I did not want to go. I was not an expert in international law and I honestly did not believe my participation could make any difference. Furthermore, I was having too much fun to run off to Istanbul: I was playing Tevye (complete with a full beard) opposite my wife, Melany, who was playing Golde in Fiddler on the Roof at the Hale Center Theater in Orem, Utah. I like teaching law. I enjoy legal scholarship. But I love acting with my family.

Nevertheless, soon after Fiddler opened, I kept waking up in the middle of the night, fretting about Istanbul. Finally, about two weeks before the conference, Melany told me that I should apply for an expedited passport and try to register as a nongovernmental delegate. As a result, I left Utah before the closing night of Fiddler— without shaving my "Tevye" beard—carrying a passport photo that did not comply with BYU's dress and grooming standards. Melany, shortly before I left, slipped a copy of the Proclamation into my suitcase with a simple explanation, "You may find this helpful," she said.

My experience in Istanbul in June 1996 was extraordinary. I was one of ten people selected from among twenty-five thousand nongovernmental delegates to address the plenary session of the conference. I discussed "International Law and the Family." With words and concepts taken from the copy of the Proclamation that Melany put in my suitcase, I urged international lawmakers to remember the importance of marriage, motherhood, fatherhood, childbearing, family, and faith.[25]

If asked about his contribution to combating the adversary's plan "to overthrow the freedom of all lands, nations, and countries," Brother Wilkins would reply that "My wife and I simply followed the Spirit." That Spirit, of course, has a great deal to do with being "anxiously engaged" in doing good things.

Following Brother Wilkins' address to Habitat II in Istanbul, some amazing and unexpected things happened. He reported that "Within thirty-six hours an international coalition had formed around concepts I had taken from the principles of the Proclamation. The conference concluded by acknowledging many of these principles and affirming that 'the family is the basic unit of society and as such should be strengthened.'"[26]

From this point, Brother Wilkins involved other Brigham Young University personnel, organized the World Family Policy Center, and began attending more U.N. conferences and committees. In 1999, the World Family Policy Center held its first international meeting in Provo with delegates, diplomats, and scholars from around the world in attendance.

> *From this gathering in 1999, an unusual international coalition of scholars, world leaders, and religious communities began to form around concepts and ideas contained not only in the Proclamation but in . . . the Universal Declaration of Human Rights . . . . This coalition emerged none too soon. As the new millennium dawned, it was becoming increasingly clear that international law could exert a powerful force on national laws relating to home and family life.*[27]

Then, in 2003, the nation of Qatar (a small country on the Arabian Peninsula) approached the World Policy Center with the intent of promoting an international conference on families. The national leadership visited Brigham Young University and met with the First Presidency of The Church of Jesus Christ of Latter-day Saints. Then, at the delegation's request, H. Reese Hansen, Dean of the Law School at BYU, and Richard G. Wilkins went to Doha (the capitol of Qatar) and began planning the Doha International Conference for the Family. Coinciding with the timing of the conference in 2004, Qatar chaired the "Group of 77:" the largest bloc within the countries of the United Nations. As an outgrowth of the 2004 conference, the Doha International Institute for Family Studies and Development was initiated to further enunciate the indispensable position of the natural family throughout the world.

A great deal has happened since the first U.N. conference attended by Brother Wilkins in 1996. Yet, it was at that conference that he was approached by an ambassador from a Middle Eastern country and asked, "Where have you been?" He was told that world leaders had been waiting for someone to speak out; to support the traditional family values that academicians within the world organization had been deriding for years. For Brother Wilkins, "Where have you been?" was a life-changing question. His experiences caused him to reflect that:

> *This question should be considered by every member of The Church of Jesus Christ of Latter-day Saints and particularly by academicians, scholars, and researchers. In 1995, the Proclamation was issued to warn and forewarn the Church and the world of a pressing need to return to the "standards, doctrines, and practices relative to the family which the prophets, seers and revelators of this church have repeatedly stated throughout its history." . . . Latter-day Saints everywhere should assess whether they have heeded the call to "promote those measures designed to maintain and strengthen the family as the fundamental unit of society."[28]*

Others may not enjoy the profound international influence that Richard Wilkins has experienced; however, the Lord's call to be "anxiously engaged" in promoting family and Constitutional ideals was given to all members of the Church. Likewise, all will painfully bear the dreaded day when we "awake to our awful situation."

The engagement admonished by the Lord is involvement in arenas that influence others. The Lord once said that his Church was the "salt of the earth" meaning that his followers would "flavor" the earth with values and ideals that might otherwise be lost in a world rejecting modern revelation. We, through "anxious engagement" are the conduits of the sorely needed ideals and principles.

Eternal consequences of neglecting freedom

How serious is the commission to stand up for our liberties, the Constitution, the Proclamation on the Family, or any of our inherent freedoms? According to President Ezra Taft Benson, our involvement in the establishment and preservation of freedom has eternal consequences.

> *Any Christian constitutionalist who retreats from this battle jeopardizes his life here and hereafter. Seldom has so much responsibility hung on so few so heavily . . . .*[29]

> *The cause of freedom is a most basic part of our religion. Our position on freedom helped get us to this earth and it can make a difference whether we get back home or not.*[30]

Working toward the preservation of freedom is not an optional part of Mormonism! Too much about it and our accountability to preserve it has been revealed. It will come at considerable effort and sacrifice and, if the price is paid here, it will be costly. If it is paid hereafter, it will be tragic.

Chapter 10— Endnotes

1   J. Reuben Clark, 1938, *Vital Speeches* 5:176-177.
         quoted in Jerreld Newquist, *Prophets, Principles and National Survival*, Publishers Press. Salt Lake City: 1964. pp. 374-375.

2   *Doctrine and Covenants* 89:4

3   Ether 8:25

4   2 Nephi 2:27

5   Alma 43:45-46

6   Alma 43:48-49

7   Alma 46:13

8   Alma 46:20

9   Alma 46:35-36

10   3 Nephi 2:13

11   3 Nephi 3:2-10

12   3 Nephi 3:1-11

13   3 Nephi 4:11

14   3 Nephi 4:21

15   3 Nephi 4:29

16   *Doctrine and Covenants* 101:76-80

17   David O. McKay, "Statements on Communism and the Constitution of the United States," p. 39, as quoted in Newquist, Op. Cit., p. 487.

18   Ezra Taft Benson, April General Conference, 1965. *Improvement Era*, June, 1965, p. 539.

19   Ezra Taft Benson, *Teachings of Ezra Taft Benson*, Op. Cit. p. 623.

20   J. Reuben Clark, *Church News*, November 29, 1952.

21   Ezra Taft Benson, September 22, 1962, as quoted in
        Newquist, *Op. Cit.* p. 236.

22   John Taylor, *Journal of Discourses* 25:349-350. October
        19, 1884.

23   *Doctrine and Covenants* 84:57

24   *Doctrine and Covenants* 84:46

25   Richard G. Wilkins, *BYU Studies*, "The Proclamation on
        the Family: Ten Years of Hope," Fall, 2005, pp. 9-
        10.

26   *Ibid.* p. 10

27   *Ibid.* p. 11

28   *Ibid.* pp. 19-20

29   Ezra Taft Benson, *Teachings, Op. Cit.* p. 591.

30   *Ibid.* p. 656

Part 2

TODAY

Introduction to Part 2

WHERE ARE WE TODAY?

The largest obstacle in writing about secret combinations is their secrecy. Fortunately, in historical writing we are able to develop a sense of perspective and examine the various pieces of the puzzle as they come together. Surprisingly, some of the main goals have not been veiled and are fairly easy to distinguish. The themes of world government and minimizing sovereignty are stated objectives that continually move to the forefront in elitist literature. Also, although war is not a stated objective, its redundant use to arrive at the goals of power and gain, is easily identifiable. Private control of printing and valuing money is another feature of the secret combination that is visible.

In much of our historical writing, we have been indebted to Dr. Carrol Quigley for his insider expose of the international bankers and to Dr. W. Cleon Skousen for his insightful review of their activities which have shaped so much of our world. Our premise throughout the text has been that secret combinations have been influential in government and world history. While their activities have certainly been prominent in world affairs, they have been especially noticeable in modern America. This was predicted by the prophets who understood that the wealth of the "promised land" would foster more attention and interest—thereby bringing more deceit to America under the control of secret combinations. Using hindsight, it is always easier to determine what has happened and to see the "big picture." Therefore, we are able to see what happened during the tumultuous times surrounding World War 1, the creation of the Federal Reserve System, and the foundations of the League of Nations, whereas those living through those experiences could not see so clearly. Likewise, during our time in history, it is sometimes difficult to put all of the pieces together and grasp the significance of the events transpiring around us. Yet, the statement about "connecting the dots" does not mean a great deal unless we are able to bring past revelations to the here and now.

There are some dangers. In identifying many of today's events that have the earmarks of secret combination activity, we invariably must name people. It is well to remember that all the players in world and national events are not part of the conspiracy of which Moroni warns. Many are innocent while others act and unknowingly give their assent—perhaps ignorantly moving the agenda of the great secret combination forward. That disclaimer given, it also stands to reason that there is a degree of complicity that others may share. At the highest levels of the secret combination, we know that the shroud of secrecy is more heavily cloaked in contrast to actions that are more observable.

We will also need to understand that—lacking the historical perspective that we have enjoyed to this point—this section of our book will view many unfinished pictures. All of the pieces have not come together yet and all of the dots haven't been positioned on the page. As the historian said, "We see through a glass darkly"—we will see enough to identify the outline of the image but we won't be able to understand all of its significance until we are able to see through the glass clearly. That will only happen with the passage of more time and we once more gain the historical perspective. At this point, however, we are able to see enough to know that events are being manipulated in secrecy for the power and gain of a few resulting in great loss of freedom for the majority.

Because of the glaring inconsistencies in so many current events, researchers have begun to explore areas that have previously been the prerogatives of "conspiracy nuts." Today, for the person interested in "making sense" of news events and understanding how so many bad decisions can be made, a plethora of scholarly material is available. Either a visit to the internet searching various key words or a visit to a local bookstore is all that is needed to study happenings beyond the 10 o'clock news.

Typical of new writings shedding light on current events is Michel Chossudovsky's book *America's "War on Terrorism."* (Second edition, 2005) Chossudovsky, a professor of economics at a Canadian university, demonstrates the interrelationships of several of today's large issues with their well-known but unpublicized nuances. A list of chapter headings will suffice to show the direction of much current research.

September 11
    Background: Behind September 11
    Where was Osama Bin Laden on 9/11?
    Who is Osama Bin Laden?
    Washington Supports International Terrorism
    Cover –up or Complicity
War and Globalization
    War and the Hidden Agenda
    The Trans-Afghan Pipeline
    America's War Machine
    The American Empire
    Disarming the New World Order
    Political Deception: the Missing Link Behind 9/11
    Doctoring Official Transcripts
The Disinformation Campaign
    War Propaganda: Fabricating an Outside Enemy

9/11 and the Iran-Contra Scandal
Providing a Face for the Enemy: Who is
*   Abu Musab Al Zarqawa?*
Protecting Al Qaeda Fighters in the War Theater
The Deportation of Civilians to the Guantanamo
*   Concentration Camp*
The New World Order
*   War Criminals in High Office*
*   The Spoils of War: Afghanistan's Multibillion Dollar*
*   Heroin Trade*
*   Foreknowledge of 9/11*
*   On the Morning of 9/11: What Happened on the Planes?*
*   America's Preemptive War Doctrine*
*   The Post 9/11 Terror Alerts*
*   Big Brother: Towards the Homeland Security State*
*   The London 7/7 Bomb Attacks*
Intelligence Based on Plagiarism: The British "Intelligence" on Iraq
The Financial Interests Behind the World Trade Center Lease
(from Michel Chossudovsky, America's "War on Terrorism." Second Edition,
2005. Global Research: Quebec, Canada.)

Many of these topics have been referred to in this book
although most have not been treated in the length they deserve.
Now we will specifically look at three recent events; all showing
inconsistency and some manipulation.   Reading these events,
remember to apply the criteria that were laid out in Ether 8:
secrecy, conspiracy, accumulation of power and gain, and
destruction of the freedom of all nations.   This part of our text
will treat specific events that have either transpired in or had their
foundation in the United States.   The unfolding episodes we will
review are the bombing of the Murrah Federal Building in
Oklahoma City; the events surrounding September 11, 2001 and
the airline hijackings; and the Iraq War.

The first two are unique in that they deal with terrorism—
virtually the only attacks in the United States that have been
labeled such.   One of the problems that we face in determining

guilt is that the very definition of terrorism includes credit for the act perpetrated. In other words, a terrorist attack will always attach the culprit's identification to the act so that group will be feared—hence the term "terrorism." Our problem in both the Oklahoma City bombing and the attack on the World Trade Center is that no terrorist group has claimed credit for the destruction and lives lost; thus, virtually defeating the usefulness of the terrorism.

In presenting these events and their significance to our review, we will frequently use a dialog format consisting of questions and answers. Because most of these events have received recent attention, a short bibliography of both publications and internet websites will follow each event.

Chapter 11

THE OKLAHOMA CITY BOMBING, 1995

A time of national unrest

Historical events, even those of modern history, must be examined in their context. As seen from other issues that we have studied, oftentimes meanings and links are clarified as we examine simultaneous events. Looking at the "big picture," we see rationale for events to transpire that frequently work upon other incidents. Isolated, an event may appear very innocuous— however, taken in context, we may find reasoning that was missed when studied individually.

Here are some occurrences that were happening or being discussed during that April of 1995 when the bombing occurred: The summer of 1992—just three years earlier—saw the tragedy at Ruby Ridge, Idaho, the deaths of Vickie and Sammy Weaver and the wounding of Randy Weaver by agents of the federal Bureau of Alcohol, Tobacco and Firearms (BATF) and the FBI. Then, just exactly one year prior to the bombing of the Murrah Federal Building in Oklahoma City, we watched the dramatic events of David Koresh and the Branch Davidians at Waco, Texas, on our television sets. Both events were still fresh in the minds of Americans and several lawsuits concerning both were making their way through the federal courts. For the most part, public sympathies were with the Weaver family in Idaho and the Branch Davidians in Waco, Texas, where 74 people lost their lives. In both cases, it was alleged that federal law enforcement personnel had used entrapment as justification for their involvement. These two events, each reinforcing the other, were constantly referred to in news reports and were the topics of books and other media. Where once the FBI had been accorded the strongest praise among Americans, because of these two tragedies federal law enforcement sunk to its lowest ebb in popularity.

Fueling public opinion that April was the projected Congressional involvement surrounding these events. The Ruby Ridge incident was set to come under investigation during the summer of 1995; and hearings on the Waco disaster were scheduled for May of 1995. Added to these emotional happenings and the BATF conduct at each were three other volatile issues also scheduled for, or undergoing then-current Congressional hearings:

(1) The Whitewater Development Corporation ("Whitewater")—A scandal involving President Bill Clinton and his wife Hillary having to do with illegal loans while the President was the Governor of Arkansas. This issue was a watershed for several other issues and created a negative attitude toward federal government. This attitude was exacerbated by document shredding and fifteen people directly related to Whitewater found guilty and convicted of crimes—none relating to Whitewater. Although this had received some prior attention from the Congress, it was officially slated for investigation beginning in May of 1995.

(2) The controversial death of White House and Whitewater Counsel Vince Foster. This was officially ruled a suicide but there were enough peculiarities and questions surrounding his death that many felt a murder had taken place. Because of the apparent investigation inconsistencies, Congress

agreed to open an inquiry on Vince Foster's death in May of 1995.

(3) There were several allegations that Mena, Arkansas, had been a place for drug smuggling into the United States. This was said to have involved some government and law enforcement officials including the then-governor of the state, Bill Clinton. As a result of certain evidence found, this was also to have become an item of Congressional investigation in May of 1995.

These issues crowded newspapers and news magazines during the spring of 1995. Then, on April 19, 1995, these topics all seemed trivial and paled in the shadow of a new calamity: the bombing of the federal building in Oklahoma City, Oklahoma, which left 168 people dead and another 500 hurt and wounded.

The Murrah Federal Building bombing

Amid the negative attitude and "bad press" given to government, the federal building at Oklahoma City became the target of a terrorist attack. This was the first of modern terrorist attacks to occur in the United States. In fact, this took place at a time when many didn't know the meaning of "terrorist;" or they understood the word to be solely applied to Palestinian or other Middle Eastern countries vying for world attention—not the context of domestic terrorism.

On the morning of April 19, 1995, we heard that a "right-wing extremist," had blown up the Murrah Federal Building in Oklahoma City. Very soon following the explosion of a rented Ryder truck packed with fertilizer explosives, Timothy McVeigh was apprehended. Shortly afterwards, an accomplice named Terry Nichols was also captured and both were eventually placed on trial and sentenced for the senseless killing of 168 people, including many children in the building's day-care center.

At the time, the whole thing seemed bazaar. McVeigh was a loner who had been a decorated war veteran from Desert

Storm, the war in Kuwait. He had evidently become disgruntled with America when he resumed civilian life; was very distraught from the events that had taken place at Waco, Texas, just a year earlier; and sought out his own personal revenge. He and Nichols had made the 4,800 lb. bomb the day before and had brought it to the Murrah Federal Building where it was left in the parking garage to ignite and demolish the building.

On June 11, 2001, Timothy McVeigh was put to death by lethal injection. Later, Terry Nichols received a life sentence with no possibility of parole. The media essentially reported that the tragic event of Oklahoma City—the worst terrorist attack to have ever taken place on American soil to date—was solved by capturing and sentencing these two men.

Were there others who might have been involved in the bombing?

To understand the grounds on which McVeigh and Nichols were prosecuted, there are certain assumptions which must be made. The most obvious is, could the Ryder truck loaded with fertilizer explosives do the inflicted damage to the building? Another question which must be posed is, could McVeigh and Nichols have concocted the bomb given their expertise and technical abilities? In answering these questions, we will also approach the possibility of other accomplices to the bombing.

The first question and the one that troubles most investigators was the damage sustained. Because Timothy McVeigh was prosecuted as the lone culprit using only a truck bomb to damage the building, any damage beyond what the truck bomb could inflict necessarily meant that there were others involved. It was not long after the bombing that military explosives expert, General Benton K. Partin, saw pictures of the damage and raised several doubts about assigning it to a single truck bomb.

Was this man really an expert, or just a person with a high rank?

Brigadier General Benton K. Partin is retired from the U.S. Air Force. He is the former commander of the Air Force Armament Technology Laboratory with 25 years experience in the design and development of bombs. He has completed all coursework towards a Ph.D. in engineering.

Why couldn't the explosives in the Ryder truck have done the damage?

Here are some of the comments made by General Partin:

> *When I first saw the picture of the truck bomb's asymmetrical damage to the Federal Building in Oklahoma, my immediate reaction was that the pattern of damage would have been technically impossible without supplementary demolition charges at some of the reinforced concrete bases inside the building, a standard demolition technique.*

> *. . . reinforced concrete targets in large buildings are hard targets to blast. I know of no way possible to reproduce the apparent building damage through simply a truck bomb effort.*[1]

Because of so much publicity by explosives experts to the effect that the McVeigh truck bomb could not have been responsible for the damage incurred at the Murrah Building, the government commissioned its own study. The Armament Directorate at the Wright Laboratory at Elgin Air Force Base in Florida was given the task of demonstrating the feasibility of an ANFO (ammonium nitrate fuel oil) bomb weighing 4,800 lbs. exploding from the parking area and significantly destroying the building. The government study, given the title of the Elgin Blast Effects Study (EBES), was just as damaging to the "McVeigh lone truck" bombing theory as prior experts had said. The conclusions of the study were:

> Due to these conditions, it is impossible to ascribe the damage that occurred on April 19, 1995 to a single truck bomb containing 4,800 of ANFO. In fact, the maximum predicted damage to the floor panels of the Murrah Federal Building is equal to approximately 1% of the total floor area of the building. Furthermore, due to the lack of symmetrical damage pattern at the Murrah Building, it would be inconsistent with the results of the ETS [Elgin Test Structure—a mock restructure of the Murrah Federal Building] test one to state that all of the damage to the Murrah Building is the result of the truck bomb.
>
> The damage to the Murrah Federal Building is consistent with damage resulting from mechanically coupled devices [explosive charges] placed locally within the structure . . . .
>
> It must be concluded that the damage at the Murrah Federal Building is not the result of the truck bomb itself, but rather due to other factors such as locally placed charges within the building itself . . . .[2]

Take note that this official evidence stating that McVeigh's truck bomb could not have done the damage that was sustained by the Murrah Federal Building was the result of a government study. Mike Smith, a Georgia-based civil engineer, was then commissioned to review the report. His statements were equally damaging to the "McVeigh lone truck" case:

> The results of the Blast Effect Test One of the Elgin Test Structure present strong evidence that a single ammonium nitrate and fuel oil device of approximately 4,800 lbs. placed inside a truck could not have caused the damage to the Murrah Federal Building experienced on April 19, 1995. . . . the air-coupled blast produced from this 4,800 lb. device would not have damaged the columns and

beams of the Murrah Building enough to produce a catastrophic failure.[3]

In essence, what these and a myriad of other studies demonstrated was that a fertilizer bomb such as used by Timothy McVeigh was incapable of severing the building's reinforced concrete. Instead, they demonstrate conclusively that explosive charges must have been set to sever the necessary columns, thus toppling the building. Both the lack of explosive force and more particularly the placement of the truck at a significant distance from the structural columns, prevented the Ryder truck bomb from causing the catastrophe. (For in-depth reporting on this and related topics shedding light on the Oklahoma City bombings, the reader is encouraged to view *The New American* of July 20, 1998, www.thenewamerican.com/tna/1998/vol4no15/vol4no15 _bombs.htm and www.whatreallyhappened.com/RANCHO/ POLITICS/OK/ok.html)

Is there any evidence of other bombs? It seems strange that all of the bombs would have gone off at the same time.

The final official story agreed upon by the media and the government was that McVeigh's Ryder truck had caused all of the damage. Initial reports, though, were somewhat contradictory. The local television station "on the spot" reported that "A bomb has gone off inside the Murrah Building and the bomb squad is clearing out rescue workers because additional bombs have been found."[4] Toni Garrett, a nurse on the scene, reported, "Four people—rescue workers—told us there was a bomb in the building with a timing mechanism set to go off ten minutes after nine." This confirms Oklahoma City Fire Marshall Dick Miller's statement that the bomb had evidently malfunctioned following the initial blast.[5] The CNN transcript of the disaster also refers to multiple bombs.

In addition to reports of other bombs, the seismographic station at Norman, Oklahoma, recorded two separate occurrences which have been attributed to the disaster. The readings showing disturbance are approximately ten seconds apart. It must be said that there are various interpretations of the readings, but one that stands out is that there were separate explosions detonated at the building.

Eyewitness reports substantiate the above findings. Jane Graham, a HUD employee working on the ninth floor and the president of the American Federation of Public Employees, Union Local 3138 in Oklahoma City (whose testimony of other events surrounding the bombing is also significant) recalls being in a meeting when an explosion was felt in the building. Many coworkers thought that it was an earthquake. Sitting at her desk

> *... she recalls, ... seven ... eight ... nine seconds later ... hearing a very large explosion and feeling it coming "up" toward them on the ninth floor from below, within the building. The last thing she remembers before she was knocked unconscious by debris was part of the roof hanging over and seeing blue sky. Her estimation of a 7 – 9 second interval between explosions is very close to the 10-second interval recorded at the Oklahoma Geological Survey seismograph at Norman ...*[6]

How could explosives have been planted without the knowledge of others in the building?

Jane Graham's testimony is also enlightening. It must be emphasized that much of her information is circumstantial, yet certainly worth pursuing. Reviewing a video release of her experiences, author Michael A. O'Camb wrote:

> *On the Friday before the bombing several persons at the Murrah Building saw three men (they took for maintenance or utility workers) "working" in a reserved area of the underground parking structure. These men had what appeared to be a set of plans of "blue*

prints," telephone wire and a large block of "clay." When the three men noticed they were being observed by one of the employees, Jane Graham, a federal government employee of the Department of Housing and Urban Development (HUD) situated in the Murrah Building, they themselves began to act somewhat suspiciously.

It was nearly a year later, while watching a video about the bombing at a friend's house, Jane was taken aback by two men she'd seen on the afternoon before the bombing and the very morning inside the Murrah Federal Building, each wearing the blue uniform (shirt and pants) of General Services Administration (GSA) employees. Jane had never seen these two men before or after this two-day period, and at the time, had thought it strange that two of the regular GSA employees would have been off on the same day, replaced by two temporaries.

The thing that really bothered her were those two men—the two she's seen the previous afternoon and the morning of the bombing—"working" inside the Murrah Building wearing their blue GSA uniforms. The video Jane was watching had been shot shortly after the bombing and here they were outside the building in street clothes accidentally caught on videotape! Why had they changed? The last time she distinctly remembered seeing them it was 8:15 A.M. on April 19ᵗʰ (approximately forty-seven minutes before the bombing.) They had just exited a stairwell that comes directly from the ninth floor down to the hallway they now briskly passed her in. As she turned to watch them they continued down the hallway and exited the building at a fast pace.[7]

Jon Dougherty summed up much of the unanswered information of the bombing in his article "Oklahoma City's Lost Information" in 2001:

Witnesses reported seeing three men in the parking garage of the Murrah Building (it had nine stories above ground and had a four-floor parking garage underneath) working with "electrical equipment and pointing at various parts of the garage in the days before the attack. Many survivors reported that some of these men were dressed in Government Services Administration uniforms but had never seen them before or since.[8]

Weren't there other people seen with Timothy McVeigh? Wasn't there a "John Doe" that the FBI was looking for? What happened to him?

In reality, there were several "John Does" because McVeigh before the bombing seemed always to have been in the company of other individuals. The sketch of the swarthy John Doe that most of us remember was given by those who rented the Ryder truck to him. The same day the bombing occurred, the owner of Elliot's Body Shop in Junction City, Kansas, with a bookkeeper and another mechanic were interviewed and agreed on a composite sketch of both McVeigh and the man who accompanied him. Timothy McVeigh was captured immediately and looked very much like the sketch. The drawing of John Doe 2 was eventually redone but still not found. Finally the FBI reported that the owner, Eldon Elliot, had mistaken John Doe 2 for another man that had been in his shop on the next day. Elliot refused to agree to that solution and was dropped from the investigation. The official answer to John Doe 2 was Elliot's mistaken identity.

Coupled with the John Doe that was advertised, there were several other eyewitness accounts of others seen with McVeigh. Ambrose Evans-Prichard has done a substantial amount of in-depth investigating about the bombing. In his article "John Doe 2" for World Net Daily, (May 31, 2001) in addition to those at Elliot's Body Shop, he documented conversations with another sixteen witnesses who saw McVeigh in the company of others following the truck rental. The interesting fact is that none were called to testify at Timothy McVeigh's trial—a trial that did not use witnesses from the local area but relied on a purchased telephone card to show that he was in Oklahoma City on April 19, 1995. Ignoring the witnesses, the verdict of the trial was that he acted alone with Nichols, his only accomplice in making the truck bomb.

Speaking of Terry Nichols, when we began this discussion, it was also said that there was some question whether McVeigh and Nichols were capable of building the bomb. Why was that so difficult?

When asked about bomb-making and delivery, former legislator Charles Key, who chaired the Oklahoma City Bombing Investigating Committee, said, "Most people don't understand the ammonium nitrate, the diesel fuel, the methane fumes, but experts will tell you you've got a potentially very, very serious problem with all those fumes in close quarters like that. So when you really consider that aspect of it, not to mention driving all those many, many miles to Oklahoma City and that bomb maintaining its integrity—which is another thing experts question—how could this really be pulled off?"[9]

Certainly, with all the public attention given to the bombing and the trials, much of this information would have come to light. Why weren't we told that others besides McVeigh and Nichols were involved?

This is an excellent point and probably the one that invites the most discussion. Few feel that McVeigh was not guilty, although many feel that he was a minor player in a much larger picture. The initial charges against Timothy McVeigh and Terry Nichols included "others unknown." Multiple eyewitnesses identified McVeigh both before and after the bombing with unknown accomplices. These, however, were not pursued by the FBI and the remaining "John Does" were dismissed.

Because of these accounts and apparent specific links of McVeigh to an Aryan supremacist group in nearby Elohim City, former deputy assistant director of the FBI, Danny Coulson, called for renewed research into the bombing in November of 2005. Although Coulson had worked earlier with the case, new information had surfaced that caused him to believe that more people were involved in the attack on the federal building. He called for additional investigative work to be done and said: "I have had significant experience conducting major investigations and in my view, this case is not over."[10]

Just prior to carrying out the death sentence, over 4,000 pages of evidence were given to McVeigh's defense attorney. Although U.S. Attorney General John Ashcroft said that the newly located "lost" information did not impact the case, Danny Coulson observed that "The totality of this information very strongly indicates there are others involved and not charged who were involved at least in conspiratorial acts."[11]

Adding to Coulson's understanding of unpursued accomplices, on May 29, 2001, the CBS 60 Minutes show also offered revealing testimonies. Just five days following the Ashcroft announcement that recently discovered material would make no difference and that the most expensive investigative work ever conducted in the United States ($85 million) was completed, four ex-FBI special agents appeared on the program to challenge the official version. *The New American* magazine gave this synopsis:

> *The four veteran agents: Rick Ojeda, Dan Vogel, Scott Jenkins, and Jim Volz, all worked on the case known at the FBI as "OKBOMB." Although the agents said they could not discuss specifics regarding the case because of a court gag order, they all expressed grave concerns about the handling of the "lost and found" FBI files. Dan Vogel said that he had taken an oath at the FBI "to protect and defend the Constitution of the United States. And as I have been reflecting over my past bureau career, I had come to the conclusion that there was a serious problem in the FBI." According to ex-agent Vogel, the so-called foul-up with the missing files was very serious business involving "possible criminal conduct" that may need "to be presented to a federal grand jury as a criminal case."*
>
> *Former agent Rick Ojeda, who received a commendation from Louis Freeh for his efforts in the bombing case, may have some*

of the most damaging information to reveal. In his CBS interview, Ojeda stated that he became concerned when reports and leads he had turned in seemed to disappear. The day after the CBS broadcast, U.S. Attorney Sean Connelly released an FBI report by Ojeda to McVeigh's attorneys that had still not been included in the DOJ/FBI "comprehensive" file release.[12]

Most of the "lost and found" evidence and the leads referred to by the agents focused on potential accomplices and others who might have acted with McVeigh in the bombing.

With the massive investigation of the bombing, did anyone get "too close" to what had really happened?

There were several people—especially those who were either in the federal building or nearby when the explosions occurred—that come to mind. Mike Loudenslager was a GSA employee who noticed a large amount of explosives brought into the building by Bureau of Alcohol, Tobacco and Firearms (BATF) and Drug Enforcement Administration (DEA) agents. He, with the operator of the day-care center located in the federal building, warned many of the workers as well as parents of children in the day-care center of the danger. As per her licensing agreement, at the completion of some remodeling in the building, the operator notified the fire marshals to come for an inspection. The fire marshals were met by federal agents and denied access to the remodeling—a peculiar situation.

Following this occurrence, Loudenslager and the day-care operator urged many parents and strongly suggested that they withdraw their children, at least temporarily, from the day-care. In his article for the *Free Republic*, O'Camb wrote:

> *Shortly after the bombing, Michael Loudenslager was actively helping in the rescue and recovery effort. A large number of those at the bomb-site either saw or talked with him. During the*

course of the early rescue efforts, however, Mike Loudenslager was seen and heard in a very "heated" confrontation with someone there. Much of his anger stemmed from the fact he felt the B.A.T.F. was in large part responsible not only for the bombing, but for the death and injury to those inside, including all the children.

To the absolute astonishment of a large number of police officers and rescue workers, it was later reported that G.S.A. employee Mike Loudenslager's body had been found inside the Murrah Building the following Sunday, still at his desk, a victim of the 9:02 A.M. bombing! This, mind you, after he's already been seen alive and well by numerous rescue workers at the bomb-site AFTER the bombing! He is also officially listed as one of the 168 bombing fatalities.[13]

Another person who was close to the unfolding events at the Murrah Federal Building was Oklahoma City Police Officer Terrance (Terry) Yeakey. On patrol close to the building, when the explosion occurred, he quickly began assisting the injured as the first law enforcement officer on the scene. What he saw is not exactly clear nor did he publicly go into the specifics about his concerns, but he telephoned his wife later that morning repeatedly saying: "It's not true. It's not what they are saying. It didn't happen that way."

Beginning on that day, Yeakey began his own investigation and eventually compiled nine boxes of files of interviews, videos, and documents pertaining to the bombing. Try as he might, however, he was unable to enlist support from his superiors to the inconsistencies of the bombing events.

As time went on, Yeakey was more and more frustrated. He wrote to a friend, Ramona McDonald, who was also one of those injured in the federal building. Here are some extracts from that letter:

I don't know if you recall everything that happened that morning or not, so I am not sure if you know what I am referring to.

The man that you and I were talking about in the pictures, I have made the mistake of asking too many questions as to his role in the bombing, and was told to back off.

I was told by several officers that he was a ATF agent who was overseeing the bombing plot and at the time the photos were taken he was calling in his report of what had just went down! . . . .

Knowing what I know now, and understanding fully just what went down that morning, makes me ashamed to wear a badge from Oklahoma City's Police Department. I took an oath to uphold the Law and to enforce the Law to the best of my ability. This is something I cannot honestly do and hold my head up proud any longer if I keep my silence as I am ordered to do. . . .

Everyone was behind you until you started asking questions as I did, as to how so many federal agents arrived at the scene at the same time.

Like Franey (a B.A.T.F. agent who claimed he was in the building) was not in the building at the time of the blast. I know this for a fact, I saw him! I also saw full riot gear worn with rifles in hand, why? Don't make the mistake as I did and ask the wrong people. . . .

If our history books and records are ever truly corrected about that day it will show this and maybe even some lame excuse as to why it happened, but I truly don't believe it will from what I now know to be the truth.

Even if I tried to explain it to you the way it was explained to me, and the ridiculous reason for having [our] own police departments falsify reports to their fellow officers, to the citizens of the city and to our country, you would understand why I feel the way I do about all of this.

I believe that a lot of the problems the officers are having right now are because some of them know what really happened and can't deal with it . . . .

I am sad to say that I believe my days as a police officer are numbered because of all this . . . .[14]

Rebuffs by his superiors, surveillance by the FBI and the Oklahoma City Police Department, and threats against himself and his family were fairly constant. Finally, on May 8, 1996,

Yeakey's dead body was found. Perhaps, not surprisingly, it was called a "suicide" by the city's chief medical examiner.

Yet, the circumstances surrounding the death seem anything but a suicide. When the car Yeakey had been driving was found, it was locked, bloody "as though a hog had been butchered" in it, and paneling was torn as though someone had been looking for something hidden. A mile and a half from his car and through rugged terrain, Yeakey's body was found in a ditch. A report by the medical examiner and other forensic evidence led a researcher to write:

> . . . *According to the report, Terry slashed himself eleven times on both forearms before cutting his own throat twice near the jugular vein. Then, apparently seeking even a more private place to die, he crawled another mile [and a half] of rough terrain away from his car and climbed [or went under] a fence, before shooting himself with a small caliber revolver. What appeared to be rope burns on his neck, handcuff bruises to his wrists, and muddy grass imbedded in his slash wounds strongly indicated that he had some help in traversing this final distance.*[15]

Others have noted that the trajectory of the shot to Yeakey's head lacked the traditional marks of a close range suicide (unless a silencer was used) and, equally disturbing, the gun used was never reported to have been found.[16]

Referring to both cases above as well as others, O'Camb wrote:

> *In an effort to cover up Mike Loudenslager's murder and to intimidate others who were there early on that morning, someone has taken out a number of internal witnesses. Dr. Don Chumley and Terry Yeakey, both, besides being at the Murrah Building that morning, shared one other commonality. Each at the time of his "death" was attempting to deliver evidence concerning the fact that*

Mike Loudenslager was alive and well after the bombing, and also to get certain other facts out about the "bombing" as well.

In Terry Yeakey's case he thought he was delivering evidence and information to a multi-county task force who would help to get the truth out. That's how he was set-up. In Dr. Chumley's case, he was killed some months earlier when his personal jet aircraft "crashed" while attempting to do the same thing.

Were the deaths of Jack Colvert, Jackie Majors and Buddy Youngblood also directly related to the cover-up of Mike Loudenslager's murder? Each of them had been at the Murrah Building that morning and each had also seen Mike Loudenslager alive and well after the bombing. Others who were there that morning have also felt threatened. Officer Gordon Martin, for one, feels at least two attempts on his life have been made. Other police officers and emergency services personnel fear for their personal safety as well.[17]

As evidenced throughout our discussions in this book, too much knowledge and information of covert activities often proves to be a liability. This is the reason that several who have been privy to insider information have determined to publish and expose themselves. By bringing the information to the attention of the public three things are accomplished: (1) eyes are focused on the individual affording him more protection; (2) the individual no longer must carry the weight of secrecy; and (3) the public is able to digest the new information and temper it to media accounts.

There were so many problems with the investigation! Were there other problems than the ones we have discussed?

Perhaps, of all the issues that have come to light in the aftermath of the bombing, nothing has been more frustrating to those who were in some way involved than the lack of objective reporting. Because Timothy McVeigh's trial was still in process six years following the bombing, several witnesses were reinterviewed over a substantial period of time. In most cases they were disturbed because they felt that they had germane information which would shed more light on the events, yet they were not called to testify. Most said that they felt the FBI or others asking them initial questions had a predetermined set of answers they were seeking. Responses outside of their expectations were dismissed as invalid.

The outcome

Because of the gravity of the events at Oklahoma City, the public's attention was shifted from the crowded Congressional docket and concerns of the presidential administration. With the destruction of the federal building by a terrorist, the nation was poised to enact the most draconian legislation in its history.

Chapter 11—Endnotes

1   Benton K. Partin quoted in "Oklahoma City Bombing
         Questions."   www.inlibertyandfreedom.com/ okc.htm

2   William F. Jasper, "Multiple Blasts: More Evidence,
         Elgin Blasts Effect Study. www.proparanoid.net/
         OK3.htm

3   *Ibid.*

4   www.brasscheck.com

5   www.apfn.org/APFN/oklahoma.htm

6   Michael A. McCamb, The Importance of Jane Graham.
         www.independence.net/janegraham.htm

7   *Ibid.*

8   John Dougherty, "Oklahoma City's Lost Information."
         April 23, 2001. www.worldnetdaily/news/article.
         asp?ARTICLE _ID =22518

9   Geoff Metcalf, "Revealing the Truth about OKC." June
         3, 2001. www.worldnetdaily/news/article.asp
         ?ARTICLE_ID=23076

10   Interview with Danny Coulson, *McCurtain Daily Gazette*,
         November 28, 2005. www.mccurtain.com/cgi-
         bin/okcscript.cgi?record=1438

11   *Ibid.*

12   William F. Jasper, "OKC Legacy of Lies Lives On." *The
         New American*: July 2, 2001. www.thenew
         american.com/tna/2001/07-02-2001/vo17no14_
         okc_legacy.htm

13   Michael A. O'Camb, "Unsolved Deaths in Oklahoma."
         Free Republic: December 10, 2000.
         www.freerepublic.com/forum/a3b2804310d68.
         htm

14   David Hoffman, "The Death of Oklahoma City Police
      Officer Terrance Yeakey." *The Washington
      Weekley*, April 21, 1997 as quoted in
      www.geocities.com/vonchloride/wwyeakey.html

15   Pat Shannan, "Who Killed Terry Yeakey?"
      www.patshannan.com/sting.html

16   *Ibid.*

17   Michael A. O'Camb, "Unsolved Deaths in Oklahoma."
      Ibid.

Chapter 12

September 11, 2001

The events of 9/11 are fresh in the minds of most Americans and will be for many years to come. We easily visualize American Airlines Flight 11 flying into the North Tower of the World Trade Center (WTC) and seventeen minutes later, United Airlines Flight 175 flying into the South Tower. Thirty-five minutes later, American Airlines Flight 77 would fly into the Pentagon taking more lives and creating further damage. Our television sets replayed over and over the crashes and the resulting horrible devastation. The WTC buildings collapsed, fire and smoke billowed everywhere, and over three thousand people were dead as a result of the worst terrorist attack to ever have taken place on American soil.

Soon we knew who was behind the attack. Within seventy-two hours we were given a list of nineteen names of hijackers and learned that they had been attending various flight training schools. The media pieced the story together for us: the hijackers had learned how to fly or at least to steer the commercial airliners; they had used boxcutters as weapons to subdue the passengers and crews; and they had piloted the planes to their prearranged crashes.

Americans were in disbelief. How could nineteen young men, many barely speaking English, have pulled-off such orchestrated devastation on a country that was so superior in intelligence and military defenses to any other country? We were glued to our television sets as the events and intrigue unfolded and eventually found ourselves cheering when our President began to take decisive action. Flushes of patriotism arose as terrorists around the world were placed on notice.

At least, that's what we saw and those were the feelings that we had—that was the official story.

That occurred just a few years ago but we've learned more about the events of that day and have seen many things that have happened since that ought to make us reflect and reevaluate what we saw.

What really happened?

The elements of secrecy and conspiracy camouflage many things that otherwise might not escape public notice. A few after-the-fact revelations have helped investigators piece together a much different scenario of the events of 9/11—one that definitely indicates Americans were misled into a false understanding.

Because of its abilities to house completely up-dated material, the internet is a helpful tool to find current thinking and information. It also has the added feature of being beyond controlled media dictates—not that the controlled media is not present, but because it can offer posts and rebuttals side-by-side with it. Consequently, it is one of the best sources of "alternative" views. Because, however, many of us still enjoy our news from "hard" sources, a plethora of books have been published which also shed light on conventional and packaged views. As seen from the chapter on *Media Control*, though, most ideas that challenge the *status quo* are not found in traditional radio and television news reports, newspapers, and news magazines. Here are some of the major inconsistencies found by researchers of events surrounding 9/11.

What about the nineteen hijackers?   Have they finally paid for their crimes?

We would have expected that the hijackers would have been quickly brought to justice and been sentenced. A year after the tragedy, Director of the FBI Robert Mueller told the nation that "We at this point definitely know the 19 hijackers who were responsible" and implied that they would speedily be brought to justice.[1] Instead, today, we find them referred to in most writings as "alleged" hijackers because several have been found to be living (not burned up in plane crashes) and, of those interviewed, all have denied that they had anything to do with the hijackings and have shown plausible alibis. To date, even with various bits of circumstantial evidence found, no convictions have been made against any of them who are living.

But the planes were hijacked and flew into the World Trade Center, didn't they?

There are some inconsistencies in the reporting, but most researchers feel that the airplanes that hit the Twin Towers were the hijacked American Airlines Flight 11 and United Airlines Flight 175. One concern that has been raised is that hitting either tower with a difficult to maneuver plane such as a Boeing 767 would be particularly difficult for novice pilots. Another interesting aside is that each of the planes "had at least one passenger who was a senior official in Raytheon's division of Electronics Warfare" aboard which, for some, opens other possibilities.[2]

But why weren't they stopped before they arrived at the Twin Towers?

This question is more difficult to answer and allows much more critical thinking about a conspiracy. Remember, a conspiracy is two or more people working together without the knowledge of another—or the knowledge of the public-at-large.

The first plane to arrive at the WTC was American Airlines Flight 11. It left Boston at 7:59 AM and fifteen minutes later its transponder (global positioning device) and radio were turned off. Six minutes later, at 8:20, it veered sharply off course and one minute later flight attendants telephoned that the airplane was under the control of hijackers who had already taken the lives of some people. At 8:46, twenty-five minutes after the telephone call, Flight 11 hit the North Tower of the WTC.

FAA regulations read that an "aircraft emergency" exists with a loss of radio contact. At 8:14, thirty-two minutes before Flight 11 crashed, the National Military Command Center was to have been notified; and they in turn were to have authorized the North American Aerospace Defense Command (NORAD) to "scramble" fighter jets from the nearest military airport. These jets should have flown to Flight 11 and forced it to accompany them back to the military base. In the event that Flight 11 would not have complied, it would have been shot down. Because all of this is built-in procedure: the calling, scrambling and arrival of the jet fighters would have taken at most, ten minutes. (The U.S. Air Force states that an F-15 jet "goes from 'scramble order' to 29,000 feet in only 2.5 minutes" and then flies at speeds to 1,850 nautical miles per hour equating to 2,150 land mph. That means that Flight 11 should have been intercepted twenty-two minutes prior to the fatal crash. Even given extraordinary delays or other interferences, there certainly should have been time to intercept the airplane. No fighter jets were scrambled and Flight 11 was allowed to fly directly to the WTC.

United Airlines Flight 175 presents a different and more compelling scenario. It left Boston at 8:14 AM, just at the time the FAA was learning that Flight 11 was possibly hijacked. (Remember that just five minutes later, at 8:21 a.m., Ground

Control was to learn from flight attendants that it had been forcibly taken-over and that people aboard the plane were dead.) So at 8:42, when Flight 175's radio and transponder were turned off and the plane changed direction, NORAD was immediately notified. At 9:03, twenty minutes after NORAD had been notified of the hijacking and seventeen minutes following Flight 11's crash into the North Tower of the WTC, Flight 175 hit the South Tower without any interference. Given the state of emergency that the entire nation felt at that time, it seems inconceivable that those charged with protecting the nation's airways would completely fail to respond.

Here are the flight breakdowns:

Flight 11	Flight 175
7:59 Left Boston	8:14 Left Boston
8:14 Radio and transponder Turned off	8:42 Radio and transponder turned off, veered off course
8:21 Flight attendants telephoned	
8:46 Hit North Tower	9:03 Hit South Tower

So the fighter jets were never scrambled to intercept the two airplanes that hit the WTC?

At least, apparently that is what happened. General Richard Myers, the Acting Chairman of the Joint Chiefs of Staff, appeared on September 13th before the Senate Armed Services Committee and said "When it became clear what the threat was, we did scramble fighter aircraft." When asked if the order was given "before or after the Pentagon was struck" (at 9:38 a.m.) General Myers responded: "That order, to the best of my knowledge, was given after the Pentagon was struck."[3] This version of the interceptor jets was repeated by both the spokesman for NORAD and Vice President Richard Cheney.

Very quickly, people began to question military competence. After all, standard operating procedure dictated that the jets should have been immediately scrambled. This, we find, was not such an extraordinary occurrence. In fact, "The Associated Press has told us that fighter aircraft were scrambled and flying beside errant commercial and private air traffic within minutes of the slightest deviation some 67 times in the calendar year preceding June 1, 2001."[4] As more information surfaced, the story changed.

In a few days, NORAD said that fighter jets were scrambled but they came too late. The NORAD spokesman said that they were not notified of the first hijacking until 8:40—long after radio communication was lost and flight 11 had veered off course. According to this new version of the story, finally at 8:46 the fighter jets were scrambled, not from the closest base but one located 180 miles away. Because Flight 11 struck the WTC at 8:46, it really would have made no difference where the F-15s took off. However, NORAD said that the alert of Flight 175 was received at 8:43 and the two fighters were redirected to intercept it—but for some inexplicable reason, they did not take off until 8:52.

However, perhaps the strangest feature of this story, from the viewpoint of the critics, involves its failure to explain, even with all those delays, why those planes did not arrive to stop the second attack on the WTC. At 8:52, there were still 11 minutes until 9:03, when Flight 175 would hit the second tower. Lieutenant Colonel Timothy Duffy, a pilot said to have flown one of the F-15s, has been quoted as stating that he "was full-blower all the way," which would mean he was going over 1,875 nmph [2,150 land mph.] At this speed, the F-15s would have been covering over 30 miles a minute. Hence, allowing the standard 2.5 minutes for them to get airborne and up to speed, they should have reached Manhattan in about 8 minutes, having a full 3 minutes left to shoot down the errant airliner. And yet, according to this second version of the official account, the

F-15s were still 70 miles away when Flight 175 crashed into the South Tower.[5]

Were NORAD's second version true and had the pilot flown at "full-blower," there would have been sufficient time to intercept Flight 175. Mathematics, however, bear out that the fighters traveled substantially slower.

Because of the conflicting stories and the lack of congruence in the second, most students of the attacks on the WTC give little credence to NORAD's second version. Whichever story one accepts, though, both are very disturbing. Added to their implausibility is that a military unit noted for exactness and strictness, has never issued a reprimand or indicated a specific break down or fault.

Senator Mark Dayton of Minnesota summed up the findings of the 9/11 Commission in regards to jets being scrambled. Directing his statements to the commission, he said that the report of the NORAD chronology that was made public after the attacks was "grossly misleading."

> The chronology said the FAA notified the military's emergency air command of three of the hijackings while those jetliners were still airborne. Dayton cited commission findings that the FAA failed to inform NORAD about three of the planes until after they had crashed.
>
> And he said a squadron of NORAD fighter planes that was scrambled was sent east over the Atlantic Ocean and was 150 miles from Washington, D.C. when the third plan struck the Pentagon—further than they were before they took off.[6]

This all may sound quite confusing, but most researchers have come to the conclusion that any scrambling that may have been done by jet interceptors was not done with the intent of preventing the airliners from hitting their targets. Given the prescribed protocol and the nation's state of emergency, the only answer for the silent fighter jets appears to be willful complicity by those who were responsible for scrambling and intercepting the airplanes.

What about the other hijacked plane? —the one that flew into the Pentagon?

American Airlines Flight 77 took off from Washington, D.C. at 8:20 a.m. Although it went "significantly off course" at 8:46, within a few minutes it was again on course. No fighter jets were scrambled when it veered from its flight pattern. At 8:56 Flight 77's transponder shut off and it disappeared from the radar screen at flight control. Again, no fighter jets were scrambled. At 9:25, air traffic controllers located at Dulles Airport reported that they saw a quickly approaching airplane going toward the capitol. At 9:35, "starting from about 7,000 feet above the ground, the aircraft made a difficult 'downward spiral, turning almost a complete circle and dropping the last 7,000 feet in two-and-a-half minutes.'"[7] At 9:38, the official account reads, Flight 77 hit the west wing of the Pentagon killing all on board and 125 military and civilian workers.

Initially, news reports did not connect Flight 77 with the Pentagon crash. It was not until that afternoon that it was generally understood that Flight 77 had turned around and reentered Washington D.C. Of all of the damage done by hijacked commercial airplanes that day, however, the connection of Flight 77 and the Pentagon Building appears the most dubious.

David Ray Griffin, PhD in his detailed book, *The New Pearl Harbor*, wrote:

> *Danielle O'Brien, one of the air traffic controllers at Dulles who reported seeing the aircraft at 9:25 said: "The speed, the maneuverability, the way that he turned, we all thought in the radar room, all of us experienced air traffic controllers, that that was a military plane." Another witness, seeing the plane from a 14th floor*

apartment in Pentagon City, said that it "seemed to be able to hold eight or twelve persons" and "made a shrill noise like a fighter plane." Lon Rains, editor of Space News, said: "I was convinced it was a missile. It came in so fast it sounded nothing like an airplane." Still another witness, who saw it from his automobile, was reported as saying that it "was like a cruise missile with wings.[8]

The various witnesses, including trained observers in air traffic control, agreed that they saw and heard something. It is beyond the purview of this book to speculate on what they saw, but it was apparently not a commercial Boeing 757. In contrast to these accounts, initially there were nineteen other eyewitnesses who reported seeing an American Airlines airplane. These people, though, upon further interviewing, either withdrew their accounts; said that they were misquoted; or could not be located. In fact, there are no currently accepted eyewitness accounts of a commercial airliner striking the Pentagon on September 11th. Further complicating the official version of the Pentagon strike was its hijacking pilot, Hani Hanjour. All who had worked with him agreed that his flying skills were inadequate and, according to CBS News, he had been reported to the FAA on numerous occasions "because his flying skills were so bad."[9] Yet, he is supposed to have accomplished the most difficult flight feat of any hijacker—to have taken the Boeing 757 from 7,000 feet to a ground parallel landing traveling from 300 to 600 mph within about two-and-one-half minutes.

Perhaps the most incredulous part of Flight 77's crash into the Pentagon, however, was its size contrasted to the damage it caused. To appreciate the problem in accepting the official account, the reader must visualize the size of a Boeing 757. It has a wingspan of 125 feet, it is 155 feet long, and the height at its tail is over 44 feet. Fortunately, following the crash, there were several pictures taken of the Pentagon—none of which, however, show any part of the plane outside of the building.

Therefore, the official story of Flight 77 is that the entire airplane went into the Pentagon structure. Countering that story is the fact that virtually all of the early pictures show a lack of damage that a person would expect to see from the impact of a 135 ton object of the above size traveling at approximately 400 miles per hour. In fact, the first pictures taken of the west side of the Pentagon show a hole approximately fifteen to eighteen feet in diameter with no part of the airplane visible. Fortunately, a team of nearby fire trucks, upon seeing the smoke from the Pentagon, came and extinguished the early fires and also took pictures. Later the façade of the west wall would fall so that the initial hole would not be as easily noticed—but none of the first pictures allow for the 125 foot wingspan nor the 44 foot tail. (An excellent website with several pictures showing the effect of the crash on the Pentagon—showing both original and retouched images—is Jack White's *911 Photo Studies* located at www.911studies.com/911photostudies.)

Well, even if there doesn't appear to be a hole large enough to accommodate the plane, surely its debris and wreckage are evidence enough that it crashed into the building.

That would be the logical conclusion, but we find that there is much that is illogical about the events of 9/11. There was neither debris nor verified wreckage of a Boeing 757 in the Pentagon. In the initial pictures taken at the Pentagon, there was virtually no debris nor signs of wreckage. The lawn in front of the building was clear and had an almost "manicured" look—despite the official report that the airliner "slid" into the building. Various airplane parts that have been brought forward following the crash have apparently been from other airplanes and, although part numbers stamped on wreckage pieces could identify them as coming from a Boeing 757, none have been made available for observation. When asked about the wreckage of the 135 ton plane, the official answer given is that the airplane parts vaporized; that the speed, impact and explosive fuel combined to make the plane disappear. So we are left with (1) a plane that was not reported as missing (2) flown by an incompetent pilot (3) that crashed completely through a wall into a hole too small for it to fit and (4) virtually disappearing without a trace. If the circumstances surrounding the events of the day were not so tragic, this flight would seem too strange to consider.

Evidence for the Pentagon may be shaky but the devastation of the World Trade Center certainly must add credibility to the effectiveness of the two hijacked airplanes that hit it.

There is little doubt as to what we saw! The South Tower (although taking the second hit) collapsed first, just fifty-six minutes—at 9:59—after being struck. The North Tower burned for one hour and forty-two minutes and collapsed at 10:28. Surprisingly, WTC-7 located two blocks away was not hit by an airplane but collapsed at 5:20 PM. These, indeed, were very strange occurrences. In the history of steel architecture never before had a steel building collapsed because of a fire—yet we saw three collapse in the same day, each officially listing fire as its cause.

Perhaps, assuming that this would be a weak link in the day's devastation, this is why the mainstream media sought to demonstrate the feasibility of the steel buildings collapsing because of fire. The NOVA program on public broadcasting channels and the History Channel aired these special programs. The problem was that the programs simply did not reveal all of the facts surrounding the fires or give the necessary information to understand steel building construction. The documentary style programs led viewers to believe that the resultant fires from jet fuel melted the steel columns causing the buildings to cave in.

Another theory—also promoted by FEMA— promoted the weakening of "angle clips" attached to the buildings' trusses. In this theory,

> *As the joists on one or two of the most heavily burned floors gave way and the outer box columns began to bow outward, the floors above them also fell. The floor below (with its 1,300-ton design capacity) could not support the roughly 45,000 tons of ten floors (or more) above crashing down on these angle clips. This started the domino effect that caused the buildings to collapse within ten seconds.*[10]

What are the problems with this? First, to melt steel a constant temperature of at least 2,770 degrees F must be maintained. The hydrocarbon fire caused by the spilled jet fuel would have reached a maximum temperature of 1,600 to 1,700 degrees—and, because of the visible black smoke from the fires, the temperature was probably much less. In addition to attaining the prerequisite heat, the fire would necessarily also need to be both large and sustained. The WTC fires were described as both small and random.

Second, as one author has rebutted the citation written above, "In order for a floor to fall, hundreds of joints had to break almost simultaneously on 236 exterior columns and 47 core columns.[11] That meant that every joint had to have the exact same amount of resistance and that the falling floors had to be completely synchronized. A virtual impossibility.

Third, to accomplish the "collapse within ten seconds," of the 1,300 foot WTC tower, (which actually happened) the floors in the building had to be very close to falling in a "free-fall" mode. This would not allow for the least bit of resistance. Even meeting a half-second of resistance on each floor would have added another forty to forty-seven seconds to the fall time. "How could the debris crush 100 steel and concrete floors while falling as fast as objects fall through the air?"[12]   Fourth, the collapse of each of the WTC buildings was total. The buildings came straight down in their "footprint," indicating that there was not one single glitch or hang-up. The stubble and debris of the buildings compacted directly over the buildings' foundations.

For the most accepted and scholarly approach to the wreckage of the WTC buildings, see Dr. Steven E. Jones' DVD of a lecture given at Utah Valley State College found in the back cover of this book. In addition, he has written, "Why Indeed did the WTC Buildings Collapse?" which may be found at http://www.scholarsfor911truth.org. Jones, a professor of physics and recognized academician, examined the various official reports relating to the WTC buildings and found them generally unscientific and wanting in plausible information. Another well done documentary comparing the official version of the WTC collapse with testimonies and evidence from scholars and field professionals is found at www.brasscheck.com/videos/911/911mysteries.html.

Couldn't we simply have the "professionals" analyze the building debris to determine the level of stress that the various structural pieces underwent? Couldn't investigators determine by the location and severity of the bends and breaks in the steel where the weak spots were and piece together the demise of the buildings?

That certainly would have made our work much easier. Unfortunately, those in control of cleaning up the damaged area quickly eliminated that possibility by removing as much of the damaged building remnants as they were able. Dr. David Ray Griffin wrote:

> *. . . after the collapse of the towers, the debris, including the steel, was quickly removed before there could be any significant investigation. The New York Times complained, saying, "The*

decision to rapidly recycle the steel columns, beams and trusses from the WTC in the days immediately after 9/11 means definitive answers may never be known." The next week, [an] essay in Fire Engineering said: "The destruction and removal of evidence must stop immediately." But it went ahead at full speed.[13]

Of the more than 300,000 tons of scrap, most was ultimately sent abroad to be reprocessed. Although very selectively distributed, there were some pieces of steel, however, from the WTC that were not immediately recycled. These were given to the National Institute of Standards and Technology (NIST) for evaluation. This was to have been a two-year program with published quarterly reports; however, following the first report of December 9, 2002, there have been no updates. Hence, there is still no information from the official body and others have been restricted from obtaining any of the steel for further research.

Nevertheless, the three buildings of the WTC did come down. Are there any theories or ideas on how this could have happened?

Most investigators of the WTC collapses have arrived at the conclusion that explosives were detonated inside of the buildings. That is surprising to many and certainly indicates collusion or conspiracy; but a great deal of testimony from people inside the towers confirms it. In an interview, Auxiliary Fire Lieutenant Paul Isaac reported that "many other firemen know there were bombs in the buildings"—in agreement with Fireman Louie Cacchioli who said that "on the last trip up a bomb went off. We think there were bombs set in the building."[14]

Just prior to the collapse of one of the towers, Ross Milanytch watched "small explosions on each floor." When it cleared "all that was left of the buildings, you could just see the steel girders in like a triangular sail shape. The structure was just completely gone."[15]

In addition to memories of recalled explosions, there is a great deal of surrounding evidence that explosives were used to bring down the massive buildings. Here are a few things to consider:

(1) Although each tower was hit by a 135 ton airplane and some damage was done in the crashes, it is interesting that each of the buildings fell straight down rather than tilting one way or another. Witnesses who had experience in explosive demolition all commented that the collapsing of the buildings looked like "classic controlled demolition."

(2) Referring to the completeness and the speed of the collapses, Peter Meyer wrote that

> . . . *this is understandable if the bases of the steel columns were destroyed by explosions at the level of the bedrock. With those bases obliterated, and the supporting steel columns shattered by explosions at various levels in the Twin Towers, the upper floors lost all support and collapsed to ground level in about ten seconds.*[16]

(3) Throughout the debris, there were several "hot spots" of molten metal that continued to burn and smolder for several weeks following the fall. As seen from the temperature of a fire fed by jet fuel, it would not be hot enough to melt steel. The use of explosives would create sufficient heat whereby the steel could maintain its high temperature in an insulated environment.

(4) The collapse of the WTC buildings was accompanied by extremely fine dust—cement dust. As we watched the buildings crashing to the ground on our television sets, most of us were surprised to see the amount of dust in the air and the

difficulty breathing experienced by those at the scene. Eric Hufschmid, author of the book *Painful Questions: An Analysis of the September 11ᵗʰ Attack*, estimated that "Perhaps 100,000 tons of concrete in each tower was pulverized to a powder." That, he said, "required a lot of energy."[17]

Jeff King of Indywest Webcast News reviewed various video clips of the tower collapses and attempted to reconcile discrepancies with the official explanations. He found that

> The biggest and most obvious problem that I see is the source is the enormous amount of very fine dust that we see generated during the collapse. . . . Where does the energy come from to turn all this reinforced concrete into dust?[18]

> [Tons of] very fine concrete is ejected from the top of the building very early in the collapsed. Since it should at most be accelerating under gravity at 32 feet per second, things would actually moving quite slowly at first. . . . It is very hard to imagine a physical mechanism to generate that must dust with concrete slabs bumping into each other at 20 or 30 mph.[19]

As King notes, "with concrete slabs bumping into each other" at slow rates of speed, the end result would be large chunks of concrete. Something had to pulverize the concrete prior to its bumping and the only thing that could do it effectively was explosives.

The power of the explosives can be seen by reviewing the various video clips of the building collapses. We most likely missed the significance of huge puffs of powder coming horizontally from the buildings while they were falling; but, knowing what we are looking for, they are clearly visible. Commenting on these powerful explosions, Dr. Griffin wrote:

> What other than explosives could turn concrete into powder and then eject it horizontally 150 feet or more? And if it be suspected

that the dust simply floated out, some of the photographs show that rather large pieces of the tower were also thrown out 150 feet or more.[20]

Coupled with the evidence of powdered concrete, the steel also showed definite signs of demolition by explosives. Whereas one would expect much of the steel to show stress by twisting and turning under the weight of the collapse; instead the steel was broken off in short sections.

Does the same hold true for WTC-7? Since it wasn't hit by an airplane, did it collapse for the same reason as the Twin Towers?

WTC-7 has been difficult to explain by official reports—in fact, there is no official version of why it fell. There were a few fires burning in the building from an insignificant amount of falling fiery debris, but they were minimal and certainly could not have generated sufficient heat to have affected the steel or the building's integrity. After all, WTC-7 was 355 feet from the North Tower—over a full football field away—and there were other buildings much closer to the Twin Towers that only suffered minimal damage. As for the use of explosives in bringing down the third building, Eric Hufschmid wrote that it was like a typical demolition.

> *When Building 7 collapsed, the interior fell first, and that caused the outside of the building to move inward. . . . The result was a very tiny pile of rubble, with the outside of the building collapsing on top of the pile. This is how conventional demolitions operate.*[21]

Apparently, the forensic research and opinions of those in the fields of demolition, explosives, and physics academia find much mutual agreement that the collapsing of the WTC buildings was a result of planted explosives rather than fire damage from spilt jet fuel.

If all of this is true, why wasn't it brought to our attention in the 9/11 Commission Report? Wasn't that commission convened to examine the problems with responses and the fatalities that occurred that day?

The 9/11 Commission has several serious flaws. For an excellent treatise on the commission, the reader is directed to *The 9/11 Commission Report: Omissions and Distortions* by David Ray Griffin. The primary problems of the commission were (1) the stated purpose of the commission; (2) the make-up of commission members; and (3) the withholding of key material from the commission.

The stated purpose of the 9/11 Commission

It was generally thought that the commission was organized to examine the events of 9/11 and determine where the various breaks in intelligence and government reaction took place; to determine where fault occurred; and to recommend reprimands or other penalties for those who were to blame.

Although the public was allowed to believe that this was a reason for the commission, Vice-Chairman Lee Hamilton more correctly gave its function when he said, "The focus of the commission will be on the future. We're not interested in trying to assess blame, we do not consider that part of the commission's responsibility."[22] In other words, limitations were placed on the commission to make sure that the breakdown did not occur again—not to make decisions or find fault about what had already happened. True to its stated purpose, with little testimony of the actual events and faults that orchestrated the tragedies of the day, the 9/11 Commission aimed its report at eliminating future like events.

The make-up of commission members

Initially, family members of 9/11 victims pled for an independent commission to examine the events of the day and to issue a comprehensive report of its findings. As the commission progressed, the Family Steering Committee assigned from victims' families were less and less satisfied that an examination into the events would be impartial. To begin with, the White House finally approved the commission with the stipulation that it would be responsible for selecting its chairman. The first choice of the Bush Administration was Henry Kissinger (CFR, Trilateral Commission, Bilderberger Group)—an unpopular choice to the Family Steering Committee because of his obvious connections to the administration and their feeling that he would not be impartial. When, however, it was time to convene a congressional hearing to approve Kissinger, he declined to reveal his multinational government contacts through his consulting firm and was forced to withdraw his name from consideration.

The next choice was Thomas Kean, the former governor of New Jersey. Besides being a CFR member, Kean was the Director of Amerada Hess Corporation. Amerada Hess was then in a joint venture with Delta Oil of Saudi Arabia, and was involved in the initial planning for a trans-Afgan pipeline—all of this just prior to 9/11. Delta Oil was owned by Khalid Bin Mahfouz, Saudi Arabia's largest banker who had prior dealings with President George W. Bush when both were implicated in the Iran-Contra Affair and the Savings and Loans scandals of the late 1980s.

His Vice-Chairman was Lee Hamilton, also a member of CFR, the Trilateral Commission and the Bilderberger Group. Hamilton had chaired the earlier commission to investigate the Iran-Contra Affair and it is interesting to note that many of the individuals that were scrutinized for criminal complicity—John Poindexter, Elliot Abrams (CFR), Richard Armitage (CFR), Dick

Cheney (CFR, Trilateral Commission), Otto Reich (CFR), Colin Powell (CFR, Bilderberger Group), and John Negroponte (CFR)—were mustered to serve again in the current Bush Administration. Although a Democrat, Hamilton also had close links to the White House.

Also chosen by the President was Philip Zelikow as the Executive Director of the commission. Zelikow was closely tied to the Bush Administration, was a member of the President's Foreign Intelligence Advisory Board, and had served on the National Security Council with Condoleezza Rice (and even coauthored a book with her.) Repeatedly, the Family Steering Committee complained that the commission was too friendly to the White House to be objective and fully independent.

Because of the leadership and make-up of the 9/11 Commission, it was felt from the beginning that little would be accomplished that would indicate complicity on the part of government.

One apparently independent member of the commission was the Democratic senator from Georgia, Max Cleland. Although not completing his term on the commission because of accepting a position with CitiBank, he was a vocal critic of the committee and of the restrictions placed by the White House. Philip Shenon in the *New York Times* reported Cleland to say, "As each day goes by, we learn that this government knew a whole lot more about these terrorists before September 11 than it has ever admitted."[23]

He was critical of various "deals" that the administration made with the commission—restriction of pertinent records that could only be shown to a couple of members of the commission; the fact that the President and the Vice-President refused to testify under oath to the commission; and that the White House "cherry-picked" the information the commission was allowed to have.[24]

Withholding key material from the commission

Timothy Roemer complained that full reports were not made available to the commission, thus often hiding salient information—receiving "only two or three paragraphs out of a nine-page report." Not given the latitude to research involvement into the events of the day, the committee was hamstrung. Any reporting is dependent on the incorporation of information and when that information is restricted or skewed, the report will necessarily show the same bias. Such was the use of the Presidential Daily Briefs from the weeks in question.

> *According to the agreement accepted by Kean, the White House would be allowed to edit these briefs before sending them to the commission. And then only a few members of the commission would be allowed to see even these edited briefs. Then, besides only being able to take notes on these edited briefs, they would have to show these notes to the White House.*[25]

Referring to the control of information by the White House, Senator Max Cleland said, "That decision compromised the mission of the 9/11 commission, pure and simple."

All of this is horrible. We evidently aren't talking about an errant group of young men on orders from a foreign government, but something that took place within our own country. Why would something like this have happened?

If this were a terrorist action as presented to the American people, we would not be surprised to see that countries promoting terrorism would have benefited from the attack and that the United States would have suffered in loss of life, finances, and reputation. If, on the other hand, there were secret groups that conspired to attack the WTC with ulterior motives, we would expect to see them emerging with added power and gain—the primary motives of secret combinations. Because these two motives appear to be distinct in the events of September 11th, they will be treated separately.

Who could financially gain from the WTC attacks?

Aside from the obvious gains: the building owner who collected $5 million in insurance benefits and the various contracts issued for demolition and rebuilding—there are those who used their "insider" knowledge that the WTC attack would occur. One of the ways that advance knowledge was useful was in the stock market. Quite obviously, both American Airlines and United Airlines stocks would lose value following 9/11. Christopher Bollyn in an article to *The American Free Press*, reported that

> *In the days following the terror attacks, suspicious and unusual stock trading activity indicated that people used inside information to make huge profits. The money made from the trades done with apparent inside information has been estimated at up to $15 billion worldwide.*[26]

One of the primary ways to take advantage of inside information is by short-selling—selling unowned stock shares at current value and then purchasing the same stocks for less money at a later time. In similar stock trading, a person can place a "put" option which allows him to sell a given stock at a specified price before a certain date. Both variations of trading earn money for the trader if the stock loses value. Opposed to the put option is the call option in which the stock trader gambles that the stock will increase in value. By foreknowledge of the hijackings of 9/11, traders who placed put options on American Airlines or United Airlines stocks could have made a great deal of money. Looking at the bids placed through the Chicago Board of Options Exchange, researcher Michael Ruppert informs us that on September 6th and 7th there were 4,744 put options on United

Airlines but only 396 call options. On September 10th there were 4,516 puts to 748 calls on American Airlines. These figures were only applicable to the two airlines involved in the WTC attacks— no other airline stocks showed significant movement. Using Ruppert's statistics, Jim Marrs continues

> . . . . *Morgan Stanley Dean Witter & Co., which occupied twenty-two floors of the WTC, witnessed the purchase of 2,157 put options during the three trading days before the 9/11 attacks as compared to 27 per day prior to September 6. Merrill Lynch & Co., which also had offices in twenty-two floors of the WTC, had 12,215 one-month put options bought during four trading days prior to 9/11 compared to the normal 252 contracts per day.*[27]

Because of the unprecedented movement in the stocks of these two airlines prior to their being used in the hijackings— virtually all for profit—Dylan Ratigan in the September 20 edition of the *Bloomberg Business News* reported, "This could very well be insider trading at the worst, most horrific, most evil use you've ever seen in your entire life, or this would be one of the extraordinary coincidences in the history of mankind, if it was a coincidence."[28]

Many of the various stock options were traced in hopes that the trail would lead to the hijackers—perhaps to the one considered the mastermind himself: Osama bin Laden. Tracing the stock trading proved useful; perhaps not so much for a bin Laden connection as for an understanding that those at the highest levels of money management evidently had prior notification of the terrorist activities. In his *American Free Press* article, "Insider Trading and 9/11," Tom Flocco wrote that

> *Extensive media reporting confirms that investors at Deutschebank-Alex Brown and their global finance entities may have profited from prior knowledge of the attacks while purchasing*

disproportionate put option contracts on targeted U.S. airlines and related insurance or investment firms.[29]

As an introduction to Deutschebank-Alex. Brown, the reader will find sufficient knowledge in learning that Deuschebank, the central bank of Germany, partnering with Alex. Brown, a banking conglomerate including Brown Brothers Harriman (the largest private bank in the United States)—has combined to form the strongest and most monopolistic bank in Europe. True to the Rothschild banking tradition, in successor combinations, links are forged with the heads of governments, wars are financed, and in many instances, international affairs are managed.

Some of the government interlinking may be seen by understanding that the Chairman of Alex. Brown—A. B. "Buzzy" Krongard—had, three years prior to the WTC attacks, received the appointment to be the counselor to CIA Director, George Tenet. Then, six months prior to 9/11, he was appointed the Executive Director of the CIA. Quoting Michael Ruppert, Flocco ties this connection together: "There is abundant and clear evidence that a number of transactions in financial markets indicated specific foreknowledge of the September 11 attacks . . . and the firm which was used to place put options on UAL stock was, until 1998, managed by the man who is now in the number three position at the CIA."[30]

Despite what seems to be a lot of money for most, the figures that we are using here are minimal amounts for the banks and families in question. The stock tradings are, however, clear links to the families and banks in question. They demonstrate without question that knowledge of the WTC attacks were known in the highest circles on a worldwide scale and that the events of 9/11 would include the use of airplanes from American Airlines and United Airlines.

As far as real gain is concerned, as elsewhere discussed in this book, war continually brings large profits. This will be discussed in greater detail in the next chapter entitled *The Iraqi War*. Of all wars fought to date, the Iraqi War is proving to be one of the most costly both in terms of weaponry and clean-up. As we have seen, lucrative military contracts have been let out without competitive bidding and, despite initial reports, our presence in Iraq will apparently continue indefinitely. The United States was also able to justify further entrance into the Middle East to establish more military bases to both capture and protect oil interests. Of these, the protection set in motion to protect the Trans-Afgan Pipeline seems most significant.

The gain from 9/11 is difficult to gage because of so many players. In our brief look at the events, for ease of explanation we have avoided many of the intrigues that other researchers have discovered. We have avoided funding provided by Pakistan; the global spy network controlled by Israel and the desire they had to bring the United States into a war with Iraq; and the financial and manpower Saudi Arabian link that profited so greatly from "Desert Storm" and the closure of the Kuwaiti oilfields. All of these interests, and perhaps others, have converged to create the 9/11 that we experienced in our country. Of the many potential participants, Jim Marrs comments:

> *Obviously, all of these players could not and did not engage in all of the elements of the crime and cover-up; perpetrators of one element might not be the perpetrators of another. At the moment, we do not yet know enough to say much more than that in effort to assign blame—although pending lawsuits and/or courageous new whistleblowers, yet to come, may soon reveal crucial evidence and connect the multiple conspiracy elements with the multiple co-conspirators in unforeseen ways.*[31]

How was the motive of power fulfilled in the events of 9/11?

To some extent, the answer above describing the extent of involvement of certain countries holds true in answering the power motive. There are some issues that we can immediately see—especially those taking place within our own country. According to pollsters, President George W. Bush went from being a President without a clear mandate from the people in his election against former Vice-President Al Gore, to becoming the most popular President in modern history. Happening during the off-year elections, his popularity also swept many other Republican politicians into Congress that may not have otherwise won their respective races.

Probably more importantly, the events of September 11, 2001 have been recognized as a modern-day Pearl Harbor—an event which galvanized the American people squarely behind their leader and allowed him to make vital national decisions that would not have been allowed under lesser circumstances. The term, "the new Pearl Harbor" has been used by many researchers of 9/11, not only because of its applicability but because various government think-tanks and papers referred to the desirability of an overt catalyst "such as Pearl Harbor" to accomplish their agendas.

Just as the events following the attack of the Japanese at Pearl Harbor in 1941 (described in more detail in the chapter *Wars and Rumors of Wars*) allowed President Franklin Delano Roosevelt broad powers to mobilize soldiers, enter into treaties, and move closer into a one-world government—the same mantle fell upon George W. Bush. Immediately following 9/11, he spoke to the American people and initiated a "War on Terrorism" and said that all terrorist nations including those that harbored terrorists would receive the brunt of our country's aggression. Reviewing some historical precedents for government deception leading the United States into war, Richard Falk, professor emeritus at Princeton University, wrote:

> *There is no excuse at this stage of American development for a posture of political innocence, including an unquestioning acceptance of the good faith of our government. After all, there has been a long history of manipulated public beliefs, especially in matters of war and peace. Historians are in increasing agreement that the facts were manipulated (1) in the explosion of the USS Maine to justify the start of the Spanish-American War (1898), (2) with respect to the Japanese attack on Pearl Harbor to justify the previously unpopular entry into World War 2, (3) in the Gulf of Tonkin incident of 1964, used by the White House to justify the dramatic extension of the Vietnam War to North Vietnam, and, most recently (4) to portray Iraq as harboring a menacing arsenal of weaponry of mass destruction, in order to justify recourse to war in defiance of international law and the United Nations. . . . In these respects, the breaking of trust between government and citizenry in the United States has deep historical roots . . . . But it does pose for all of us a fundamental, haunting question. Why should the official account of 9/11 be treated as sacrosanct and accepted at face value, especially as it is the rationale for some of the most dangerous undertakings in the whole history of the world?*[32]

Voicing similar sentiment of the cause and the far-reaching consequences of the attack, Michael Ruppert told the normally liberal Commonwealth Club on August 31, 2004, that

> *The 9/11 attacks were the result of deliberate planning and orchestrated efforts by identifiable leaders within the U.S. Government, and the energy and financial sectors, to see a Pearl Harbor-like attack which would provide the American Empire with a pretext for war, invasion, and the sequential confiscation of oil and natural gas reserves, or the key transportation routes through which they must pass.*[33]

Wielding the power of a wartime President, domestic controls were also flexed. Increasing the power of federal government (while significantly reducing rights of individuals) he spearheaded the passage of the USA PATRIOT Act through Congress. (USA PATRIOT is an acronym for the Uniting and Strengthening of America by Providing Appropriate Tools Required to Intercept and Obstruct Terrorism.) The 342-page act was brought to Congress for a vote before it could be read and debated; and quickly passed under the cloak of "expediency." (Congressman Ron Paul said, "It is my understanding that the bill wasn't printed before the vote—at least I couldn't get it. . . . Maybe a handful of staffers actually read it, but the bill definitely was not available to members before the vote."[34]) Others who later spoke out against provisions of the act that appeared unconstitutional were rebuffed by White House spokesman Ari Fleischer who said, "To those who scare peace-loving people with phantoms of lost liberty, my message is this: Your tactics only aid terrorists."[35] What were some of the "lost liberties" he was talking about? Alisa Solomon wrote in *The Village Voice* a year following 9/11:

> *Thanks to these maneuvers in the name of combating terrorism, the government can now freeze the release of public records, monitor political and religious gatherings, and jail Americans indefinitely without trial and without legal representation. As Bush and Cheney ready the country for war against Iraq, they have established a climate that stifles dissent—and put laws in place enabling them to clamp down on those who ask too many questions.*
>
> *Meanwhile, Attorney General Ashcroft granted himself and the agencies he oversees a spate of new powers. By decree, he suspended attorney–client privilege. Soon after, he unilaterally removed restraints on the FBI that had been put in place after the excesses of the 1960s and 1970s, unleashing agents to sniff around community meetings, political gatherings, religious services, and*

even your email messages and website visits, without having any evidence, nor even a good hunch, that anything illegal is afoot.

> *Not to be outdone, Bush issued a few executive orders of his own. One called into being military tribunals in which "enemy combatants" could be arrested, tried, convicted, and sentenced to death entirely in secret and with no opportunity for judicial overview. Another rescinded the planned release of the papers of former presidents, effectively closing the public record.*[36]

This is power in its rawest sense—not the kind of power given to a person but to a government intent on control. Because the United States has always been "the land of the free," encroachments to personal liberties are more glaring than under totalitarian governments.

Summary

The apparent terrorist activities of 9/11 have, probably more than any single event in modern history, galvanized the overt posture of the United States. America was reminded of her vulnerability and has been constantly rereminded by various alerts, travel and baggage searches, and forfeitures of certain privacy rights. In addition, because our nation was attacked by terrorists, as Americans we felt justified in following our leaders and retaliating with a war against terrorism—including Iraq. Unquestioning, we allowed preemptive warfare against a nation that, we believed, had weapons of mass destruction to use against the United States and that harbored terrorists.

These entanglements all occurred because of the events of 9/11—the catalyst for much of America's foreign and domestic policy.

In the event that the research contained in this chapter is correct however, and that the official version of the destruction of the World Trade Center buildings and the Pentagon was not as we have been led to believe, a new set of answers must be found.

This, perhaps more than any issue in modern times, is such a pivotal issue that every American must make at least preliminary conclusions based on correct information.

Chapter 12—Endnotes

1 "Playing the 9/11 Unity Card." Associated Press, November 3, 2002. www.nomoregames.net/ Index.php?page=911&subpage1=unity_card

2 David Ray Griffin, *The New Pearl Harbor*. Olive Branch Press: Northampton, MA, 2004. p. 209.

3 Ibid. p. 8

4 "Address of Michael C. Ruppert for the Commonwealth Club—San Francisco." August 31, 2004. www.fromthewilderness.com/PDF/Common wealth.pdf#search=%22ruppert%20common wealth%22

5 Griffin, *Ibid*. p. 10.

6 Ruppert, *Op. Cit.*

7 Griffin, *Op. Cit.* p. 25.

8 *Ibid*. P. 26.

9 Ibid. p. 41.

10 *Ibid*. p. 16.

11 *Ibid*.

12 *Ibid*. p. 16.

13 *Ibid*. p. 20.

14 Jim Marrs, *Inside Job: Unmasking the 9/11 Conspiracies*. Origin Press: San Rafael, CA, 2004. p. 33.

15 *Ibid*. p. 34.

16 Griffin. *Op. Cit.* p. 17.

17 *Ibid*. p. 18.

18 *Ibid*.

19 *Ibid*.

20 *Ibid*. p. 19.

21   *Ibid.* p. 22.

22   *Ibid.* pp. 150-151.

23   "9/11 Commission: The Official Cover-Up Guide."
      www.911truth.org/article.php?story=2004052510
      4145424

24   Griffin, *Op. Cit.* p. 155.

25   *Ibid.*

26   Christopher Bollyn, "Revealing 9/11 Stock Trades could
      Expose Terrorist Masterminds." American Free
      Press, April, 2004. www.globalresearch.ca/
      Articles/BOL412B.html

27   Marrs, *Op. Cit.*, p. 89.

28   *Ibid.* p. 88.

29   Tom Flocco, "Profits of Death: Insider Trading and 9/11."
      Pt.1. www.tomflocco.com/fs/ProfitsOfDeath.htm

30   *Ibid.*

31   Marrs, *Op. Cit.* p. 135.

32   Richard K. Falk, Foreword, *The New Pearl Harbor. Op.
      Cit.*

33   Ruppert, *Op. Cit.*

34   "Damage Control: Selling Patriot Act on Road Show."
      www.newswithviews.com/NWV.exclusive/
      exclusive8.htm

35   Alisa Solomon, "Things We Lost in the Fire." *The
      Village Voice*, September 11—17, 2002. www.
      villagevoice.com/news/0237,solomon,38225,1.
      html

36   *Ibid.*

Chapter 13

THE IRAQ WAR

A war is a military operation with a military objective that can be achieved and then you declare victory. . . . but getting Osama bin Laden, destroying the al Qaeda in Afghanistan is not a victory, it doesn't end terrorism. In fact, the very actions we've taken may intensify and perpetuate the causes of terrorism.

Retired U.S. Admiral Eugene Carroll, December 27, 2001

For many, the Iraq War began on March 20, 2003, with preemptive military strikes and the bombing of Baghdad. The justification for American involvement in Iraqi affairs was (1) that democracy could not exist under the cruel dictatorship of Saddam Hussein; (2) that there were weapons of mass destruction (WMD)—primarily biological weaponry hidden throughout the country; and (3) that Iraq was pursuing the development of nuclear warheads. These issues were presented in a way that evoked emotional response and were quashed through the militarily action "Operation Iraqi Freedom."

For those with longer memories, however, confrontation with Iraq began in August of 1990 with the Iraqi invasion of Kuwait. "Operation Desert Shield," a military campaign involving over one-half million service personnel, was joined by several countries to free Kuwait. This, unlike any other previous armed conflict, played out on our television sets with ongoing commentaries by the media, political analysts, and military strategists. Having watched the drama unfold and having been given a full briefing on Saddam Hussein, many viewers felt a sense of surrealism as the "Gulf War" unfolded in their living rooms.

Some Iraqi history

There is still much that we do not understand about American presence in Iraq, although with the passage of time, more is coming into focus. A glaring reason for lacking understanding of events surrounding involvement in Iraq is an order of secrecy imposed by President George W. Bush. In his order, he granted former presidents, vice presidents, and their surviving families immunity from releasing records relating to "military, diplomatic or national security secrets" under the Freedom of Information Act. This effectively placed records from the 1980 Reagan-Bush administration and successive administrations off-limits for research and has hampered an understanding of historical antecedents. Were this information known in greater detail, undoubtedly we would have a better grasp on issues which have precipitated current events.

But certain things are known. Recent history points toward a different Saddam Hussein and Iraq than we generally hear of through the news media. Although always considered somewhat rough and a "thug," in 1959 while Saddam was still in his early twenties, he was designated as one of six by the Central Intelligence Agency (CIA) to assassinate the then-prime minister of Iraq. Escaping from a botched assassination attempt, the CIA then paid for Saddam's housing in Syria and gave him further training. This relationship apparently persisted through an eight-year war with Iran while he received CIA updates on Iranian positions.

Not only was the CIA involved with Saddam Hussein but U.S. exports to Iraq stemming from the Reagan-Bush years offer a more sinister link. After U.N. weapons inspectors entered Iraq following the first Gulf War, they reported to the U.S. senate committee that oversees American export policy that they had "identified many U.S.-manufactured items exported . . . that were used to further Iraq's chemical and nuclear weapons development and missile delivery system development programs."[1] As the senate committee continued their investigations, they found that eighty batches of biological materiel had been sent to Iraq during the Reagan-Bush years.

> *These included two batches of anthrax and two batches of botulism being sent to the Iraq ministry of higher education on May 2, 1986; one batch each of salmonella and e.coli sent to the Iraqi state company for drug industries on August 31, 1987.*
>
> *As well as anthrax and botulism, the USA also sent West Nile fever, brucella melitensis which damages major organs, and clostridium perfringens which causes gas gangrene. The shipments went on after Saddam ordered the gassing of the Kurdish town of Halabja in which some 5,000 people died in March of 1988.*
>
> *Other items which were sent by the U.S. to Iraq included chemical warfare agent precursors, chemical warfare agent production facility plans and technical drawings, chemical warfare filling equipment, biological warfare-related materials, missile fabrication equipment and missile system guidance equipment.*[2]

Politically, the United States also intervened on behalf of Iraq. In March of 1988 it was reported that Iraq had used chemical weapons against the Kurds in Halabja (using helicopters purchased earlier from the U.S.) killing over 5,000 people. When the senate sought to place sanctions on Iraq for violation of the Geneva Protocol on Chemical Weapons, the Reagan administration prevented them. Likewise, the U.S. voted against a U.N. Security Council statement to condemn Iraq's use of chemical weapons.

Despite interaction between U.S. government entities and Iraq, however, American ties were stronger with Kuwait in 1990. Ending in 1988, the eight-year war with Iran left Iraq's resources severely depleted and their only access to rebuilding their economy was oil production and sales. This had been a full-scale war with access to modern weaponry and eventually an estimated loss of a million lives. It was at that time that Kuwait had placed a huge surplus of oil on the international market and brought prices so low that it was difficult for Iraq to obtain additional needed income. This dilemma, as well as Kuwait's encroachment over the Iraqi border and tapping into oil reserves that Iraq felt were unquestionably theirs, precipitated plans of aggression against Kuwait.

At the time, April Glaspie was the U.S. Ambassador to Iraq. On July 25, 1990, at Saddam Hussein's request, she had an interview with him and made the following statement concerning the potential dispute between Kuwait and Iraq:

> *I admire your extraordinary efforts to rebuild your country. I know you need funds. We understand and our opinion is that you should have the opportunity to rebuild your country. But we have no opinion on the Arab-Arab conflicts, like your border disagreement with Kuwait.*
> *I was in the American Embassy in Kuwait during the late 60's. The instruction we had during this period was that we should express no opinion on this issue and that the issue is not associated with America. James Baker [Secretary of State] has directed our official spokesmen to emphasize this instruction. . . . All that we hope is that these issues are solved quickly.*[3]

Apparently, from Ambassador Glaspie's statement, the United States would not intervene should Iraq initiate a reprisal against Kuwait. Just a week later, supposedly with little concern to be shown by the United States, Iraq invaded Kuwait with 120,000 soldiers and 300 tanks.

Manufacturing a war mentality

Earlier, Iraq had been an ally with the United States against Communism; Saddam Hussein had been a CIA asset; the U.S. had freely exchanged military and biological materiel; and political leaders had openly defended Iraq in both the national and international arenas. What happened to turn the one-time ally into such a bitter enemy?

It couldn't have been because Kuwait was a model nation for other Arab nations to emulate. On the contrary, the 25-year old independent nation had disbanded the National Assembly and placed all authority in the Emir—the ruling al-Sabah family. It had both quashed fledgling attempts at democracy and had a history of intimidated and censured journalism. In fact, it was quite evident that efforts on the part of the United States were decidedly more against Iraq than they were in favor of Kuwait. Apparently, as seen by recent moves to build more military bases, Iraq's strategic location in the midst of the oil-rich Middle East was a larger part of the equation.

For the United States to engage Iraq in confrontation, however, there had to be perceived justification. Kuwait was a tiny nation in comparison to Iraq and would be the obvious underdog in a clash between the two countries. To be certain that the U.S. population had the perspective of an evil, aggressive tyrant attacking a small, defenseless nation, public relations firms were enlisted and paid well by the Kuwaitis. There were

> *. . . 119 H&K [Hill and Knowlton, then the world's largest public relations firm] executives in 12 offices across the U.S. overseeing the Kuwaiti account. "The firm's activities, as listed in its report to the Justice Department, including arranging media interviews for visiting Kuwaitis, setting up observances such as National Free Kuwaiti Day, National Prayer Day (for Kuwait), and National Student Information Day, organizing public rallies, releasing hostage letters to the media, distributing news releases and*

information kits, contacting politicians at all levels, and producing a nightly radio show . . . . Citizens for a Free Kuwait also capitalized on the publication of a quickie 154-page book about Iraqi atrocities titled The Rape of Kuwait, copies of which were stuffed into media kits and then featured on TV talk shows and the Wall Street Journal. The Kuwaiti embassy also bought 200,000 copies of the book for distribution to American troops.[4]

In hindsight we are able to see the impact of public relations work in breeding a war mentality. Similar to Edward Bernays, who was previously discussed pioneering such work during World War 1, Hill and Knowlton brought Americans in line with administration designs. Following the war, the Canadian Broadcasting Corporation produced the documentary, *"To Sell a War"* in which interviews were conducted with some of the PR gurus at the forefront of the Gulf War. One public relations leader explained that audience surveys were used to determine the clothing and hairstyle of the Kuwaiti ambassador so that he would be likeable to American viewers. He said that the job of the public relations agency was

. . . "to identify the messages that really resonate emotionally with the American people." The theme that struck the deepest emotional chord, they discovered, was "the fact that Saddam Hussein was a madman who had committed atrocities even against his own people, and had tremendous power to do further damage, and he needed to be stopped."[5]

Documenting the effectiveness of Hill and Knowlton's manipulation of America's perception of Iraq, John MacArthur wrote *Second Front: Censorship and Propaganda in the Gulf War*. In his book he recounted the history of the Congressional Human Rights Caucus—another public relations front group. The committee was made up of members of Congress but had no official role; therefore, as MacArthur wrote, "The Human Rights

Caucus is not a committee of Congress, and therefore is unencumbered by the legal accouterments that would make a witness hesitate before he or she lied. . . . Lying under oath in front of a congressional committee is a crime; lying from under cover of anonymity to a caucus is merely public relations."[6]

> *In fact, the most emotionally moving testimony on October 10 [the day the caucus convened for hearings] came from a 15-year-old Kuwaiti girl, known only by her first name of Nayirah. According to the Caucus, Nayirah's full name was being kept confidential to prevent Iraqi reprisals against her family in occupied Kuwait. Sobbing, she described what she had seen with her own eyes in a hospital in Kuwait City. Her written testimony was passed out in a media kit prepared by Citizens for a Free Kuwait. "I volunteered at the al-Addan hospital," Nayirah said. "While I was there, I saw the Iraqi soldiers come into the hospital with guns, and go into the room where . . . babies were in incubators. They took the babies out of the incubators, and left the babies on the cold floor to die."*
>
> *Three months passed between Nayirah's testimony and the start of the war. During those months, the story of babies torn from their incubators was repeated over and over again. President Bush told the story. It was recited as fact in Congressional testimony, on TV and radio talk shows, and at the U.N. Security Council. "Of all the accusations made against the dictator," MacArthur observed, "none had more impact on American public opinion than the one about Iraqi soldiers removing 312 babies from their incubators and leaving them to die on the cold hospital floors of Kuwait City."*
>
> *At the Human Rights Caucus, however, Hill & Knowlton and Congressman Lantos had failed to reveal that Nayirah was a member of the Kuwaiti Royal Family. Her father, in fact, was Saud Nasir al-Sabah, Kuwaiti Ambassador to the U.S., who sat listening in the hearing room during her testimony. The Caucus also failed to reveal that H&R vice president Lauri Fitz-Pegado had coached Nayirah in what even the Kuwaitis' own investigators later confirmed was false testimony.[7]*

The invasion of Kuwait took place on August 2, 1990. Four and one-half months later, on January 17, 1991, the U.S. led coalition entered into the undeclared war with a "shock and awe" bombing campaign which lasted for 74 days. Less than a month and a half later, Iraq complied with the demand that it retreat to its pre-war position; however, the combined air forces of the United States and Great Britain continued bombing for another month. Much of the bombing was directed toward Iraqis who were retreating on "the 'Highway of Death' between Kuwait and Basra. In this single largest massacre since the firebombing of Tokyo in the night of March 9 to 10, over 100,000 Iraqi soldiers and Iraqi, Palestinian and Kuwaiti civilians were incarcerated by DU [depleted uranium] and other bombs."[8]

The same month that Iraq invaded Kuwait, the United Nations placed a "blanket ban" on both imports and exports except medicines and humanitarian food supplies. This embargo would continue until May of 2003. The restriction of supplies entering Iraq was controlled by the U.S. and the U.K. and prevented Iraq from receiving necessities and, in most cases, from repairing damage to water supplies and sewage systems caused by the 1991 bombings.

Based on declassified documents, researchers have attempted to tabulate the impact of the bombings and embargo on the Iraqi people. Christian P. Scherrer wrote:

> *The documents prove that the United States officials knew that the U.S.-U.K. bombing devastated the water treatment system of Iraq, they knew what the consequences would be, such as increased outbreaks of disease and high rates of child mortality, and they intentionally designed the sanctions regime and its enforcement to increase mortality among Iraqis in order to keep 'conditions favourable for communicable disease outbreaks.' [this partly declassified document can be found at http://www.gulflink. osd.mil/declassdocs/dia/ 19950719/ 950719_60500007_91r.html]*

[In] 1991 the U.S. air force deliberately hit reservoirs, dams, pumping stations, pipelines, and purification plants. The U.S. then tried to limit the definition of "humanitarian goods" to food and medicine alone, preventing the import of items needed to restore water supply, sanitation, electrical power, and medical facilities.[9]

In other words, Iraq was bombed severely after Saddam Hussein felt that he had assurance that the United States would not interfere with his attack upon Kuwait. The bombing continued for over a month after the Iraqis had met the terms of "surrender," and was followed by a 13-year embargo preventing Iraq from rebuilding its own necessary services. In November of 2000, former U.S. Attorney General Ramsey Clark said that "the sanctions against Iraq have killed more than 1.5 million people, more than half of them children under the age of five, an especially vulnerable segment of the population."[10]

The sanctions against Iraq received some attention because of their apparent inhumanity. On the CBS "60 Minutes" program of May 12, 1996, Madeleine Albright—at that time the U.S. Ambassador to the United Nations and soon to be appointed Secretary of State—was interviewed by CBS reporter Leslie Stahl. Albright was asked, "We have heard that a half a million children have died. I mean, that's more children than died in Hiroshima. And—and you know, is the price worth it?" Albright replied, "I think this is a very hard choice, but the price—we think the price is worth it." Fortunately, most viewers were appalled at her response.[11]

During the import/export restriction placed upon Iraq, another door was opened to meet the critical needs of the country. An Oil-for-Food program was initiated that allowed Iraq to export oil in exchange for food and other vital necessities. This, however, failed to import enough of the needed supplies because all goods had to be approved through a committee—the United

States and Great Britain being the key players. Viewing the Oil-for-Food program, a researcher wrote:

> *"The scandal is that in most cases Iraq had already paid with its oil revenues for shipments of life-saving medicine and water purification equipments, which [were] blocked from being delivered. By the time of the U.S.-U.K. invasion in March 2003, huge masses of shipments of goods valued [at] U.S. $5.2 billion—prepaid by Iraq's oil revenues filling the U.N. administered accounts—were delayed or simply blocked for years under any pretext by the U.N. representatives of the U.S. and British governments of the day.*[12]

Therefore, even though Iraqi exports had paid for needed supplies, they were not delivered and the health hazards and unsanitary conditions prevailed. With all of the pressure placed upon the people of Iraq, though, the country still managed to survive. To be sure, there was internal strife and the Iraqi leadership was often more self-serving than benevolent. But the bottom line still found Iraq in control of its oil and its country while the United States could only act as an advisory nation. There was apparently no pretext or justification for usurping Iraq's government. At least that was the case until September 11, 2001.

The smoke settles from 9/11

Despite Iraq's posture as a country struggling for survival, it surfaced very quickly as a prime suspect in the tragic events of 9/11. CBS News carried a report on September 4, 2002, that ". . . barely five hours after American Airlines Flight 77 plowed into the Pentagon, Defense Secretary Donald H. Rumsfeld was telling his aides to come up with plans for striking Iraq—even though there was no evidence linking Saddam Hussein to the attacks."[13] The news report continued from the original notes of a Rumsfeld aide: ". . . best info fast. Judge whether good enough [to] hit S.

H. [Saddam Hussein]." The article concluded with, "Now, nearly one year later, there is still very little evidence Iraq was involved in the Sept. 11 attacks. But if these notes are accurate, that didn't matter to Rumsfeld."

So very quickly, without evidence, Iraq was implicated in the Twin Towers disaster. This was soon dispelled by government intelligence reported to the administration just ten days later that there was no credible link between Iraq and the events of 9/11.[14]

Despite any evidence, the Bush Administration continued to wed the attacks to Saddam Hussein. A year and one-half after 9/11, a commonly held attitude was that Iraq definitely had a hand in the terrorist activities that were responsible for the airliner hijackings and ensuing disasters. Linda Feldman of the *Christian Science Monitor* reported in an article entitled *"The Impact of Bush Linking 9/11 and Iraq"* on March 14, 2003, that:

> *In his prime-time press conference last week, which focused almost solely on Iraq, President Bush mentioned Sept. 11 eight times. He referred to Saddam Hussein many more times than that, often in the same breath with Sept. 11.*
>
> *Bush never pinned blame for the attacks directly on the Iraqi president. Still, the overall effect was to reinforce an impression that persists among much of the American public: that the Iraqi dictator did play a direct role in the attacks. . . .*
>
> *Sources knowledgeable about U.S. intelligence say there is no evidence that Hussein played a role in the Sept. 11 attacks, nor that he has been or is currently aiding Al Qaeda. Yet the White House appears to be encouraging this false impression, as it seeks to maintain American support for a possible war against Iraq . . . .*
>
> *The administration has succeeded in creating a sense that there is some connection [between Sept. 11 and Saddam Hussein] says Steven Kull, director of the Program on International Policy Attitudes (PIPA) at the University of Maryland.*[15]

The false understanding persisted long after Iraq had been exonerated. A September 2003 poll conducted by *USA Today* found that 69% of Americans believed that the attacks of 9/11 were linked to Saddam Hussein. A Harris Poll in October of 2004 found that 62% of all voters and 84% of those favoring George W. Bush in the upcoming election believed that Saddam Hussein had strong links to al Qaeda. The same poll found that 52% of the American public actually felt that Iraqi leadership had helped to plan the airline hijackings. A sampling of 944 U.S. military respondents in Iraq taken in the beginning months of 2006 was even more disturbing: "Almost 90% think the war is retaliation for Saddam's role in 9/11."[16]

The latter figure dealing with U.S. troops engaged in Iraq may be more easily understood in light of President Bush's letter sent to both the Speaker of the House and the President Pro Tempore of the Senate on March 18, 2003 justifying American actions in Iraq. He wrote that acting against Iraq was consistent with "continuing to take the necessary actions against international terrorists and terrorist organizations, including those nations, organizations or persons who planned, authorized, committed, or aided the terrorist attacks that occurred on September 11, 2001."[17]

Even though the White House would eventually state publicly that there was no connection between Iraq and the Twin Towers disaster, old beliefs die hard. A sampling from the President's press conferences may explain why:

September 25, 2002—"The war on terror, you can't distinguish between al Qaeda and Saddam when you talk about the war on terror."

October 7, 2002—"We've learned that Iraq has trained al Qaeda members in bomb-making, and poisons, and deadly gases. . . . We know that al Qaeda and Iraq have had high-level contacts that go back a decade."

November 7, 2002—"He's [Saddam's] a threat because he is dealing with al Qaeda."

May 2, 2003—"Imagine a world in which Saddam Hussein was there stirring even more trouble in a part of the world that, uh, that had so much resentment, so much hatred, that people came and killed 3,000 of our citizens . . . ."

Unfortunately, despite all evidence, a mindset fostered by the Bush Administration was in place that was difficult to dislodge. The mindset began early and only after the bulk of the damage was done and the United States was committed to the Iraq War, was the admission made that Saddam Hussein had no culpability. On May 1, 2005, a document was found that seems to bear out the administration's intent. What has become known as the "Downing Street Memo" is a set of minutes of a meeting held in England on July 23, 2002 between members of Prime Minister Tony Blair's cabinet. Under the heading, "This record is extremely sensitive," is the following excerpt from a meeting with George W. Bush:

> . . . *Military action was now seen as inevitable. Bush wanted to remove Saddam, through military action, justified by the conjunction of terrorism and WMD. But the intelligence and facts were being fixed around the policy.*[18]

So the preplanned conclusion or "policy" was that the Bush Administration wanted to justify a military attack on Iraq based on both terrorism and weapons of mass destruction. That neither of these were valid issues was not a concern because "the intelligence and facts were being fixed around the policy."

Weapons of Mass Destruction

For several months prior to the bombing of Baghdad, Americans became used to the phrase "weapons of mass destruction" usually written as WMD. These warheads typically fall under the classification of biological, chemical and nuclear, and have the potential impact of devastating the populations of entire cities and large geographical areas.

Four months prior to the events of 9/11, Secretary of State Colin Powell reported to the Senate that:

> *The Iraqi regime militarily remains fairly weak. It doesn't have the capacity it had 10 or 12 years ago. It has been contained. And even though we have no doubt in our mind that the Iraqi regime is pursuing programs to develop weapons of mass destruction— chemical, biological and nuclear—I think the best intelligence estimates suggest that they have not been terribly successful.*[19]

Somehow, following 9/11 and the desire to implicate Iraq, the intelligence sources determined that Iraq was successful after all in rebuilding its WMD and war machine. The issue of WMD, probably more than any other, was given as justification for the preemptive invasion of Iraq. As Paul Wolfowitz, then the Deputy Secretary of Defense, explained, "For bureaucratic reasons we settled on one issue, weapons of mass destruction, because it was the one reason everyone could agree on."[20]

This justification found its way into most White House press conferences, news channels and newspapers, and was a constant theme for several months. To refresh our memories, here is a sampling of statements that were frequently reiterated:

> *Right now Iraq is expanding and improving facilities that were used for the production of biological weapons.*
>
> *President George W. Bush*

Our intelligence officials estimate that Saddam Hussein had the materials to produce as much as 500 tons of sarin, mustard and VX nerve agent.

> *President George W. Bush*

Simply stated, there is no doubt that Saddam Hussein now has weapons of mass destruction.

> *Vice President Dick Cheney*

We know for a fact that there are weapons [of mass destruction} there.

> *White House Press Secretary Ari Fleischer*

We have sources that tell us that Saddam Hussein recently authorized Iraqi field commanders to use chemical weapons—the very weapons the dictator tells us he does not have.

> *President George W. Bush*

Well, there is no question that we have evidence and information that Iraq has weapons of mass destruction, biological and chemical particularly . . . all this will be made clear in the course of the operation for whatever duration it takes.

> *White House Press Secretary Ari Fleischer*

We know where they are. They are in the area around Tikrit and Baghdad.

> *Secretary of Defense Donald Rumsfeld*[21]

The danger is already significant and it only grows worse with time. If we know Saddam Hussein has dangerous weapons today—and we do—does it make any sense for the world to wait to confront him as he grows even stronger and develops even more dangerous weapons.

> *President George W. Bush*[22]

While this dialog emanated from the presidential administration, Iraq steadfastly denied that such weapons existed. Because of U.N. sanctions, they said that all such weaponry was destroyed following the invasion of Kuwait in 1991. That response was met with disbelief and credence was instead given to "intelligence sources." As Prime Minister Tony Blair said, "We are asked to accept Saddam decided to destroy those weapons. I say that such a claim is palpably absurd."[23] Finally in October of 2004, a lengthy report was delivered to the government. Following the announcement of the report, an article from CNN under the heading "No WMD Stockpiles in Iraq" said:

> Saddam Hussein did not possess stockpiles of illicit weapons at the time of the U.S. invasion in March 2003 and had not begun any program to produce them, a CIA report concludes.
> In fact, the long-awaited report, authored by Charles Duelfer, who advises the director of central intelligence on Iraqi weapons, says Iraq's WMD program was essentially destroyed in 1991 and Saddam ended Iraq's nuclear program after the 1991 Gulf War.[24]

This corroborates a 1995 debriefing of Hussein Kamel— the highest-ranking Iraqi official to defect from Saddam Hussein's inner circle. Hussein Kamel was Saddam's son-in-law, a general, and had been the head of the weapons industries in Iraq. The full debriefing can be found on a website compiled by Glen Rangwala—a Middle East specialist at Cambridge University: http://traprockpeace.org/glenrangwalaindex .html. (This scholarly website is a goldmine of information on the background and the actual events surrounding the war in Iraq.) In the debriefing, General Hussein Kamel explained:

> We gave instructions not to produce chemical weapons. . . . there was no decision to use chemical weapons for fear of retaliation. They realized that if chemical weapons were used, retaliation would be nuclear. . . . All chemical weapons were destroyed—biological, chemical, missile, nuclear were destroyed.[25]

Hussein Kamel's debriefing was quite in-depth with information unknown prior to his defection. Apparently, all that he said was true. This is the reason that the weapons inspectors were given free access to virtually anything they wanted to see. Hans Blix, the person in charge of inspecting Iraqi weapons and finding the illusive WMD, reported on February 4, 2003 that:

> *Since we arrived in Iraq, we have conducted more than 400 inspections covering more than 300 sites. All inspections were performed without notice, and access was almost always provided promptly. In no case have we seen convincing evidence that the Iraqi side knew in advance that the inspectors were coming. . . . we note that access to sites has so far been without problems, including those that have never been declared or inspected, as well as to Presidential sites and private residences.*[26]

Alan Simpson and Glen Rangwala wrote about the various weapons inspections in their insightful article, *The Absence of Truth—Government Propaganda and the War on Iraq*. Continuing from the Blix report of February, they wrote:

> *Over the next month, the assessment of the inspectors became more positive. Hans Blix told the Security Council on 7 March that Iraq was taking "numerous initiatives . . . with a view of resolving long-standing open disarmament issues," and this "can be seen as 'active,' or even 'proactive'" cooperation. Iraq had destroyed 72 of its 120 medium range missiles on the request of the inspectors, and was ahead of the timetable to destroy the entire stock. The regime had passed a law prohibiting the production or retention of any chemical, biological or nuclear weapons, as the inspectors had asked. They had verified that they had destroyed bombs containing anthrax in 1991 by excavating the destruction site.*[27]

The authors, using their full stock of information, then asked sarcastically, "Could it be that the main fear of the U.S. and U.K. governments was not Iraq's weapons, but that the inspectors would declare Iraq clean of prohibited weapons before they had a chance to invade?[28]

This knowledge did little to change the direction of the Iraq War. Senator Carl Levin of the Senate Armed Services Committee said that "1,750 experts have visited 1,200 potential WMD sites and have come up empty handed." Since "the administration's case for going to war against Iraq rested on the twin arguments that Saddam Hussein had existing stockpiles of weapons of mass destruction and that he might give weapons of mass destruction to al Qaeda to attack us," the entire war in Iraq should be questioned.[29]

During the various inspections that took place, some of the earlier chemical and biological warheads that were used in the Iran-Iraq war were found. Those who were hoping to find WMD to justify America's preemptive intervention initially felt vindicated; however, the WMD of earlier vintage (mostly originating from U.S. complicity) were not the weaponry that inspectors were looking for. They continually identified the older weapons as not fitting the criteria they were seeking. In fact, most of the earlier warheads that were found were in ill-repair, corroded and unusable.

The War on Terrorism

Just nine days after the Twin Towers were taken down, President George W. Bush addressed a joint session of Congress. He said that "our 'war on terror' begins with al Qaeda, but it does not end there. It will not end until every terrorist group of global reach has been found, stopped and defeated." The war on terrorism—really the war on terrorists—was formally introduced.

As an extension of the war on terrorism and to provide a rationale for future entanglement, in 2002 President Bush delivered his State of the Union address and referred to the "axis of evil." The countries included in the axis were North Korea, Iran and Iraq. He said:

> *Iraq continues to flaunt its hostility toward America and to support terror. The Iraqi Regime has plotted to develop anthrax, the nerve gas, and nuclear weapons for over a decade. This is a regime that has already used poison gas to murder thousands of its own citizens—leaving the bodies of mothers huddled over their dead children. This is a regime that agreed to international inspections— then kicked out the inspectors. This is a regime that has something to hide from the civilized world.*
>
> *States like these and their terrorist allies constitute an axis of evil, aiming to threaten the peace of the world. By seeking weapons of mass destruction, these regimes pose a grave and growing danger. They could provide these arms to terrorists, giving them the means to match their hatred. They could attack our allies or attempt to blackmail the United States. In any of these cases, the price of indifference would be catastrophic.*

So very quickly, a literal war was declared on terrorists and all nations that might harbor terrorists—a war unlike any other. The U.S. had called for wars against things and situations—not countries—before. There was the war on drugs, the war on poverty, and in earlier history, wars on slavery, polygamy and alcohol. The war on terrorism was different because it included as enemies those countries harboring and dealing with terrorists—countries that had never threatened or shown any pretense of war toward the United States.

Unfortunately, because the war on terrorism lumps many countries together, it precludes negotiation and peaceful approaches. Essentially, it calls the United States an innocent victim while Muslim and many Middle Eastern countries are labeled as violent perpetrators. So when President Bush announced, "Bring 'em on, we're plenty tough," the Iraqis retaliated by showing videos of executions. The United States responded by torturing captured insurgents; the Iraqis escalated car bombings; and the United States increased troop numbers and house-to-house searches. The war on terror leaves no middle ground for negotiation. The capitulation of Iraq is not the goal— the eradication of terrorists is.

This, as George W. Bush has admitted, will be an ongoing, never-ending war. As some have observed, "How do we know who's winning?" "How do we know if we are accomplishing what we set out to do?" "Will we ever know if we have been successful?" These are all valid questions because, in reality, terrorism is an unnamed foe. If a war is fought against a country and the government of the country cedes its will to the conquering country, then we say that a war has been won. This will never be the case with loosely organized terrorist cells whose mobility takes them from country to country and either striking or remaining silent at will.

Another facet of the war on terror that must be referred to before drawing this chapter to a close is the penchant of the U.S. to initiate and engage in terrorist activities. Terrorism, according to an army definition is "the calculated use of violence or the threat of violence to attain goals that are political, religious, or ideological in nature . . . through intimidation, coercion, or instilling fear."[30] Although Americans traditionally feel that definition only applies to the "other guys," many throughout the world have seen a different side of U.S. foreign policy that is generally withheld from national scrutiny.

Surely the bombing and subsequent deaths of tens of thousands of civilian Iraqis in Baghdad and other cities throughout the Middle East constitute the definition of terrorism. Likewise, American activities already documented throughout the pages of this book in South and Central America, the Balkans, Vietnam and Cambodia are defined as terrorism—the random killing of people to instill fear and compliance. Of all nations, the United States has been a chief leader in employing terrorist tactics. One author observed:

> *The most obvious place to look is Latin America, which has had considerable experience with international terrorism. The crimes of 9-11 were harshly condemned, but commonly with recollection of their own experiences. One might describe the 9-11 atrocities as "Armageddon," the research journal of the Jesuit University in Managua observed, but Nicaragua has "lived with its own Armageddon in excruciating slow motion" under U.S. assault "and is now submerged in its dismal aftermath," and others fared far worse under the vast plague of state terror that swept through the continent from the early 1960s, much of it traceable to Washington. A Panamanian journalist joined in the general condemnation of the 9-11 crimes, but recalled the death of perhaps thousands of poor people when the President's father bombed the barrio Chorillo in December 1989 in Operation Just Cause, undertaken to kidnap a disobedient thug [Manual Noriega] who was sentenced to life imprisonment in Florida for crimes mostly committed while he was on the CIA payroll. Uruguayan writer Eduardo Galeano observed that the U.S. claims to oppose terrorism, but actually supports it worldwide, including "in Indonesia, in Cambodia, in Iran, in South Africa, . . . and in the Latin American countries that lived through the dirty war of the Condor Plan," instituted by South American military dictators who conducted a reign of terror with U.S. backing. (31)*

This is why, although the atmosphere in the United States was quite hawkish following 9/11, an international Gallup Poll taken the week of the attack showed that most other countries were in favor of the United States seeking a diplomatic rather than a military solution. (32) "In Europe, figures [for countries condoning military retaliation] ranged from 8% in Greece to 29% in France. In Latin America, support was even lower: from 2% in Mexico to 16% in Panama." (33)

Although we may think of ourselves as the "good guys" against a sea of ugly terrorists from abroad, there is a perception among foreign nations that the United States is the salient offender of the practice of terrorism. So, rather than the innocent country that is hated because of its love of freedom and sense of fair play, the United States has brought upon itself much of its unpopularity. As far as tactics are concerned, terrorism has been used and initiated by our country as well as other countries.

Summary

The war on terror and its immediate extension, the Iraq War, have changed the course of modern warfare. Beginning with the faulty premises that the attacks of 9/11 were in part the responsibility of Saddam Hussein, and that Iraq had weapons of mass destruction and was prepared to use them against the United States—the United States initiated a preemptive attack on Iraq. Although both premises proved to be wrong, massive destruction of Iraq and its occupation by mostly American forces ensued. Military bases have been constructed and apparently Iraq will remain a U.S. military stronghold.

The war on terror, however, neither begins nor ends with Iraq. It exists wherever terrorist cells are found and brings any country into war that knowingly harbors those with aggressive attitudes towards the United States. It is fought with all of the treachery and inhumanity befitting warfare in a hi-tech world.

Chapter 13—Endnotes

1   "How America Armed Iraq." *The Sunday Herald*,
     Glasgow Scotland. June 14, 2004.
     www.unknownnews.net/ saddam.html.

2   *Ibid.*

3   *The New York Times International*, Sunday, September
     23, 1990.

4   www.prwatch.org/books/tsigfy10.html

5   *Ibid.*

6   John R. MacArthur, *Second Front: Censorship and
     Propaganda in the Gulf War.* Berkeley:
     University of California Press, 1992. p. 58.

7   www.prwatch.org/books/tsigfy10.html

8   Ramsey Clark, et. Al., *War Crimes: A Report on United
     States War Crimes Against Iraq.* Washington,
     DC: Maisonneuve Press, 1992. pp. 90-94

9   Christian P. Scherrer, "The US-UK Engineered Genocidal
     Sanctions Against Iraq, 1990-2003." June, 2003,
     revised September, 2003. www.icti-e.com/ Generated
     Items/Scherrer%20Speech.pdf.

10   *Ibid.* p. 4.

11   *Ibid.* p. 3

12   *Ibid.* p. 5

13   www.cbsnews.com/stories/2002/09/04/september11
     /main520830.shtml.

14   www.msnbc.msn.com/id/10164478

15   www.csmonitor.com/2003/0314/p02s01-woiq.html

16   www.zogby.com/NEWS/ReadNews.dbm?ID=1075

17   www.whitehouse.gov/news/releases/2003/03/20003031
     9-1.html

18   www.timesonline.co.uk/article/0,,2087-1593607,00.html

19   www.thememoryhole.org/war/powell-no-wmd.htm

20   Paul Wolfowitz, *Counterpunch.* May 29, 2003.
        www.counterpunch.org/wmd05292003.html

21   *Ibid.*

22   www.cnn.com/2004/world/meast/10/06/iraq.wmd.report

23   *Counterpunch, Ibid.*

24   *CNN, Ibid.*

25   www.casi.org.uk/info/unscom950822.pdf

26   www.traprockpeace.org/latw030703.html

27   *Ibid.*

28   *Ibid.*

29   *CNN, Ibid.*

30   "U.S. Army Operational Concept for Terrorism
        Counteraction," TRADOC Pamphlet No. 525-37,
        1984.

31   Noam Chomsky, "Terror and Just Response," July 2,
        2002. www.chomsky.info/articles/20020702.htm

32   www.gallup.international.com/terrorismpoll-figures.htm
        data from September 14-17, 2001.

33   Chomsky, *Op. Cit.*

Conclusion

As of the writing of this book, the three events examined in Part 2 are inconclusive. The motives and actors in the highest echelons who planned and carried them out are still unknown to the public. Through the passage of time more facts will surface and historical perspective will give students a better grasp of their significance. What is known now, however, is that media and government accounts veer sharply from first-hand information, leaving the critical observer to ask "why?"

Historically, we have seen that other events have been engineered either to lay foundations or to reinforce agendas distinct from the desires of the public at large. Staged emotional actions have frequently nurtured public support to rally around preconceived establishment goals. Thus, wars, educational ideals, and curtailment of certain freedoms, are often seen as popular movements while, in reality, they are often reactions to manufactured stimuli.

Because, in the Lord's words, much of what transpires in these echelons of power is included in the phrase "the hidden things of darkness,"[1] many observations are not readily apparent. And, because Latter-day Saints and Christians are generally honest and open, they assume that government and other entities are also honest in reporting events. It is against our natures to be suspicious and to search out ulterior motives that are not obvious. Yet, in the preceding pages we have learned that:

1. Constitutional safeguards have been broached by government under the guise of expediency and preserving freedom.

2. Engineered emotional fervor under false pretenses has been used to propel America into foreign wars.

3. Wars have been intentionally used to siphon the wealth of nations and to consolidate it into establishment control.

4. In most instances, the content of media and formal education is controlled.

5. Sovereignty and the right to determine national standards and ideals among individual nations is being relinquished to the United Nations.

6. Although vociferous denial to the contrary, evidence demonstrates that government individuals and agencies have fostered the drug trade in the United States and positioned other countries to comply with illicit drug demand.

7. The motives and methods of today's power usurpers parallel those of the Gadianton Robbers of Book of Mormon times.

Unfortunately, the intent of this book is not to provide answers but only to document the reality of our "awful situation." Moroni already told *Book of Mormon* readers how to avoid the pending catastrophe by describing the fall of the Jaradite and Nephite civilizations and explaining that he did so (1) "that thereby ye may repent of your sins; and (2) suffer not that these murderous combinations shall get above you."[2]

Repentance is an individual endeavor and one that is beyond the prerogative of this book to discern. Suffering or upholding "murderous combinations" to "get above" us, however, is apparent. As we have seen, Moroni's description of conspiracy and methodology is surprisingly close to similar activities in the 21st century.

And, most painful of all, since the accuracy of his description of the latter-days is undeniable, his prophecy of the future looms even larger.

> . . . *and the work, yea, even the work of destruction come upon you, yea, even the sword of justice of the Eternal God shall fall upon you, to your overthrow and destruction if ye shall suffer these things to be.*
>
> *Wherefore, the Lord commandeth you, when ye shall see these things come among you that ye shall awake to a sense of your awful situation, because of this secret combination which shall be among you . . . .*[3]

Conclusion—Endnotes

1   *Doctrine & Covenants* 123: 13

2   Ether 8:23

3   Ether 8:23-24

Bibliography

Current affairs

Nafeez Mosaddeq Ahmed, *The War on Freedom: How and Why America was Attacked September 11, 2001.* Tree of Life Publications: Joshua Tree, CA. 2002.

Scott Armstrong, Malcolm Byrne and Tom Blanton, *Secret Military Assistance to Iran and the Contras: A Chronology of Events and Individuals.* National Security Archive. 1987.

James Bamford, *A Pretext for War.* Doubleday: NY. 2004.

James Bamford, *Body of Secrets: Anatomy of the Ultra-Secret National Security Agency.* Anchor Books: NY. 2002.

Ben Bradlee, Jr., *Guts and Glory, the Rise and Fall of Oliver North.* Donald. I. Fine: NY. 1988.

Jean-Charles Brishard and Guillaume Dasquie, *Forbidden Truth: U.S.—Taliban Secret Oil Diplomacy and the Failed Hunt for Bin Laden.* Nation Books/Thunder's Mouth Press: NY. 2002.

Zbigniew Brzezinski, *The Grand Chessboard: American Primacy and Its Geostrategic Imperitives.* Basic Books: NY. 1997.

Michel Chossudovsky, *War and Globalisation: The Truth Behind September 11.* Global Outlook: Canada. 2002.

Richard A. Clarke, *Against All Enemies: Inside America's War on Terror.* Free Press: NY. 2004.

Steve Coll, *Ghost Wars: The Secret History of the CIA, Afghanistan, and bin Laden, from the Soviet Invasion to September 10, 2001.* Penguin: NY. 2004.

Tony Collins, Open Verdict, *An Account of 25 Mysterious Deaths in the Defense of Industry.* Sphere Books: London. 1990.

B. K. Eakman, *Educating for 'The New World Order.'* Halcyon House, Portland, OR. 1991.

Drugs, Law Enforcement and Foreign Policy: Report of the Subcommittee on Terrorism, Narcotics and International Operations of the Committee on Foreign Relations. United States Senate.

David Ray Griffin, *The 9/11 Commission Report: Omissions and Distortions*. Olive Branch Press: Northamption, MA. 2005.

David Ray Griffin, *The New Pearl Harbor: Disturbing Questions about the Bush Administration and 9/11*. Olive Branch Press: Northampton, MA. 2004.

Daniel Hopsicker, *Welcome to Terrorland: Mohamed Atta and the 9/11 Cover-up in Florida*. Eugene: MacCow Press. 2004.

Chalmers Johnson, *The Sorrows of Empire: Militarism, Secrecy, and the End of the Republic*. Henry Holt: NY. 2004.

Peter Lance, *Cover Up: What the Government is Still Hiding about the War on Terror*. Harper-Collins: NY. 2004.

Michael Levine, *The Big White Lie: The CIA and the Cocaine/Crack Epidemic*. Nation Book/Thunder's Mouth Press: NY. 1993.

John MacArthur, *Second Front: Censorship and Propaganda in the Gulf War*. University Presses of California, Columbia and Princeton: Berkeley. 1992

Rahul Mahajan, *Full Spectrum Dominance: US Power in Iraq and Beyond*. Seven Stories: NY. 2003.

Jim Marrs, *Inside Job: Unmasking the 9/11 Conspiracies*. Origin Press: San Rafael, CA. 2004.

Alfred W. McCoy, *The Politics of Heroin: CIA Complicity in the Global Drug Trade*. Chicago Review Press: Chicago. 1991.

Thierry Meyssan, ed., *9/11: The Big Lie*. Carnot Publishing: London. 2002.

Thierry Meyssan, ed., *Pentagate*. Carnot Publishing: London. 2002.

Greg Palast, *The Best Democracy Money Can Buy: The Truth about Corporate Cons, Globalization, and High-Finance Fraudsters*. Plume: NY. 2003.

Allen Quist, *FedEd, The New Federal Curriculum and How It's Enforced*. St. Paul: Maple River Education Coalition. 2002.

Dan Raviv and Yossi Melman, *Every Spy a Prince: The Complete History of Israel's Intelligence Community*. Houghton Mifflin: Boston. 1990.

Terry Reed and John Cummings, *Compromised: Clinton, Bush and the CIA*. Shapolsky Publishers, Inc.: NY. 1994.

Peter Dale Scott and Jonathan Marshall, *Cocaine Politics, Drugs, Armies, and the CIA in Central America.* University of California Press: Berkeley. 1991.

Joel Skousen, *World Affairs Brief* (www.worldaffairsbrief.com)

Ron Susskind, *The Price of Loyalty: George W. Bush, the White House, and the Education of Paul O'Neill.* Simon & Schuster: NY. 2004.

Rodney Stich, *Defrauding America.* Diablo Western Press: Alamo, CA. c1997.

Webster Griffin Tarpley and Anton Chaitkin, *George Bush: the Unauthorized Biography.* Executive Intelligence Review: Washington DC. 1992.

Craig Unger, *House of Bush, House of Saud: The Secret Relationship between the World's Two Most Powerful Dynasties.* Scribner: NY. 2004.

Joan M. Veon, *The United Nation's Global Straitjacket.* Hearthstone Publishing: Oklahoma City. 1997.

Gore Vidal, *Dreaming War: Blood for Oil and the Cheney-Bush Junta.* Nation Books/Thunder's Mouth Press. 2002.

Bob Woodward, *Veil: the Secret Wars of the CIA, 1981-1987.* Simon and Schuster: NY. 1987.

Historical References

Edward Bernays, *Propaganda.* Liveright: NY. 1928.

Samuel L. Blumenfeld, *NEA: Trojan Horse in American Education.* The Paradigm Co.: Boise, ID. 1984.

Ken Bowers, *Beneath the Tide: Who Really Rules the World.* Private Printing. 2005.

William Guy Carr, *Pawns in the Game.* Private Printing. 1956.

J. Reuben Clark, *Memorandum on the Monroe Doctrine.* Department of State Publication No. 37: Washington DC. 1930.

John Coleman, PhD, *Conspirator's Hierarchy: The Story of the Committee of 300.* American West Publishers, Bozeman, MT. 1992.

Count Egon Caesar Corti, *The Rise of the House of Rothschild.* Western Islands: Boston. 1972.

Virginia Cowles, *The Rothschilds: A Family of Fortune.* Weidenfield and Nicolson: London. 1973.

Dennis Laurence Cuddy, PhD, *The Globalists.* Hearthstone Publishing, Ltd.: Oklahoma City. 2001.

Richard Deacon, *The Truth Twisters.* McDonald: London. 1987.

Thomas J. Dodd, *Freedom and Foreign Policy.* McFadden Paperback: NY. 1962.

William F. Engdahl, *A Century of War: Anglo-American Oil Politics and the New World Order.* Paul and Co.: MA. 1992.

Worthington Chauncey Ford, *The Writings of George Washington.* 14 volumes. G. P. Putnam's Sons: NY. 1889.

Col. Elisha Garrison, *Roosevelt, Wilson and the Federal Reserve Law.* Christopher Publishing House: Boston. 1931.

David Lloyd George, *Is it Peace?* Hodder and Stoughton: London. 1923.

E. M. House, *Philip Dru: Administrator.* B. W. Huebsch. 1912.

William F. Jasper, *Global Tyranny . . . Step by Step: the United Nations and the Emerging New World Order.* Western Islands: Appleton, WI. 1992.

Thomas Jefferson, *The Works of Thomas Jefferson.* 12 volumes. G. P. Putnam's Sons. 1904.

William H. McIllany, *The Tax-Exempt Foundations.* Arlington House: Westport, CT. 1980.

Ralph MeGehee, *Deadly Deceits: My 25 Years in the CIA.* Sheridan Square Publications: NY. 1983.

George Morgenstern, *Pearl Harbor: the Story of the Secret War.* Institute for Historical Review: Costa Mesa, CA. 1991.

Frederic Morton, *The Rothschilds: A Family Portrait.* Secker and Warburg: London. 1963.

Eustace Mullins, *The Secrets of the Federal Reserve.* Bankers Research Institute: Staunton, VA. 1983.

George A. Peek, Jr., ed., *The Political Writings of John Adams.* Liberal Arts Press: NY. 1954.

Carroll Quigley, *The Anglo-American Establishment.* Books in Focus: New York. 1981.

Carroll Quigley, *Tragedy and Hope.* Macmillan, New York. 1966.

Report of the Congressional Committee Investigating the Iran-Contra Affair, 100th Congress, First Session. Report No. 100-433. 1987.

Charles Seymour, *The Intimate Papers of Col. House.* 2 Volumes. Houghton Mifflin: Boston. 1926.

Holly Sklar, ed., *Trilateralism: The Trilateral Commission and the Elite Planning for World Management.* South End Press: Boston. 1980.

George P. Schultz, *Turmoil and Triumph, My Years as Secretary of State.* Charles Scribner's Sons: NY. 1993.

W. Cleon Skousen, *The Making of America.* The National Center for Constitutional Studies: Washington DC. 1986.

W. Cleon Skousen, *The Naked Capitalist.* Ensign Publishing: Salt Lake City. 1970.

William Strauss and Neil Howe, *The Fourth Turning.* Broadway Books: NY. 1997.

Robert B. Stinnett, Day of Deceit: *The Truth about FDR and Pearl Harbor.* Free Press: NY. 2000.

Antony C. Sutton, *Wall Street and the Bolshevik Revolution.* Arlington House: NY. 1974.

Antony C. Sutton, *An Introduction to the Order; How the Order Controls Education; and How the Order Creates War and Revolution.* Research Publications: Phoenix. 1983.

Antony C. Sutton and Patrick M. Wood, *Trilaterals over Washington.* Scottsdale: The August Corporation. 1981.

Tax-Exempt Foundations. Hearings Before the Special Committee to Investigate Tax-Exempt Foundations and Comparable Organizations, House of Representatives. United States Government Printing Office: Washington DC. 1954.

Tax-Exempt Foundations. Special Committee to Investigate Tax-Exempt Foundations, House of Representatives Staff Report. United States Government Printing Office: Washington DC. 1954.

Ernst H. Van der Beugel, *From Marshall Aid to Atlantic Partnership.* Elsevier Publishing Co.: NY. 1966.

George Sylvester Viereck, *The Strangest Friendship in History: Woodrow Wilson and Colonel House.* Liveright: NY. 1932.

David Wise and Thomas B. Ross, *The Invisible Government.* Random House: NY. 1964.

Rene Wormser, *Foundations: Their Power and Influence.* Covenant House Books: Sevierville, TN. 1993.

LDS References

Ezra Taft Benson, *An Enemy Hath Done This.* Parliament Publishers: Salt Lake City. 1969.

Ezra Taft Benson, *God, Family, Country: Our Three Great Loyalties.* Deseret Book Co.: Salt Lake City. 1975.

Ezra Taft Benson, *The Teachings of Ezra Taft Benson.* Bookcraft: Salt Lake City. 1988.

Ezra Taft Benson, *This Nation Shall Endure.* Deseret Book Co.: Salt Lake City. 1977.

Christopher S. Bentley, *The Hidden Things of Darkness.* Sunrise Publishing: Santa Teresa, NM. 2001.

J. Reuben Clark, *Stand Fast by Our Constitution.* Deseret Book Co.: Salt Lake City. 1962.

Neil J. Flinders, *Teach the Children: An Agency Approach to Education.* Book of Mormon Research: Provo. 1990

Frank W. Fox, *J. Reuben Clark: The Public Years.* Brigham Young University: Provo. 1980.

Robert E. Hales, *Secret Combinations Today: A Voice of Warning.* Horizon Publishers: Bountiful. 1996.

Ray C. Hillam, *J. Reuben Clark, Jr.: Diplomat and Statesman.* Brigham Young University Press: Provo. 1973.

Jerome Horowitz, *The Elders of Israel and the Constitution.* Parliament Publishers: Salt Lake City. 1970.1886.

Journal of Discourses, 1851-1886. 26 volumes. F. D. Richards: Liverpool. Photomechanical reprint, 1966.

David O. McKay, *Statements on Communism and the Constitution of the United States.* Deseret Book Co.: Salt Lake City. 1964.

Jack Monnett, *Revealed Educational Principles & the Public Schools.* Archive Publishers: Grantsville, UT. 1999.

Jerreld L. Newquist, ed., *Prophets, Principles and National Survival.* Publishers Press: Salt Lake City. 1964.

D. Michael Quinn, *J. Reuben Clark: The Church Years.* Brigham
    Young University: Provo. 1983.

W. Cleon Skousen, *The Majesty of God's Law.* Ensign Publishing:
    Salt Lake City. 1996.

Speeches of the Year. Brigham Young University: Provo.

John Taylor, The Government of God. Richards: Salt Lake City. 1852.

Index